OPEN SHELVES AND OPEN MINDS

ALSO BY C. H. CRAMER

ROYAL BOB: THE LIFE OF ROBERT G. INGERSOLL
NEWTON D. BAKER: A BIOGRAPHY

OPEN SHELVES
AND
OPEN MINDS

A History of the
Cleveland Public Library

C. H. CRAMER

THE PRESS OF
CASE WESTERN RESERVE UNIVERSITY
CLEVELAND & LONDON
1972

*This book has been brought to publication
with the generous support of the
Friends of the Cleveland Public Library.*

The photographs illustrating this volume are reproduced with the kind permission
of the Picture Collection of the Cleveland Public Library.

Printed in the United States of America.
International Standard Book Number: 0–8295–0219–X.
Library of Congress Catalogue Card Number: 70–170150.

TO
THE FRIENDS OF
THE CLEVELAND PUBLIC LIBRARY

CONTENTS

PREFACE

THIS HISTORY, as well as divers other projects, has been made possible by reason of the dedicated effort and financial support of the Friends of the Cleveland Public Library.

The first group with that name, organized in the late 1930s, did not survive the turbulence of the Rush–Library Board imbroglio and the distractions of the Second World War. The current association of Friends began its operations in 1956 with nine members; by 1970 the roster numbered 1,400 individual and corporate memberships. In 1956 the first order of business for the revived Friends was to defray promotional costs for the bond issue which would ensure the purchase of the *Plain Dealer* building. Since that time the organization has provided upwards of two hundred thousand dollars in support of many estimable activities. Among them have been the purchase of rare books, furnishing the lounge in the Business and Science building, the purchase of photographic prints of famous Clevelanders, and the provision of attractive furniture in the Eastman Garden. Funds have been made available for the Annual Book Fair, speakers at special events, the underwriting of National Library Week in Cleveland, and tuition scholarships for staff members completing degrees in library science. The inspiration provided by the Friends also brought "seed" money to the library. As a result of their work on the library's centennial celebration the Kulas Foundation made a large grant, and an anonymous donor made a substantial contribution to ensure installation of the humidity control that is essential for the preservation of the White Collection.

For all of these reasons the total achievement of the Friends has been an impressive one.

An author always approaches a large research project with a feeling of awe and fright, hoping that in due course some light will appear at the end of a tunnel of ignorance. In this case the illumination appeared quickly because the entire staff of the library was cordial and assiduous in providing essential information. In the process this author also established an intellectual companionship that was most rewarding.

Some institutional histories become encyclopedic by reason of the inclusion of names in profusion and departmental data ad infinitum. From the standpoint of an archival record this pattern has achieved some recognition, but it has been lethal if narrative history is intended to hold the attention of its readers. In this volume the prime purpose has been to attract interest in the major events, whether they are triumphs or failures, in the record of the Cleveland Public Library.

The author is grateful to three knowledgeable persons who read and commented on the manuscript in its early stages. They were Miss Fern Long, deputy director of the library, Mrs. Ruth Helmuth, the archivist of Case Western Reserve University, and the past president of the Friends, Mrs. Harley C. Lee, whose continuing enthusiasm provided an essential incentive. At the Press of Case Western Reserve University the editing of the manuscript has been achieved through the assistance of Director William R. Crawford.

The narrative which follows, covering the first century of the Cleveland Public Library (1869–1969), marks the completion of the last item in an extensive program planned by the Friends in celebration of the institution's centennial. At this point our attention and interest turn naturally to the continuing history of the library in its second hundred years. I extend to the Friends and to the library staff every good wish as they meet the problems and the challenges of the future.

C. H. C.

Cleveland, Ohio
November, 1971

OPEN SHELVES AND OPEN MINDS

CHAPTER ONE

OUT OF SMALL BEGINNINGS

SMALL BEGINNINGS IN OHIO

THE IDEA behind the mighty Cleveland Public Library, like that of Plymouth Plantation, came "out of small beginnings . . . as one small candle may light a thousand." In 1811, when Cleveland was the tiniest of settlements on a rude frontier, sixteen of its sixty-four inhabitants subscribed to its first library, a short-lived reading circle established to distribute the hard-to-come-by printed word. In this literary round the members read such books as a history of Rome, Johnson's *Lives of the English Poets*, Goldsmith's *Greece*, and Cervantes' *Don Quixote*. This list would constitute a respectable cultural showing in any intellectual milieu; it was astounding for a wilderness village on a riverbank.

All early libraries in the United States were similarly supported, by subscriptions or charity. The first one in Ohio had been founded in 1796 before statehood was achieved; this library was established by Colonel Israel Putnam, son of the general who achieved renown at the Battle of Bunker Hill. In order to share his books with the community of Marietta, Putnam organized a company whose subscribers each paid ten dollars. It was known as the Belpre Farmer's Library. For a time the books appear to have been kept in a large rush basket under the Colonel's bed, a unique repository indeed. Nearby, the better-known Coonskin Library was founded a few years later by the Western Library Association after its incorporators had attended what was described by one member as a "libery meaten." In the early 1800s hard money was scarce on the frontier but pelts of raccoons and "she bares" were abundant; of

3

the two, raccoon pelts had a better market with the agents of John Jacob Astor. The cash-poor organization was known to have sold coonskins in Boston to raise money for the purchase of books. In spite of its zoological nickname, the association's books were restricted to those considered suitable for Christians; the Reverend Thaddeus Harris and the Reverend Manasseh Cutler selected the first fifty-one volumes for the only library in the world named for the irreligious raccoon.

During the early 1830s in Cleveland there was a Cleveland Reading Association with one hundred members. There was also a Young Men's Literary Association with eight hundred volumes; its first president was Charles Whittlesey, the scientist and historian often designated as Cleveland's first literary man. Both of these societies were the victims of the Panic of 1837 and the economic depression that followed it. In the same decade sailors from Lake Erie could find relaxation in the privately financed Bethel Reading Room which was open two evenings a week. This operation had an unusual come-on, one wonders whether by design. For the sailors a red signal-light indicated that the library was open. The same illumination also certified that other dwellings in Cleveland were available for a different kind of relaxation.

By the middle years of the nineteenth century the most influential cultural organization in the Western Reserve was the Cleveland Library Association, which offered interesting books, a reading room, a museum, and a lecture series for those who could buy shares of stock at ten dollars each. The book collection continues to the present day. In 1880 its name was changed to the Case Library. Until 1924, when it became affiliated with Western Reserve University, it was still an endowed subscription library, charging its members a nominal fee to use its 100,000 books and 300 periodicals (although it did permit students at the Case School and at Western Reserve University, and all clergymen, to enjoy its privileges without charge). The librarian for the association in the mid-1850s was a talented Negro. He was William Howard Day, who had come to Cleveland after graduation from Oberlin College in 1847, and in time would become the editor and publisher of the first newspaper in the United States published especially for Negroes—the *Aliened American.*

The Cleveland Library Association could never have flourished without the support of the Case family, which contributed as mightily to the intellectual and cultural history of Cleveland as it did to its business development. The members of this family were blessed with great wealth, were most generous in their benefactions, and were all cursed with wretched health.

The senior Leonard Case came from western Pennsylvania, where one of his earliest recollections was the excitement of the Whiskey Rebellion of the 1790s. In 1800 his family moved across the border to northeastern Ohio where Leonard came down with a fever, probably the result of exposure from ranging the surrounding forests for cattle owned by the family. After two years of intense suffering he rose from his bed a cripple, without hope of recovery and requiring continual use of cane and crutch throughout the rest of his life. Undaunted, he studied mathematics and surveying and law. He was admitted to the bar in 1814. Ultimately he became a banker, a railroad promoter, and the final agent who liquidated land debts in the Western Reserve for the state of Connecticut. Case foresaw the prosperity and importance of Cleveland and, as fast as he obtained money beyond his immediate needs, invested it in land either in the city or in its environs, thus laying the foundation—for himself and his two sons—of great future wealth. In the public sphere he served as auditor of Cuyahoga County and as president of Cleveland Village. He was instrumental in ornamenting the streets of his adopted city with shade trees, to the point where Cleveland became widely known and praised as "the Forest City."

Leonard Case's eldest son William continued the family's business ventures and introduced it into new cultural enterprises. As a railroad entrepreneur he was instrumental in developing lines south and east from Cleveland to Cincinnati and Ashtabula, both of which later became a part of the New York Central System. But it was his abiding interest in the political, intellectual, and scientific affairs of Cleveland that was unusual. William served well for four years as a member of the City Council, and as mayor of Cleveland from 1850 to 1852. He was a major leader in the development of the Cleveland Library Association. Possessed of exemplary literary and artistic tastes he was also fond of hunting and fishing, and developed a great interest in natural history and horticulture. As a child he had been far from robust and rather than chance the uncertainties of a college career took to the outdoors, becoming a first-class woodsman, hunter, and taxidermist. Out of this experience he developed what was called "The Ark," a reference to its alleged resemblance to the contents of Noah's famed vessel. The Cleveland "Ark" was housed in a small, wooden, two-room structure adjacent to the ancestral home of the Case family at the corner of Public Square. Originally it was a social club; in time it became a museum filled with specimens of birds, eggs, rocks, shells, and other natural "curiosities" collected by its members as they tramped through what was still a very wild country. The intellectual interests of the members were broad, leading some of them into the pursuit of local history and the collection of books. In due course, from the initial influence of the "Arkites" and of the Cleveland Library Association, would come the Cleveland Academy of Natural Science, the Western Reserve Historical Society, and the Rowfant Club of book lovers and collectors.

William Case also conceived the idea for a magnificent Cleveland cultural center in Case Hall (on the easterly portion of the present Federal Building site at East Third and Superior), construction of which was begun in 1859 and completed in 1867—after a long delay due to the vicissitudes of the Civil War. In planning the four-story building he visited Faneuil Hall in Boston, then considered the nation's civic and architectural gem. When it was opened in 1867, Case Hall had a grand concert in its public auditorium; Signora Peralta and Signori Steffani and Bellini sang before a capacity house where reserved seats commanded the high price of two dollars. The hall seated fifteen hundred people, featured a "patent opera chair," plus decorations on the walls and ceiling by the Italian artist Garibaldi. In time, great musicians and orators of the world appeared on its stage; it was to ring, inter alia, with the eloquence of the Reverend Henry Ward Beecher and the agnostic Robert G. Ingersoll. Case Hall was the largest and finest building in the city, but it failed as a profitable cultural investment and after a score of years was turned into business offices. Unfortunately, William Case did not live to see even the dedication of the building. He died of tuberculosis in 1862, some five years before the structure was completed. Large-hearted and generous, shrinking from notoriety, he made a huge contribution to the development of Cleveland.

Leonard Case, Jr., attended the schools of Cleveland and in 1842 was graduated from Yale with a record that was creditable but not exceptional, save in the field of mathematics where he achieved honors. That he did not distinguish himself in college was not due to lack of talent. It was because the delicacy of his health forbade the intellectual or physical exertions necessary for prominence in either the academic or athletic programs. After his return to Cleveland he developed a library, studied on his own, read law, and was admitted to the bar although he never practiced the profession. An admirer of the strength and physical symmetry which he lacked, his only real luxury was a stable of fast horses, which he purchased at fabulous prices although he neither rode nor handled them. Instead he delighted in the comfort of the easygoing but slow family carriage, and was quite willing to watch his coachman skim rapidly past, driving the fast horses. He continued his interest in mathematics and spent hours poring over problems; E. W. Scripps would note that he took great delight "in their intricacies and gloried in his triumph over them." Beyond this, his tastes were literary and scholarly; he wrote essays and poems. One of the latter, a seriocomic poem entitled "Treasure Trove," was published in the *Atlantic Monthly*. A loner, he shunned both marriage and notoriety. With a few close friends he played billiards and whist and cribbage in his own home, but that was the limit of his social life.

Unlike his father and elder brother, Leonard Case had a positive distaste for business and public office. For that reason he turned his business affairs over to an agent and never occupied a governmental position. As the last bachelor survivor of his family line, he had inherited a fortune of $15 million at the time of his father's death in 1864. By reason of the postwar decline in prices and his own exceptional generosity, this inheritance had declined to $10 million by the time of his death in 1880. His benevolent heart was responsive to all appeals for charity, and he also gave to public institutions with a bountiful hand. Even so, his wealth continued to be impressive; at his death he owned three hundred acres of land in the heart of Cleveland, one thousand acres to the west in what is now Lakewood and Rocky River, and vast mining properties near Marquette in Michigan.

As a businessman the junior Leonard Case may have allowed a considerable family fortune to decline, but on the cultural side he accelerated the pace of giving and accentuated the reputation which the family already enjoyed. In 1870 he gave the Cleveland Library Association an endowment of $25,000 and a perpetual lease of rooms on the second floor of Case Hall. Six years later he gave the association the entire building valued at $300,000. In 1877 he made possible the Case School of Applied Sciences by contributing real property in the center of Cleveland which was valued at upwards of $2 million. Because of the donor's dislike of publicity, the knowledge of this gift was withheld until after his death at sixty in 1880 from emphysema and a variety of other ailments. E. W. Scripps paid him this tribute in the *Penny Press*:

> Since Case's death instances of his great openhanded generosity are being talked of, which shows him to have belonged to a species of mankind almost entirely extinct in this age, i.e., he was a man who, miserable in everything pertaining to his own life, lived with the determination of making just as many people happy as he could with the opportunities fortune and the Almighty had furnished him.

SMALL BEGINNINGS IN THE UNITED STATES

All these developments in Cleveland were but a reflection of what was happening in the rest of the country through subscription and mercantile and apprentice libraries. The first subscription organization had been that of the Philadelphia Library Company established by Benjamin Franklin in 1732; he would claim forty years later that this company was "the mother of all the North American subscription libraries, now so numerous." From this initial venture, more than fifty similar libraries had been established in the next half-century in New England alone, in part because they were encouraged by exemption from taxation. In Ohio the first subscription library chartered by the state was the Dayton

Library Society in 1805. In Cuyahoga County the first similar charter was granted to the Euclid Literary Society in 1814. By 1840 Horace Mann would find that Massachusetts had almost three hundred libraries of this kind, with a total of 180,000 books. In time mechanics and apprentices came to believe the principle was sound, and established their own book collections on a subscription basis; there were also mercantile libraries which substituted ink-stained young clerks for grimy apprentices. There were even joint-stock organizations for the purchase of general culture which included pianos; female employees of the cotton mills of Massachusetts, most of them recently from rural areas, subscribed to joint-stock pianos for their boarding houses, perhaps to accompany their broadening study of German and their reading of British reviews. Although subscription libraries were not supported by taxation they were public in the sense that they were open without discrimination to all who could pay a modest fee.

To this general movement, designed to provide education for an adult population, the national lyceum movement made a considerable contribution. Lyceum membership was open to anyone for an annual sum of two dollars or, for a life membership, twenty dollars. The original intention of the lyceum was to provide its members with libraries, lectures, concerts, debates, and scientific demonstrations through museums. The first such group, established by Josiah Holbrook in 1826, became so popular that the movement spread to nearly every state in the Union, and by 1890 there were some three thousand lyceums. In the early days the emphasis was on libraries; it was felt that the possession of a book collection should be the primary object of the movement. Later the program spent most of its efforts on lectures. In its day, this technique was an important force in adult education and social reform and political discussion. Aided by the powerful support of such men as Henry Barnard, Edward Everett, and Daniel Webster—and favored by the contemporary zeal for the improvement of the common man—the organization spread rapidly. Crowded audiences listened to Emerson, Dickens, Thackeray, and Garrison. To rapt listeners Wendell Phillips was said to have delivered his discourse on "The Lost Arts" two thousand times, and Emerson would say, "The Ly-

ceum is my pulpit." Interest in the lyceum movement declined after
the Civil War, but its forensic activity was reborn in the Chautau-
qua movement a few decades later.

In Cleveland, at midpoint in the nineteenth century Charles
Dickens, William Lloyd Garrison, Horace Greeley, Henry Ward
Beecher, and Susan B. Anthony—among others—were on the lyceum speaking circuit. The average price received by Emerson for
an evening lecture was ten dollars and traveling expenses; on one
occasion when he received the maximum of fifty dollars, he expressed grave doubt as to the morality of accepting such excessive
remuneration. The humorist Artemus Ward, who then reviewed
these lectures for the Cleveland *Plain Dealer*, thought there was
another reason why Emerson should not receive that much money.
He wrote:

> He is a man of massive intellect . . . but his lecture last night
> was rather a sleepy affair. For our part . . . we would as lief
> see a perpendicular coffin behind a lecture desk as Emerson.
> The one would amuse as much as the other.

Ward also took a dim view of Horace Greeley, with the comment:

> A great many persons think he is a great man, and Greeley
> inclines to that opinion himself. Long may he wave.

SHOULD LIBRARIES BE FREE?

Because of this activity in the private sector, there were many
people who thought the idea of a publicly supported library to be
comparable in absurdity with the then-novel concept of tax-supported public schools. It was claimed that taxes were already too
high and that public support for libraries would be inequitable because it would subsidize book readers at the expense of those not
so inclined. It would also represent an extension of governmental
functions that was both socialistic and contrary to free enterprise.

Many felt it was wrong to favor one special section of the community—the book readers—at great cost to all the rest. If one man
could have his hobby paid for by his neighbors, why not all? Were

"theatre-goers, . . . amateurs of music, and others to have their earnings confiscated, and their capacities for indulging in their own special hobbies curtailed, merely to satisfy gluttons of gratuitous novel-reading?" As late as 1902 a prominent businessman of Detroit would decry the necessity of spending half a million dollars for libraries. He asserted:

> Men who have no money of their own, who do not expect to have any of their own, and who, if they had it, would not know how to take care of it are delirious with desire to spend the people's money.
>
> An influenza of extravagance has attacked the officialdom of the city.

It was also claimed that free libraries would be godsends for town loafers, who would find themselves housed at public expense in comfortable surroundings provided by the tax-paying public. In both England and the United States it was observed that the mistake of publicly supported libraries was an unfortunate outcome of the disaster of tax-supported schools; in Spencerian rhetoric one British writer would lament that

> while State education is manufacturing readers for books, State-supported libraries are providing books for readers. The two functions are logically related. If you may take your education out of your neighbor's earnings, surely you may get your literature in the same manner. Literary dependency has the same justification as educational dependency. . . . Those who have been compelled to accept a semi-gratuitous education, . . . can hardly be expected to relish paying the market value for their books and newspapers. They have been taught to read at other people's expense, and why should they not be provided books in the same easy way? It is not at present proposed to supply them with foolscap, etc., in order that they may "keep up" their writing proficiency, but no doubt this is a luxury reserved for the future.

Free libraries, as "socialists' continuing schools," were reprehensible extensions of the basic function of government, a function which should be restricted to the protection of the property of men *and* the protection of the virtue of women. Like all state socialism, such tax-supported libraries would represent the "negation of that liberty which is the goal of human progress." For that reason every opposition to them was encouraged as a "stroke for human advancement."

In spite of such Cassandras the battle for free public education and for free public libraries had been won by the middle of the nineteenth century. Advocates of new tax-supported educational facilities convinced the electorate that they were essential for political and economic and moral reasons. On the political side it was obvious that a democracy could not function without an educated electorate, and the library could play a major role in developing this society of the intellect. Thomas Jefferson put it this way: "If a nation expects to be ignorant *and* free, . . . it expects what never was and never will be." A century later his point of view was reflected accurately by the president of the Library Board of Cleveland, who used Jeffersonian language to assert: "We might as well expect to have good citizens without good books and good schools, as to make bricks without straw." Daniel Webster had once called the little red schoolhouse the "sentry box of American liberty"; using the same figure of speech the public libraries could very well be called the "arsenals of American democracy." President Francis Wayland of Brown University, who was a clergyman and educator and an advocate of free libraries, would contend that libraries provided a leveling influence because all citizens could begin on an equal footing in the society of the intellect; there the prizes went to the wise. In this competition, as Wayland saw it, "Poverty . . . works no exclusion, and wealth furnishes no recommendation. . . . The man who is denied admission to the aristocracy of property, is welcomed into the prouder and nobler aristocracy of talent." Wayland was happy to cite the example of Elihu Burritt. Burritt was the learned blacksmith without formal schooling who distinguished himself as a linguist and who was outstanding in the peace movement. He and other self-educated scholars were proof that books in many languages could reach the homes of those with, and those without, formal education and college degrees. On the basis of such examples, the possibility of universal knowledge seemed assured;

even a "heavy ploughboy" had the potential for creativity and aspirations which could be realized by the right kinds of opportunities. If it was the intention of the United States to preserve political democracy and to prevent the government from becoming a farce, its people must be intelligent and virtuous and informed. In reaching this goal, the free public library would be an important factor.

On the political side, schools and libraries would provide the intelligent electorate which was essential in a democracy; they would also protect the restive masses from the lures of radical socialism and communism. There was a faith that educated workers would not be led, like stupid cattle, to these revolutionary panaceas. In the 1870s the library at Brookline, Massachusetts, was proud of the fact that readers increased in depression years, in part because it demonstrated that the institution was performing a great human service by providing a rendezvous for the unemployed. The town, it stated, was fortunate to have such a "safe asylum for hands and brains that might, through forced idleness and discouragement, be led to harm." Librarians in Worcester were gratified to see "rude manners and vulgar practices" disappear, albeit slowly, from their popular reading room. The "uncultured" learned to speak in low tones and even to remove their hats on entering the library. The sobering experience of the Paris Commune was interpreted as a result of man's essential ignorance of both his rights and the rights of others; for this reason it was assumed that "books are better than bayonets." In the United States the railroad strikes of 1877 and additional labor unrest in the 1880s gave the advocates of libraries convincing arguments on which they could base their claims; they advertised their institutions as antidotes against "excitements, disturbances and violence based on ignorance and idleness." Libraries, they said, would go far to avoid, in future years, such excesses. Furthermore, extensive reading would turn most socialists into the moderate Fabian type; public libraries would thus make a great contribution toward "socializing the socialists."

On the economic side, there is no question that an educated labor force, brought into being through libraries and schools, has been vital in this country's development. In 1890, when President Benjamin Harrison spoke at the dedication of the Allegheny Public

Library, he testified that it was only through the mental development of the men who ran the mills that local industrial advances, as well as the prosperity of the country as a whole, could be achieved. His faith was fully justified. It soon became apparent that the major part of economic growth lay more in investment in the development of human resources through free education than in capital expenditures for buildings and equipment and inventories. Jean-Jacques Servan-Schrieber has made this point in his best-selling book, *The American Challenge*. He states that the reason for lagging technology in Europe is not so much due to American attempts at domination, as the Europeans like to claim. Instead it is a reflection of the weaknesses of the European educational system; its libraries and schools are limited to the few rather than the many.

There was also a "missionary" aspect to the public library movement of a century ago, typified by the argument on behalf of a proposed public library at Hartford, Connecticut. It ran as follows:

> The utility of Public Libraries consisting of well chosen Books under proper Regulations, and their smiling Aspect on the interests of Society, Virtue and Religion are too manifest to be denied.

The Cleveland Board of Education had the same belief. In 1868 it announced that the "power for good" of its about-to-be-established public library would increase year by year, and that "as a conservator of the public morals and a preventive of crime, its value cannot well be overestimated." At the turn of the century when applications were being made for Carnegie funds, the "Patron Saint of Libraries" was puzzled by the logic—or illogic—of some of the requests. The mayor of Berlin, Wisconsin, asserted that the town had more than twenty saloons but not one place where a fellow could spend an evening away from the influence of liquor; he therefore claimed that a library would provide nothing but good. On the other hand responsible citizens of Bloomfield, Iowa, were proud of the fact that they had had no saloons for more than three decades; such virtue, they declared, obviously qualified them for a gift from Carnegie.

Advocates of public libraries were constantly stressing their importance in soothing the young and savage breast. At the open-

ing of the Cleveland Public Library in 1869 Mayor Stephen Buhrer
said that the new institution would be

> an attractive place of resort for young men, withdrawing them
> from expensive and vicious amusements.

Shortly thereafter, the directors of the Lowell Library in Massachusetts stated:

> Let the library be free to all, and then, perhaps there will be
> one young man less in the places where intoxicating drinks
> are found. . . . Make the library free to all and then, perhaps,
> there will be one young woman less to fall from the path of
> purity and goodness down to that depth of degradation and
> misery to which only a woman can fall.

THE FIRST PUBLIC LIBRARIES

In their study of the development of tax-supported libraries, anti-
quarians are inclined to point to Salisbury (in Connecticut), Peterborough (in New Hampshire), and both West Cambridge and Wayland (in Massachusetts) as the lineal ancestors of modern public
libraries. Early libraries in these towns were highly experimental
and uncertain in their financial support. In 1803 Caleb Bingham,
a Boston publisher and bookseller, created the first of these institutions, a children's library. He hoped to provide an opportunity
for reading which had been denied to him as a boy and for that
reason sent a collection of 150 titles to his native town of Salisbury, on condition that the town accept the quixotic gift. It did,
with initial but waning enthusiasm. From time to time it supple-
mented his donation with grants from tax money, but this support
was sporadic at best, and by mid-century the library no longer
existed. Nonetheless, it received dubious distinction as the first example of a free public library. In 1835 at West Cambridge, Massachusetts, a Dr. Ebenezer Larned gave a similar library; the town
supported it with annual appropriations until 1872 when it merged
with a standard public library there.

In the early 1830s the state of New Hampshire distributed a portion of the state-bank tax among its towns for literary purposes,

with the instruction that they devote their shares for free schools or for "other purposes of education." Most municipalities used the money for free schools, but the town of Peterborough interpreted the law broadly enough to establish in 1833 a library which it maintained with annual appropriations of $100 for the next sixteen years. It was the first town library (established two years before the one at West Cambridge) to be continuously supported over a period of years. In 1847, during the commencement proceedings of Brown University, President Francis Wayland announced his intention to give $500 for a library in the town of Wayland, provided the town matched the donation. As a result a public library went into operation in 1850, supported by an assessment *optional* with the *individual* taxpayer—rather than from regular tax funds. A university president would scarcely be in a position to claim much initial credit for a system of library support which was so ineffective and illusory. Strangely enough, Wayland's inchoate donation did inspire legislation that empowered towns to support libraries by taxation which was standard and regular rather than optional.

The libraries at Salisbury, West Cambridge, Peterborough, and Wayland were all small-scale ventures and, left to themselves, would never have set in motion the idea of universal public libraries. This task was accomplished by two state-supported schemes: school-district and town libraries. New York was first in establishing the school-district type, in 1835. By the end of the century similar legislation had been passed in twenty-one states; this was usually done through permissive legislation authorizing a maximum tax which might be levied for such book collections. The most dramatic support for this type of library came from two famous educators: Horace Mann in Massachusetts and Henry Barnard in Rhode Island. School-district libraries, in spite of the name, provided free reading for the public in general as well as the school pupils. Many contained adult collections for adult readers and were not necessarily housed in school buildings. Although adopted with considerable enthusiasm at the beginning, these libraries fell into disfavor and declined in importance except in Michigan, where income from penal fines was used to promote these educational institutions. In other states ultimate dissatisfaction came because most school-district libraries represented geographical units which were too small, were poorly housed, and were badly supervised by inadequate school trustees and by librarians who were both untrained and uninterested.

The school district was too minuscule for efficient library work, and for that reason the next experiment, quite logically, took the town itself as a more suitable unit. New Hampshire led the way. This state had never experimented with school-district libraries; in 1849 it permitted its municipalities to tax themselves for the creation of libraries "open to the free use of every inhabitant of the town or city . . . for the general diffusion of intelligence among all classes in the community." This act was a model because of the idealism of its language and the absence of limiting restrictions. Other states followed the example although none approached its positive educational philosophy or its potential generosity as far as possible taxes were concerned. In giving New Hampshire credit for passing the first general town-library act, it must also be noted that one year earlier (in 1848) Massachusetts had passed a similar, if very special, act applicable only to Boston. The Great and General Court of Massachusetts had authorized the city to establish a special public library, provided the appropriation for this institution did not exceed the sum of $5,000 in any one year. This was actually the first statute ever passed authorizing the establishment and maintenance of a public library as a municipal institution supported by taxation. In retrospect, it turned out extremely well. Within a quarter of a century, by reason of the leadership of authentic scholars and teachers like George Ticknor and Edward Everett and Justin Winsor, Boston Public had become the leading library in the United States—in size, use, imagination, and leadership.

In Ohio several school-district laws were passed, but the early ones were ineffective. The basic act was that of 1853 which provided for a mandatory tax of one-tenth of a mill to provide libraries in the schools, theoretically for pupils *and* the general public. This was to be carried out by a state commissioner who was to select and distribute the books. The reaction of pupils to this system is not recorded, but the citizenry was less than enchanted by the privilege of going to school buildings at odd hours to withdraw reading material. In 1860 the tax of one-tenth of a mill was abolished, after the state had distributed more than 300,000 volumes. This left schools with valuable libraries in storage, but no funds for their administration. The operating burden became so acute that the state of Ohio actually begged schools to give the books away. In 1867 the state commissioner noted the general puzzlement about the disposition of the stored books and suggested that they should be transferred almost anywhere—to existing subscription libraries or "to others that may yet be formed." In Cleveland the volumes were deposited at the Central High School, which was kept open on Saturday afternoons for withdrawals. Because no one was really responsible for security and maintenance, the volumes "wasted away"; there were only 2,200 remaining in early 1869.

Reform proposals were the only natural and forthcoming result of such a chaotic system. In 1867 the Boards of Education of Cincinnati, Cleveland, and Dayton petitioned the General Assembly of Ohio for authority to levy a tax for the maintenance of public libraries free to all citizens. This was enacted in a law which permitted boards of education in cities with populations over 20,000 to levy a tax of one-tenth of a mill for each dollar evaluation of their taxable property; such boards could also appoint a librarian and make all needful rules and regulations for the institution. In support of this law the chief protagonist in Cleveland was the incumbent superintendent of schools of the city. He was the Reverend Anson Smyth, whose career meandered between the pulpit and the classroom, and who has been dubiously called the "Father of the Cleveland Public Library." He had worked his way through Williams College and Yale Theological Seminary, graduating with honors. After early Congregational pastorates on the "frontier" of Michigan and in Toledo, he became superintendent of the Public Schools of Cleveland, and in that capacity helped in the development of the new law for libraries in 1867. Immediately after this successful municipal service he again returned to the church, and served Cleveland's North Presbyterian Church until the failure of his voice forced retirement.

The new law provided for a Cleveland library that was a part of the school system and would therefore be controlled by the Board of Education. The board did so directly (through a subsidiary library committee consisting of its own members) throughout the first decade of the library's existence, except for an unfortunate two-year period from 1871 to 1873. Beginning in 1878, the Ohio legislature placed control of the library in a committee of not less than three nor more than seven members who were chosen by the Board of Education. In 1883 the name of this committee was officially changed to the Public Library Board, a name it has since retained. In the same year the name of the institution was changed from Public School Library to Cleveland Public Library, as it is known today. It is apparent that the school-district concept has lasted a long time.

A CLEVELAND PUBLIC LIBRARY

And so it was that the Cleveland Public Library opened on 17 February 1869 on the third floor of the Northrup and Harrington Block on West Superior Avenue, near the present entrance to the garage of the Sheraton-Cleveland Hotel; in due course the first two floors would be occupied by the Hower and Higbee department store. The *Cleveland Herald* noted happily that the city had "at last got what it long needed—a public library free to all. The library room was adjacent to the Board of Education. The newspaper reports indicated that the space (twenty by eighty feet) was "fitted up in splendid style." The floor had a covering of matting, and the bookcases, with a capacity of 12,000, were considered sufficient for "some time to come." In actual fact, they proved adequate for only two years! The cost of bookcases, floor covering, desks, chairs, and other essential furniture amounted to the modest sum of a bit more than a thousand dollars.

At the formal dedication there were appropriate ceremonies. The president of the Board of Education (a banker named E. R. Perkins) talked about the tax structure and then got around to what he thought were weightier matters. He quoted Bacon's observation that "a library is a shrine to contain the names of deceased saints of literature," and manifested some concern that it might also include the remains of "not a few sinners." It was apparent that Perkins had no comprehension of the prominent role the library was to play in presenting authors and ideas, both living and dead. The Reverend Anson Smyth, who had sponsored the necessary state legislation for city libraries, bespoke his hope that the "library would grow and prosper for a thousand years under the fostering care of the board, who . . . ought always to put their very best men on the library committee." This turned out to be a pious, if sincere, aspiration which was not infrequently honored in the breach. Stephen Buhrer, the contemporary mayor of Cleveland who had little formal education, applauded the noble future of the library and hoped that it might retard "the descending cycles of damnation" into which the youth of the land were plunging.

The new Cleveland Public Library opened with 5,800 books, give or take a few—depending on who was doing the counting. Twenty-two hundred volumes were inherited from the old school-district library, plus 3,600 purchased with the proceeds of the new tax authorized by the state legislature in 1867. One reporter hailed the collection as a "wilderness of books." The new librarian was bold enough to say that they "covered the whole field of literature from grave to gay, from lively to severe." Actually the number of books in the Cleveland institution, as in many other libraries in the nineteenth century, was not impressive. The University of Vermont, founded in 1791, had accumulated only 30 books by 1803. At the University of North Carolina, founded in 1795, the president kept his institution's library in an upstairs bedroom of his home. Elsewhere academic libraries were placed in stray belfries or dormitories or museums. Most college libraries consisted of small and miscellaneous collections, which were open only an hour a week for withdrawals and returns, simply because there were not enough books to go around. As late as 1864 the prestigious Library of Congress had only 82,000 volumes in its collection; thirty years later it possessed no system of classification, no shelf list, no suitable catalogue, and a staff which was inadequate in both quantity and quality. The Cleveland Public Library had a long way to go, but it had company.

CHAPTER TWO

THE FIRST FIFTEEN YEARS:
Two Librarians Succumb to Pressure

TWO LIBRARIANS, 1869–84

DURING THE FIRST FIFTEEN YEARS of the Cleveland Public Library, from 1869 to 1884, two librarians resigned following investigations which were humiliating and demeaning for all concerned. Both librarians were the victims of governing boards, or subsidiaries thereof, which decided to go beyond the establishment of policy to actual day-by-day operation of the library. These encroachments by boards were generally ineffective; sometimes they were hilarious. Early in 1875, as an example, the minutes of the Board of Education reveal the following recommendation and action on a report from the Committee on the Library:

> That there is need of four spittoons in the reading room and your committee requests the privilege of purchasing the same. Granted.

A decade later the minutes, by this time of the Library Board, divulge that

> Mr. Kennedy reported that, pursuant to a vote of the Committee on Employees, he had requested the Janitor to light up the rooms of the Library and put out the lights and close the doors every evening. The request was complied with.

It was soon obvious that while assemblies and committees could legislate, appoint the president or director, raise money, and if nec-

21

essary investigate—they could not govern effectively. When they tried to do so, for example, by selecting books and personnel for the library, misunderstanding and distress were inevitable for both the board and the librarian. Beyond this basic difficulty Luther Melville Oviatt, the first librarian who served from 1869 to 1875, was a scholar who antagonized those board members who believed in the gospel of business efficiency *and* the concept that a library, like Sunday and trade schools, should purchase only those books which provided inspiration or vocational utility. The second librarian, Irad Beardsley (1875–84), was a businessman who tried desperately to support the inspirational and vocational role he thought was in demand, but who failed because he did not succeed in convincing the public, or a majority of the Library Board, that this was really the prime function of a library.

LUTHER MELVILLE OVIATT

Oviatt was born in Connecticut, as were many early settlers of the Western Reserve; he came west with his family to Dover (now Westlake) in Cuyahoga County. He attended Western Reserve College at Hudson where he graduated in 1857 with honors and a knowledge of literature and classical languages of which he was always proud, and justifiably so. A century later some of his writing would be classified as ornate, but in his day it was both acceptable and admired. As an example, when the new building for the Cleveland Central High School was dedicated in 1856 Oviatt would be on hand with a poem, which was declaimed as follows:

> Hail, glorious day—so long expected,
>   How many hearts beat high with pride
> To see that stately fane erected,
>   To shed a hallowed influence wide.
> Away with ignorance, all debasing,
>   Away with prejudice and hate—
> Live—ev'ry meaner trait effacing,
>   Shake off each fetter ere too late.

From college Oviatt had gone directly into the public school system of Cleveland, serving at various times as teacher, principal, and for two years as superintendent of instruction. Along the way, two of his students were John D. Rockefeller and Laura Spelman, who in time would become Mrs. Rockefeller. Oviatt classified John as a poor student with a disagreeable disposition who had to be whacked over the knuckles from time to time; his future wife was quite the opposite—slender, attractive, studious, a good scholar, and liked by everyone. He regarded it as a mystery that Miss Spelman could ever marry anyone like John D. Rockefeller. With a trained and well-stored mind, along with an abiding love for books plus intensive reading and a pleasant manner, Oviatt appeared to be more than adequately qualified for the position of librarian—the precise duties of which no one (including the board which hired him) understood. This was to be his undoing.

By the close of the first year the library had become so successful that its achievement provided some embarrassment; the demand for books had been so great that it could not be met as fully as desired. Families were restricted to one book each for a period not exceeding two weeks, and the same volume could not be renewed immediately. Because of limited personnel, library hours were restricted: the institution was open from 10:00 to 12:00 in the morning, 8:00 to 5:00 in the afternoon, and 7:00 to 9:00 in the evening on all "secular" days of the year. Oviatt's beginning salary was $1,500 a year, considerably less than he had received as principal or superintendent in the public schools. When the library opened there was one assistant with an annual salary of $400. Beyond these restrictions, made necessary by limited dollars and books, the board imposed a "closed shelf" system which made no sense in the absence of a catalogue. Rule 7 read that "Officers of the library shall alone be entitled to take books from, or replace them on, the library shelves." This meant that borrowers could ascertain what books the library had by word of mouth or by peering as best they could through the glass doors of the locked cases. The system of organizing books by subject matter in general fields of knowledge—created by Melvil Dewey, the testy genius of global reforms that included classification and new spelling systems and the adoption of the metric system—would not appear until 1876. It was therefore not possible for Oviatt, as the poet put it,

> To tag upon each author in large labels
>   that are gluey
> Their place in Thought's great Pantheon in
>   decimals of Dewey.

Oviatt adopted the only system in common use at the time. It was based on shelves. Each book was given two numbers, the first showing the consecutive order of the book on the shelf, and the other corresponding to that of the shelf on which the book had been placed. This signified, as the librarian explained it, that "Thackeray's *Vanity Fair* is marked No. 4, Shelf 282, showing that it is the 4th book on the 282nd shelf." This also meant that, once a shelf was full, additional or duplicate books purchased on the same subject had to be placed on other shelves and separated from similar or identical ones already in the library, a very serious disadvantage. But Oviatt applauded the system, which he claimed was so simple that "it was within the comprehension of a child." Perhaps the young understood it; his elderly critics did not. Later they would characterize the "shelf-number" system as "the most peculiar that was ever invented, and in some respects the most fantastic that was ever imagined."

In spite of restrictions, necessary or not, the number of withdrawals from the library was remarkable. Almost half of the entire number of volumes was in constant circulation; readers borrowed more than sixty-five thousand books during the first year, an average of more than eleven borrowers per book. Some relief was made possible by a gift from the German citizens of Cleveland, who had recently celebrated the hundredth anniversary of the birth of Alexander von Humboldt, the famous scientist and explorer. They decided that they could best honor the memory of their countryman by making a contribution for the purchase of standard German works for the Cleveland Public Library. The gift amounted to $1,000, a considerable sum when it is recalled that the entire receipts for the library in its first year were less than $6,500.

WHAT SHOULD PEOPLE READ?

It is apparent that no library can contain all the books in the world; even if it did, it could not bring all of its offerings to the attention of its readers. Librarians in every age have had to make hard decisions on what books should be purchased. Lyman Bryson once observed that librarians have never been able to avoid the exercise of "a certain amount of choice as to what intellectual experiences other people should have." It follows that the optimum objective of every librarian is to present, "without arrogance to the ignorant and without flattering the learned," the best reading for the greatest number at the least cost, as Melvil Dewey once phrased it. In this regard Oviatt was progressive; he wanted to provide books which would interest the mechanic, the businessman, the scholar, *and* the reader—child or adult—who wanted entertainment and diversion. He believed firmly that the standard books of instruction must be provided; he was just as certain that those who wanted adventure and whimsy and fancy should be served. In this philosophy he was not only ahead of his time—he completely outdistanced the conservatism of some members of his governing board. This ideological gap would be productive of pain and anguish for all concerned.

On the subject of children's literature, Oviatt was completely modern. He had the highest regard for the publishers of his day who were turning out books for juveniles that were attractive in style, illustration, and content—so much so that many adults were reading them. He manifested courage in criticizing the *Uncle Tom's Cabins* and the *Godey's Lady's Books* which had been adored in the past and were still venerated by the Establishment in Oviatt's time. He wrote:

> There may be some persons who estimate all books by the standard of Gradgrind in Dickens' *Hard Times*. "Facts, Sir! We want nothing but facts. They are the only things of any value in the world"; and the question in their view is forever settled. Yet is there nothing valuable in the cultivation of fancy—of imagination—of all those fairy illusions of grace and

beauty, glorious and fleeting, which shed a golden glow over the prosaic realities of life? Without these, what would become of poetry, sculpture, painting and music. . . .

True it is that all the children's books may not contain "facts," such as would satisfy the soul of a Gradgrind. Yet those who, without examining them, measure the literary standard of juvenile books now by what it was twenty or thirty years since, must have enjoyed a Rip Van Winkle sleep since that time. Then, those remarkable biographies of impossible children, "who always died young," as it was meet they should do to avoid contamination, in a world where their very incomparable excellence repelled all inclination to rival their lives—or their early deaths—constituted the chief staple of our Sunday School and Christmas books, out of which categories they were seldom found.

In 1874 he was ready and willing to defend books purchased during the past year (40 percent of which had been novels), because their acquisition was "for the express purpose of popularizing the institution and making it an attractive center of resort for all classes of readers." He went on to point out:

It is indisputably the fact that most persons—probably seven-eighths of all readers—read for amusement, or at least entertainment merely, rather than instruction; and it would certainly seem to be slightly verging on assumption, at least, for the remaining one-eighth, who may wish to read nothing but scientific or standard works, to claim that the latter classes exclusively, or chiefly, should be placed in the Library, regardless of the wishes or preferences of the great majority of general readers, when the institution in its entirety is controlled by the public voice, and subject to such modifications of its character as the public may demand.

Oviatt's antagonists, then and now, are in a position to cite evidence, convincing to them, that works of imagination—including novels—leave a great deal to be desired. To the surprise of modern liberals, Thomas Jefferson was of the opinion that girls should not read novels because they produced "a bloated imagination, sickly judgment, and disgust toward all the real business of life." In the nineteenth century *Tom Jones* as well as the works of Hardy and Zola would be closed out of some libraries. Many of the clergy would conclude that a public library, with its undesirable novels, was "an evergreen tree of diabolical knowledge." In Detroit the Library Commission believed fiction to be an instrument of the devil which tended to corrupt and degrade. The Detroit *Free Press*, belying its name, was in agreement; in 1877 it solemnly related that it

> could tell of one young woman . . . of fine education, who gratified a vitiated taste for novel reading till her reason was overthrown, and she has, in consequence, been for several years an inmate of an insane asylum.

The members of the commission were pained by the expense of placing "romantic trash" on the shelves of the Detroit Public Library, and their suffering became more acute as they saw borrowers passing the classics by as they lugged fiction home by the armful. They waged a constant but losing battle in an attempt to wean readers away from light fiction to the heavier intellectual fare that only "worthwhile" books would provide.

The Cleveland Board of Education reflected the same philosophy. In 1870 it decreed that the number of books allowed to each family would be increased from one to two, "*provided* at least one of them was a standard or instructive work"; it was apparent that the board was attempting to increase the circulation of the "worthwhile" books. A prominent member of the board, its president for several years, was worried about both the library and its librarian. This board member was Moses G. Watterson, then a clerk in the mayor's office who later became the treasurer of Cuyahoga County. In Watterson's opinion it was apparent that Oviatt's "extensive literary researches had disqualified him for ordinary business . . ."; he knew too much about books and not enough about practical methods of accounting and controlled instruction. The library was popular but for the wrong reason; more than half the books read were fiction—and most of the readers were impressionable youth between ten and twenty years of age. Watterson was convinced that this encouragement, for which the new library was responsible, developed "an unnatural appetite for exaggeration, without regard for the lesson sought to be impressed," which in time would result in "intellectual dissipation rather than intelligence." In his judgment the library was undermining the school; he was convinced that "this constant and indiscriminate reading of fiction" would usurp the place of the classroom—that this "increase of appetite would produce not minds disciplined and equipped for work, but [minds] untrained, seeking and only satisfied with unprofitable amusement."

If Watterson had known that in 1940 the Cleveland Public Library would own 651 copies of *Gone With the Wind* (plus 4 more in Braille) without satisfying the popular demand for that robust and lusty novel, he might have suffered his first coronary occlusion. He could very well have concluded, as would-be critics do in every generation, that "the trash they're writing these days isn't what it used to be."

OVIATT VS. BOARD OF MANAGERS

Because some members of the Board of Education did not agree with Oviatt's concept of what a library should be and should do, it was inevitable that there would be disagreement over matters of policy. There were also differences over administration when a Board of Managers attempted to take over the direction of the institution as well as the selection of books and personnel. Among other things, the managers employed the director of the Cincinnati Public Library to select books for its Cleveland counterpart! At this point the position of librarian in Cleveland became superfluous, requiring the parent Board of Education to make a decision whether it wanted to keep its librarian or its Board of Managers.

During the first two years, the Cleveland Public Library was the direct responsibility of the Board of Education through its Committee on the Library. Then in October 1871, it created and elected a Board of Managers of the library, consisting of six citizens who were not members of the Board of Education. The reason given was that the annual selection of books was too great a task for the librarian, a responsibility that would now be assumed by the Board of Managers; in practice, as has been noted, the managers were not equal to this challenge and needed rescue by Cincinnati. By August of the next year (1872) this administrative body, backed by Watterson on the Board of Education, asked for the dismissal of Oviatt and the promotion of a "Miss Merriam," the assistant librarian and cataloguer, to the top position (her given name remains a mystery in official reports and newspaper accounts). The Board of Managers supported its recommendation by citing several minor reasons and one major objection to Oviatt. Among the minor reasons were the following: the classification system was "fantastic"; the administration of accounts was "bewildering"; Oviatt had hired his nephew as an evening assistant at a cost of fifty dollars taken from the salary of another library assistant; and he had violated the "one-man, one-book" rule by lending seven books at one time to one person. The major charge was that the librarian had violated Rule 7, which prohibited the opening of bookcases to the public, with the result that "the books were wholly unprotected against the careless or the dishonest." Three hundred ninety volumes had been lost in the past fiscal year. The managers stated that in no library did the public have access to the books, lest the taxpayer suffer the unnecessary expense of paying for books that had disappeared.

Oviatt met this attack with a rebuttal that was complete in coverage and robust in language. He stated that the report against him was a "work of fiction" written by two antagonists on the Board of Managers who, "with an apparent reckless indifference to the truth or falsity of their allegations, and a kaleidoscopic coloring and perversion of simple fact, . . . rushed their imaginary bantering to the midnight press to be printed, and, as it was hoped, read and believed by those who prefer fiction to fact, and accusation to refutation." He said that the classification system was not a fanciful one of his own but had been adopted only after consultation about the practices in other libraries. He found nothing that was abstruse or bewildering in his accounts. His nephew had been engaged because he spoke German and was willing to work at night, and the assistant librarian was delighted to be relieved of night duties—even at a price. He had indeed made an exception by issuing seven books to one person; she was a teacher in the public schools, who needed them for a temporary period in her classes.

On the question of Rule 7 and the missing books, Oviatt asserted that overcrowding and the absence of a catalogue were responsible. The library room was frequently so thronged that it was difficult to pass through the crowd. Without a catalogue the only way potential borrowers could ascertain what books were available was to look at them. Shelves were therefore opened, with the librarian or assistant standing by—unless temporarily called away —to lock the cases after a selection had been made. There was obviously some undesirable exposure of books, a problem which had also confronted the public libraries in Boston and St. Louis in their earlier days. In Cleveland one volume was missing for every 1,660 withdrawn, and most of the lost books were in the juvenile category. Their highest average value would not exceed 60 cents each, or $234 for the whole, if none of the 390 were returned—and experience showed that one-third of them would ultimately reappear. Oviatt concluded that this was not "a very alarming showing, certainly, when by the very arrangement of our cramped library room the public must, and do, have a certain amount of access to the books, which the attendants are handling, which no rules, however stringent can entirely obviate, till a printed catalogue is prepared, and the books are selected from that alone, with a railing and desks between the visitors and attendants."

In normal circumstances one would expect these charges and countercharges to be confined to appropriate board meetings. In this instance they were not, and Oviatt found himself involved in a furious newspaper controversy in which every allegation and innuendo was published, for the edification of the public and his own discomfiture. On the journalistic side the institutional antagonists were two Republican newspapers (the *Herald* and the *Leader*) against a Democratic one (the *Plain Dealer*). Editorially the contest pitted J. H. A. (John Herbert Aloysius) Bone of the *Herald* and Edwin Cowles of the *Leader* against Thomas A. Stow of the *Plain Dealer*. Additionally Stow, as a member of the Board of Education, supported Oviatt—and Bone as one of the Board of Managers asked for the dismissal of the librarian. Bone was an Englishman who came to Cleveland in 1851 and at one time or another filled virtually every position on the editorial staff of the *Herald* from reporter to editor in chief. Later, when the *Herald* was absorbed by the *Plain Dealer* (1885), he was one of the "assets" incorporated into the newspaper that had previously been his bitter rival and, as chief of the editorial forces of the *Plain Dealer*, remained an asset for the last two decades of his life. Bone's pen dripped vitriol. Once when Stow questioned the competence of a music teacher named Stewart, Bone questioned both the integrity and the musical virtuosity of Stow in this language:

> Undoubtedly, Mr. Stow, in his juvenile days, was wont to jerk the gentle jews-harp, and we understand that he is an accomplished artist on the accordian, besides being a capital whistler, and no doubt Professor Stewart would gladly avail himself of the opportunity to take a course in music from Professor Stow.

Stow had begun his career on the *Plain Dealer* as a compositor, became foreman of the shop, and spent the rest of his days as one of the editors on the paper. He had a yen for politics but, except for the Board of Education, the public looked the other way when he ran for office. Edwin Cowles worked all his life under a serious physical disability; it was a deafness that would have discouraged those of weaker character. In spite of his handicap, as historian Elbert J. Benton once noted, he became an editor "of remarkable courage, unchangeable convictions, and relentless dogmatisms. . . ." He was prominent as a founder of the Republican party and as the editor of the most prestigious paper in Cleveland; in his day the *Leader* measured up to its name. Its political bias was so pronounced that, according to a knowledgeable contemporary, it "rated most Democrats as traitors and canonized even the least worthy of the Republican leaders of the period." It did so in such strong language that Cowles sometimes found it necessary to apologize in order to forestall suits for libel. As an example, in 1876 the *Leader* published the following commentary on the editor of the *Plain Dealer:*

When the snarling, ill-conditioned editor of the Cleveland *Plain Dealer* gets drunk and falls out of the third story window of his boarding house, people in the street who catch a glimpse of his florid face and sanguinary hair cry out: "Behold, that blazing meteor!" They afterward gather up the quivering, glutinous, odorous mass on the pavement, sweep it up and carry it in the house and put it to bed.

In regard to the library, journalistic charges and countercharges were exchanged in great profusion during the summer of 1872. The *Leader* and the *Herald* published in fulsome detail the charges of the Board of Managers against Oviatt and its recommendation that he be replaced by Miss Merriam. From his defensive position on the *Plain Dealer*, Stow "stripped down to his suspenders" (as Bone reported it) and charged that this publicity was partisan, incompetent, and untruthful. In Stow's judgment Oviatt had established an excellent record; "he is a man," said Stow, "of literary tastes and culture, of remarkable memory, a very cyclopedia of book information." By contrast with other public libraries, the record of Cleveland, with its small staff and slender budget, was enviable in its service to the populace. Boston Public Library, with fifty-four employees and 131,000 volumes had only 231,000 books withdrawn during the past year; Cleveland's library, with four employees and but 13,000 volumes, had 100,000 withdrawn. Twenty employees of the Cincinnati Public Library, whose salaries totalled $12,362, had circulated 190,000 books; the cost for Oviatt and his three assistants was $2,650. Stow and the *Plain Dealer* were particularly bitter about the two "prime movers" on the Board of Managers; they were Bone and the Reverend Samuel Wolcott, pastor of the Plymouth Congregational Church. This duo was following a policy of "anything to beat Mr. Oviatt" and were more interested in the persecution of the librarian than in the good name and character of the library. In their efforts they "had descended to the lowest trickery of a Tombs lawyer to carry a point in their favor." Bone was dubbed "the valiant Don Quixote of the *Herald*." To satisfy a grudge against the librarian he had seized every opportunity "of airing his spite, and by magnifying molehills into mountains [of] distorting images by his convex mirror of thought" he had caused the Board of Education much trouble. Stow employed the rapier (rather than the customary bludgeon) against the Reverend Mr. Wolcott. He said that in the course of his life he had never seen such a vindictive report made by men, "some of whom had the reputation of being Christian gentlemen." In his younger days, he added, he had been taught that "no one should bear false witness against his neighbor, and these gentlemen had in their distortion of the facts . . . virtually broken the commandment."

In early August 1872 Stow, who was then chairman of the Library Committee of the Board of Education, characterized the Board of Managers as a "fifth wheel" that ought to be abolished. The extra wheel was not only superfluous; it was also insubordinate. Stow said that some members of the Board of Managers, particularly Messrs. Bone and Wolcott, had assailed seven members of the Board of Education, both in public and private. Apparently the "seven" were not pleased; by a vote of seven to five the parent Board of Education agreed to ask for the resignations of the Board of Managers—"because of the insubordination of the managers, and on account of the disrespectful language which part of the managers had used of late respecting the board." Nonetheless, the "insubordinate" members maintained their status and did not submit their resignations for almost a year.

In October 1872 a motion to dispense with the services of the librarian was lost by a "decided vote" of the Board of Education. In March 1873 Miss Merriam resigned; Stow had employed a curious xenophobic argument in opposing her candidacy. He said that she might be a lady of genius but had not demonstrated such brilliance to this point; furthermore "she comes here from the East and from a people very unlike in many respects our people, having tastes and customs dissimilar to a certain extent." In late June 1873 the moribund Board of Managers, holding on in spite of the request for its resignation, recommended Andrew Freese for librarian in place of Oviatt. Freese was an able but ailing educator who had preceded Oviatt as the superintendent of schools. The Board of Education defeated this proposal by a vote of eleven to five. Following this action four members of the Board of Managers, including Bone and Wolcott, resigned in high dudgeon; their resignations happened to be submitted, quite interestingly, on Bastille

Day, 1873. Because the Board of Managers now had no quorum, Stow logically and joyfully asked for its abolition. His motion carried by a vote of nine to four. The action meant that the Board of Education resumed its former direct control through the small Library Committee. This type of governance remained in force until 1879 when, by state law, responsibility was vested in an appointed library board—the pattern that has been followed to this day.

By this time Oviatt had every reason to breathe easily; instead he let out a hyperbolic emanation that was infuriating to his enemies and embarrassing to his friends. In the Annual Report of 1873 he thanked the Board of Education for its support and pledged that from this point:

> The Library will prove to be a perennial literary fountain, with abundant and never-failing resources for the thirsty travelers in the boundless fields of knowledge which know no horizon. Let them partake of this fount freely, and renew again and again the draught, till they rise at last refreshed and invigorated from the influence of this noblest elixir, and go forth to fight the battle of life with a power like that which the earth-born Antaeus felt at the touch of his mighty mother.

In spite of a decided tendency toward orotundity which occasionally led him to effusions of this kind, Oviatt merited praise as a gentle scholar and book lover who performed quite well in a most difficult assignment with few precedents for guidance and direction. His victory, over powerful opponents, was both temporary and Pyrrhic. Because of illness in the summer of 1874 he missed the annual two-week inventory of the library (until 1884 the library was closed for a fortnight each August to take stock and count the books). In late June 1875 Oviatt resigned with regret. His letter read as follows:

> For months past I have struggled against a depressing physical languor, the result, in the opinion of my medical advisor, of long confinement, anxiety, and overwork in my vocation. At its commencement, thinking it only temporary, I resolved to overcome it, and believed that I could. Fate or nature has

proved stronger than will or belief. I am convinced by my own feelings, as well as by medical advice, that my health can only be regained by a long interval of exemption from all care, labor, and responsibility.

The Board of Education accepted the resignation with comparable regret, expressing its "earnest hope that his health, impaired as we feel in our service, may be speedily restored."

Alas! several years were required to bring the hoped-for recovery, and when some degree of health was restored Oviatt had no interest in returning to an educational career—in either school or library. During some of his remaining years he sold real estate. Death came in 1889, when he was sixty-eight years of age. The obituary in the *Plain Dealer* stated that he succumbed to old age. One can only wonder, as Oviatt had stated, whether it was "fate or nature" that had "proved stronger than will or belief." Had he lived a few years longer he would have enjoyed Sam Walter Foss' ode to the head librarian, which reflected so accurately the problems Oviatt himself had encountered:

> Sing, O Muse! the Head Librarian and the joy
>   that's her'n or his'n.
> See him, see her, his or her head weighted
>   with the lore of time,
> Trying to expend a dollar when he only
>   has a dime.
>
> . . . .
>
> See him 'mid his myriad volumes listening
>   to the gladsome din
> Of the loud vociferant public that no book
>   is ever "in";
> And he hears the fierce taxpayer evermore
>   lift up the shout
> That the book he needs forever is the
>   book forever "out".
> How they rage, the numerous sinners, when he
>   tries to please the saint,
> When he tries to please the sinners hear the
>   numerous saints' complaints;

And some want a Bowdlered Hemans and an
    expurgated Watts;
Some are shocked beyond expression at the
    sign of naked thoughts,

. . . .

Oh, the gamesome glad Librarian gushing with
    his gurgling glee!—
Here I hand my resignation,—'tis a theme too
    big for me.

IRAD L. BEARDSLEY

Irad L. Beardsley, who was the librarian from 1875 to 1884, was
the antithesis of Oviatt in background, philosophy, and experience.
He was a businessman with no college education who was engaged
in a great variety of enterprises and activities during the course of
his life. Born in western New York he had come at the age of twenty
to Cleveland, where he was involved in the wholesale grocery
business. Gold in California beckoned in 1849, and Beardsley went
off to find it; as was the case with most of the "forty-niners," he returned with loads of experience and no money. For the next fifteen
years he first kept books for the *Plain Dealer* and the *Cleveland
Leader*, and then returned to his first occupation as a wholesale
grocer in foreign and domestic fruits. After his tenure as librarian
in Cleveland he became an auditor of the Standard Oil Company
with headquarters in New York. His son became private secretary
to Henry M. Flagler, the financier who put Florida and Key West
on rails. For this reason Beardsley began to spend his winters in the
South; he died in St. Augustine, at the age of eighty-two in 1901.

On the basis of this curriculum vitae, one can only marvel over
his selection as librarian of the Cleveland Public Library. No satisfactory explanation for the appointment has ever been offered—
unless it is the discouraging one that the Board of Education was
more interested in a bookkeeper who could count the volumes in
and out, than it was in a librarian who read and appreciated the
books which are the basic material of all libraries. When Beardsley
succeeded Oviatt in 1875, the *Cleveland Leader* observed that the
Plain Dealer could no longer howl about nepotism because the new

librarian was Editor Tom Stow's father-in-law, and Stow was not only with the *Plain Dealer* but was the chairman of the Library Committee of the Board of Education. Unfortunately, the *Leader's* basic charge was wrong and it had to "eat crow"; Stow's family connection with the librarian was not a close one—he had married a niece of Beardsley. The *Leader*, presumably fearful of a suit for libel, therefore acknowledged its error, admitted that the new librarian was not appointed primarily because of his relationship to Stow, and stated that Beardsley would serve well in the library. This journalistic sparring did not answer satisfactorily what real qualifications the new librarian had for the position. Beardsley himself did nothing to explain the mystery. In his first annual report he was honest enough to admit that he had entered upon his duties "under peculiar circumstances, and unfamiliar with the workings of the Library. . . ."

OVIATT AND BEARDSLEY: A COMPARISON

Beardsley and Oviatt were poles apart in their basic philosophy about the kind of service a public library should provide. Oviatt had been inclined to interpret Rule 7 broadly and allow borrowers to handle books, he approved of those who wanted to read for diversion or amusement, and he had a tolerance for fiction that was unusual in its day. Beardsley proposed to keep books out of borrower's hands until they had been formally withdrawn, he thought the library should concentrate its efforts on the stern purposes of enlightening and improving the mind, and he disapproved of the reading of fiction.

On the question of access to books, Oviatt's nemesis, Moses G. Watterson (as president of the Board of Education) was still fretting—as Beardsley assumed office—about the opportunities which had been provided for unscrupulous persons to carry books out of the library with no record whatsoever. Beardsley got the message and took a firm stance against anything approaching the open shelf. In his Annual Report of 1880 he said:

> So far as I am informed none of the more important libraries of the country permit indiscriminate access to books and for

reasons that are forcible: it prevents keeping the books in order, the assistants are interrupted in their duties and the losses by pilfering become serious. The safety of property is only assured by denying general access to the shelves.

Beardsley therefore barred the public from the shelves and allowed them to handle the books only after an assistant had brought them to the registration desk for withdrawal by the borrower. Books were no longer placed upon the ledges of cases for public scrutiny, a procedure Beardsley claimed had involved the handling of as many as 500 volumes per day. Restrictions on public access also reduced the loss of books—although the librarian was still trying to explain, in his third year on the job, why there was a deficit of 151 books under his new system of supposedly foolproof surveillance. Beardsley liked to count books in and out, and would have appreciated the story about the stern and serious Harvard librarian, John Sibley. He is supposed to have met President Charles W. Eliot while crossing the Yard. The president could not help but notice that his librarian had an unaccustomed smile on his face. Asked the reason for his happiness, Sibley replied: "The Library is locked and every book is in it but two, and I know where they are and I am going after them." The University of Michigan solved this problem in another way; from 1856 to 1906 no books were permitted to be taken out of its library.

Beardsley had an aversion for novels and tried to discourage them while maintaining patronage of the library. It was an impossible goal, given human nature and interests as they are, and he did not succeed in his attempt to make the library a "true educator." Nonetheless he tried, by reducing the purchase of fiction and by "condemning" as many books as possible in this category among those already on the shelves. He delighted in homilies against the evils of light and frivolous reading. As far as children were involved he was convinced that most juvenile books were not productive of good "because they inculcated exaggerated ideas, and put out of view the stern realities of life to the rising generation." There were also the adults, who had arrived at years of maturity but were just as fickle as their children. They read novels whose teachings were false because their tendencies were "demoralizing, calculated to dwarf the minds of the ignorant, to invite ephemeral and sensual ideas which are diametrically opposed to religion, to morality, and to the discipline necessary to fill an honorable position in life." He was also certain that readers of fiction took less care of books and that they were notorious for their delinquency; Beardsley claimed that novels comprised seven out of eight books not returned on time. He did not believe that readers of novels "progressed" to more demanding and desirable material, as he defined it. "Having observed closely for several years," he wrote, "I am prepared to say that of the class we designate as novel readers, and who are steady drawers of sensational books, few or none advance to a better class of literature."

NEW QUARTERS AND FINANCIAL CRISIS

In the 1870s the library suffered the misfortune of moving three times in four years. Two of the moves occurred in 1875, certainly something of a record for a library of a major city. In January of 1875, while Oviatt was still librarian, the Board of Education had leased rooms for the institution in the new Clark Block on West Superior Street, at an annual rental of $2,500. At the same time, Leonard Case erected the block named for him at East Third and Superior, a building that was ultimately razed to make room for the present main library. The Case Block was a large structure that cost almost a million dollars, a huge sum in those days. Municipal officials leased it as the City Hall for twenty-five years at an annual rental of $36,000. The building was so large that excess space was sublet by the city to retail stores on the ground level, to artists in studios on the top floor, and to the Cleveland Public Library. The last move was taken by the library because the available quarters in the new City Hall were much more convenient for the public. The Board of Education therefore negotiated a release from its recent contract with the owners of the Clark Block but had to pay a bonus of six months' rent in order to achieve a discharge from the long-term contract. The anguish and travail suffered by Oviatt (who supervised the first move) and by Beardsley and especially by their staffs, from the traumas of two moves in one year, were not calculated in dollars by the Board of Education or by any other authority at the time.

The "commodious and elegant apartments" now available to the library in the City Hall (one reading room on the ground floor and four rooms on the second level) made possible for the first time a separate reference department and newspaper room as well as the circulation department with which the institution had begun its operations in a single room. The first "Library of Reference" was large enough (twenty-two by fifty-two feet) for 2,500 volumes; Beardsley boasted that it attracted the "attention of many culti- vated and refined persons" and that there was no place in Cleveland "where a leisure hour could be more pleasantly and profitably spent." The newspaper room began with thirty dailies and twenty- six weeklies in English, plus foreign newspapers which included three in German and two in Bohemian. Beardsley was disturbed by the mutilation of papers which soon became a serious evil, defying detection in spite of the vigilance of the attendant in charge. His only solution was to offer rewards for informers, a suggestion which was fortunately not endorsed by the Board of Education.

In spite of all the advantages offered by the Case Block, four years later the library moved again. It followed the Board of Educa- tion to the second and third floors of the old Central High School building at 850 Euclid Avenue, just west of Ninth Street on the future site of the Citizens Building. Central High School had been built in 1856 at a cost of $20,000. Visitors came long distances to see its marvels, and many taxpayers then considered it "a piece of vicious extravagance." By 1879 it was no extravagance, but the library remained there for twenty-two years (1879–1901). In this building, the reference department and the general reading room were placed on the third floor. On the second was the circulation department protected from the public by a high counter running the entire width of the room, in front of which borrowers stood while waiting for books. Back of the counter stood the tall book- cases, which were not available to the public; the aisles between these cases formed alcoves which were dimly lighted by smoky windows and gas jets.

Unfortunately Beardsley found himself with this additional space but a restricted budget. For almost a decade the Cleveland library had been operated, as were the libraries in Cincinnati and other Ohio cities, on the assumption that the one-tenth-of-a-mill property tax could be used for the purchase of books and their bindings and that the Board of Education would pay salaries and costs of administration. In May 1877 the city solicitor of Cleveland ruled that no expenses of the library could be paid from the school fund. This created a first-class crisis which the library met by juggling accounts as best it could, at the same time closing the institution completely for more than two months, reducing the librarian's salary from $2,100 to less than $1,500, and cutting the staff from fourteen to two—which meant that the new reference and newspaper rooms had to be closed. During the next year the Ohio State legislature authorized an additional levy for administration which rescued the library from this impossible situation. Nonetheless, during the brief and unnecessary period of severe fiscal drought the library was hardly able to function at all.

BRECKENRIDGE VS. BEARDSLEY

During his last four years as librarian, criticism of Beardsley increased. In 1880 the *Penny Press* charged that his staff was regularly tardy, to the inconvenience of patrons. There had been numerous complaints that the library was not open for withdrawal of books until 10:00 A.M. instead of the stated time of 8:00 A.M. When asked for an explanation Beardsley replied that he and his assistants had to spend two hours each morning rearranging the books; the reason was "that the books and shelves were so mixed during the day that they could not be handled before this two hours' hard labor in the morning from 8 to 10 o'clock." The *Penny Press* had some suspicion about this claim and sent a reporter to verify the "two hours' hard labor" of Beardsley's assistants. On the first morning he found that the four "overworked assistants" arrived at the library rooms, not at 8:00 A.M. but at the following morning hours: the first at 9:15, the second at 9:18, the third at 9:50, and the fourth at 9:55. The reporter's surveillance on the second day revealed the same pattern. He also ascertained that on the first day forty-eight potential patrons had arrived in the early hours to withdraw books but had found the library's doors locked; on the second day the number so turned away was thirty-six. Noting that the average of those turned away was forty-two per day, the *Penny Press* estimated that with the library open 290 days in the year, a total of more than twelve thousand taxpayers "are deprived of their right by their servants." The newspaper had an explanation which was found in its concluding "punch" line:

Cause: pure laziness.

Four years later on 23 June 1884 a member and former secretary of the Library Board, a lawyer named Louis Breckenridge, presented fourteen charges against Beardsley, who was brought into the meeting to hear the accusations. The librarian asked for a week in which to make a formal reply in his defense, and in subsequent hearings before the board was represented by his own legal counsel. There were five long hearings over a period of more than a month, and the last of the sessions went on for six hours from 2:00 P.M. to 8:00 P.M. During these confrontations, counsel for Beardsley were seated at one end of a long table with a formidable array of books and documents before them; Library Board member Breckenridge was at the other end surrounded with a similar collection of carefully assorted manuscripts, all within easy reach. John Griswold White, a lawyer who was the greatest patron the Cleveland Public Library has ever had, was in the chair as moderator during the hearings; he had been appointed to the Library Board for his first term less than two months earlier and was now receiving a baptism of fire.

The first twelve of fourteen charges involved inconsequential if controversial details of administration concerning the ordering of books from abroad, the accounting for monies received, the procedure for ordering certain periodicals, and the problem of taking reference books out of the library. A majority of the Library Board acquitted Beardsley on ten of these twelve charges. The members felt, by a vote of four to three, that he had been lax in ordering periodicals and in permitting reference books to leave the library. The most interesting of this first group of charges involved the ordering of books from abroad, in the name of the library, which were not really destined for that institution. It soon developed that Beardsley had done so only because three members of the Library Board at that time—the Reverend John W. Brown (then its president), Justice of the Peace L. F. Bauder, and lawyer Henry C. Ranney—had looked over catalogues of secondhand books and had asked that he order them from Europe. Beardsley had wondered about the propriety of his action and had queried the Customs House about it. He had been told that there would be no violation unless the volumes ordered were less than twenty years old; those of greater age entered duty-free in any case. The books that interested the three board members were of considerable vintage and would be free of duty. Ultimately the Library Board decided that Beardsley had not acted in this connection for his own personal gain; it also came to the conclusion that the board members involved at that time were less than discreet and circumspect. In due course it therefore resolved:

> That while the Board sees no wrong in the practice formerly prevailing of permitting non-dutiable books, not intended for the Library, to be enclosed with books imported by the Library. Yet as this practice is liable to misconstruction, and has given rise to suspicion and disputes, it is the opinion of this Board that nothing not intended for the Library should be consigned to, or imported by the Library.

At this point the clergyman, the lawyer, and the justice of the peace —who had been involved as board members in the exercise—had obviously been consigned to the penalty box.

The newspapers again covered the charges and countercharges in full detail, as they had with Oviatt; by contrast, this time all of them were friendly to Librarian Beardsley rather than board member Breckenridge and inserted editorial comments in their news stories which were indicative of their bias. The *Plain Dealer* and the *Leader* referred to the "hair-pulling" and "hammer-and-tongs" activity that was going on as Breckenridge and Beardsley sat with glaring eyes and flushed cheeks across from one another, differing only in that Breckenridge had an "additional glitter in his one good eye which foretold evil for some one." At one point in the confrontation, Breckenridge had actually dubbed his opponents as representatives of the "missing link," a sophisticated and highly contemporary reference to the brand-new Darwinian concept. The reporter from the *Plain Dealer* noted that Breckenridge was so sanguine that Beardsley would be declared dishonest as well as incompetent, that he asserted that if he did not carry his point the reporter could claim his (Breckenridge's) head. In the light of the ambivalent ultimate decision—which adjudged Beardsley incompetent but not dishonest—the reporter stated that it was his intention to call the Cleveland Medical College to ascertain if they needed a good specimen of a sorehead, like Breckenridge's, for their museum.

As noted earlier, the board found Beardsley guilty, by a vote of four to three, on only two of the first twelve charges—and these two dealt with minor accusations concerning the withdrawal of reference books and the purchase of certain periodicals. Beyond these initial dozen charges, however, the board (by a similar vote of four to three) sustained the charges in the final two, which were both vital and critical. These accused the librarian of lacking executive ability, of gross carelessness, of a disposition to usurp authority and of a tendency to disobey the rules of the board. The *Penny Press* tried to excuse Beardsley by pointing out that Breckenridge had the "finest, most unadulterated . . . 'gall' ever exhibited in this part of the country." It went on to say that in such a close vote "not only did this intellectual giant act as prosecuting witness, attorney for L. Breckenridge, judge and jury, but also as executioner." Although Breckenridge had a legal right to vote, the newspaper said that "common decency" should have prevented him from sitting in judgment on charges which he had brought himself; Beardsley had therefore been the "victim of a very broad farce." The only thing wrong with this argument was that Breckenridge was not one of the majority of four which finally condemned Beardsley for incompetence. He voted in the minority of three, presumably because he believed that the librarian should have been found dishonest as well as incompetent. In the final tally, had Breckenridge abstained from voting as the *Penny Press* suggested, the result of four to two against Beardsley would have been even more conclusive.

In this unfortunate imbroglio there was fault on both sides. Breckenridge was a domineering board member who wanted to personally administer the library as well as to establish policy for it. At one point he admitted, "I consider Beardsley . . . merely as a hired hand"; under the circumstances it is not surprising that Beardsley did not hold Breckenridge in high regard. On the other hand, there is no question that a majority of the board—exclusive of Breckenridge—did not find Beardsley qualified to be a librarian. After this, his only recourse was resignation, which he accomplished with an illogicality embarrassing to all concerned. He thanked the board for a "vindication" which could only have been apparent to him, but he nonetheless thought it best to depart. His final statement, which was injudicious and understandable and sad, read as follows:

> At the close of the malicious investigation instituted against me by a member of the Board, and my conduct as a man and as a librarian having been vindicated, I came to the decision that to continue in a service where a portion of those who manage the Library were at enmity toward me, would be too distasteful to my feelings to continue longer an employment which has extended over a period of nine years. What has been done during that time to build up the institution under your control is left to the judgment and verdict of the public.

CHAPTER THREE

THE FIRST OF THE GREAT TRIUMVIRATE:
William Howard Brett

ALWAYS A BOOKMAN

In 1884, when the Cleveland Public Library reached the age of fifteen, it was a poor institution indeed. For one reason or another the first two librarians, and the boards which were supposed to give them support and encouragement, had achieved the dubious distinction of making it one of the worst metropolitan libraries in the nation. After that, in its middle fifty-four years from 1884 to 1938, the Cleveland Public Library became the preeminent institution it is today—not only in the United States but in the world. For this transformation a remarkable triumvirate was responsible: its members were William Howard Brett, John Griswold White, and Linda Eastman.

Brett was the son of idealistic parents. His father, a descendant of John Alden, came west to participate in a short-lived utopian experiment known as the Trumbull Phalanx, one of the more than forty ventures in communal living which sprang up in the United States during the 1840s based on the doctrines of a French social philosopher named Charles Fourier. The Fourierist phalanx at Brook Farm in Massachusetts was the best known; the one at Braceville in Ohio's Trumbull County was organized with 150 members in 1844. Among those who settled in the community was a recently married young couple, Morgan Lewis and Jane Brokaw Brett. Their first child was born on 1 July 1846 in Braceville. They named him William Howard Brett.

In due course their son turned out well, but the Trumbull Phalanx was both disappointing and disillusioning for the young par-

46

ents. Many other members shared their point of view, largely because of a bumbling administration plus fear that the region was unhealthy and would be the cause of much illness and death. As a result, the Trumbull Phalanx itself expired in 1848. Before this termination of a noble concept, Morgan Lewis Brett had withdrawn his family and had gone to nearby Warren. There he settled in a modest house on a narrow street facing what was then the clear and clean Mahoning River—now, alas! a polluted cesspool. It was to be the family home for a quarter century.

Their son loved books, learned to read on his own before he began his formal schooling, soon was spending much of his time in the small bookshop of William Porter in Warren. Porter was a cultured bibliophile who had once started a subscription library, not unlike the better-known Coonskin one, because payment could be made in kind. In December 1842, the *Western Reserve Chronicle* carried the following advertisement:

> Wheat, corn, hay, oats, wood, butter, tallow, and most kinds of produce will be received for subscriptions to Porter & Ide's circulating library.

In the high school, Brett was proud that he was reading books not on the approved list, and justified his behavior by stating:

> I am quite sure that I really got more of history from the Waverly novels, and from Cooper than I did from the textbooks; but my acquaintance with them was made in small part from the few books which my good father was able to buy for me, it was made very much more from the kindness of "good Samaritan" neighbors . . . and as a boy I cultivated the acquaintance of most of the people in town who owned books.

At fourteen he became librarian of his small school library and remained in the position until he graduated from the Warren High School. In those surroundings there was no card catalogue; the librarian knew every book on a limited list, understood its exact place on the shelves, knew who had borrowed it. The salary was the fines, an early and impressive example of the incentive system.

From the high school in Warren, Brett entered the University of Michigan as a medical student, but became disenchanted with the program. He completed a second year at Western Reserve College in Hudson where Oviatt and White had been stellar students, but after one year there Brett ran out of money and his brief college career came to a close.

When Brett came to Cleveland, because the opportunities in Warren in the book field were limited, his good friend William Porter got him a job with the Cobb and Andrews Company, wholesale and retail book dealers. The firm, originally J. B. Cobb and Company, was a fascinating one founded by siblings with classical names; there were three Cobb brothers named Caius Cassius, Brutus Junius, and Junius Brutus Cobb. That their father had strong literary tendencies was indicated by the intriguing names of his other children—Lucius Marcius, Marcius Lucius, Lucia Marcia, Cassius Caius, Marcia Lucia—and Daniel! The original store on Superior Avenue grew, and soon there were branches in other cities. When it left Superior Avenue in 1875 and invaded the residential thoroughfare known as Euclid Avenue, the firm had become Cobb, Andrews and Company. In 1888 it would be purchased by Charles H. and Harris B. Burrows who were also prominent booksellers and stationers. At Cobb and Andrews, Brett had the reputation of being the most knowledgeable bookman in Cleveland. He came to enjoy his job, but in his earlier years in Cleveland had thought of going West to grow up with the country. He told a friend: "If I could only get a little money ahead I would go west and join a surveying party on the railroads." The friend's observation was: "It was force of circumstances that prevented 'Buffalo Bill' growing up on the great plains, and not choice that produced the greatest librarian of his time."

In 1884, after the Beardsley fiasco, the Library Board offered Brett the position as librarian of the Cleveland Public Library. John Griswold White, who was serving his first term on the board, would testify later that no one on it had much idea about the qualifications of a librarian. One member, who was opposed to Brett's appointment, said that he could get a bookkeeper for a great deal less than it would be necessary to pay Brett—and "what was a librarian but a bookkeeper?" Fortunately six of the seven members of the board, admitting their ignorance about the qualifications of a librarian, still thought he should *know* as well as *keep* books. For this reason they offered the position to Brett, the chief and most popular employee of the largest bookstore in the city—and indeed the largest bookseller west of Philadelphia. Brett hesitated; he had family obligations, the library at that time was not nearly as prestigious as Cobb and Andrews, and the small salary offered was no enticement. He finally decided to take the new position because he felt he could render a larger service in the public library, whatever the cost in labor and remuneration might be.

The labor turned out to be unremitting. In the Cleveland Public Library, Brett's working habits would ultimately keep him at his job six full days a week, with many long evenings at the office and usually a visit to some part of the system on Sunday. The salary was hardly alluring. Brett began at $2,100 in 1884, and by 1895 had been raised all the way to $2,700. By comparison with other cities, Brett was grossly underpaid; in 1895 Pittsburgh and Providence paid their public librarians $4,000, in St. Louis the salary was $3,600, in Minneapolis and Milwaukee and Newark the compensation was $3,000. By contrast, Cleveland was niggardly in its monetary recognition of an outstanding librarian, and this situation continued throughout Brett's tenure. In 1918, more than three decades after he had joined the Cleveland Public Library, his compensation was $7,000 per annum.

THE OPEN SHELF

The transition from a bookstore to a public library presented a very real challenge for Brett. To his eternal credit he pondered the situation with understanding and was not only receptive to new ideas but courageous in putting many of them in force—to the point where John Griswold White would contend that the Cleveland Public Library had "more new ideas, more sane ideas, than any other library in the world." Among the new departures which Brett either initiated or adopted enthusiastically were the open shelf, children's libraries, extension work through branches and schools and industrial plants, a cumulative index to periodicals, a catalogue that was a marvel, departmentalization of the library, and the development of a library school.

The open shelf had been introduced first in small libraries, notably the one at Pawtucket, Rhode Island, where a "dear Mrs. Sanders" had taken the daring plunge. But Brett was the first librarian of a metropolitan library with enough fortitude to inaugurate it in the face of adverse admonitions from the Cassandras of his day. The critics were convinced that the innovation would produce general pandemonium and the loss of books. In a discussion of free access at a conference of librarians held in London in 1877, the opposition included Dr. Melvil Dewey, soon to become the patron saint of classification. Still later, a British librarian stated he was certain that the open shelf could only be introduced "in praise of anarchy." It will be recalled that Irad L. Beardsley, Brett's predecessor in the Cleveland Public Library, would not consider the idea because it would "muss up" those books that were not stolen.

Brett supported the open shelf because of his faith in humankind and his belief that borrowers from libraries must be presented with the maximum of choice. From his own background in bookstores he understood fully the value of direct handling of books by customers if purchases were to follow. As a result of this early training he realized that borrowers in libraries must be relieved of the high counters, which were formidable barriers, if a real choice was to be offered to them. Before the institution of free access to books, potential readers had to consult a shelf list and then make out a call slip. When the book came they saw it for the first time and on quick perusal frequently found it a disappointment, with the result that several call slips were required before the patron was reasonably satisfied. These same call slips sometimes provided amusement for librarians—particularly when puzzled would-be readers asked for any book by "anon," or when a despairing man would write, "Please pick out a good love story for my wife." Brett knew that many people who entered a library had at best one or two books in mind; if those books were not available the borrower should be able to visit the shelves and choose for himself. In Brett's opinion, "In so far as he compares books and exercises his judgment in reaching a choice, he is educating himself." In this regard the "open alcoves of the free library" would become "broad highways." Brett was in essential agreement with the observation that the fundamental objective of a library is "not how to make people wise, but how to make them want to be."

Brett also believed that borrowers must not only be trusted but should be challenged to prove their integrity. He did not think that those entering a library should be treated as were undergraduate borrowers at Harvard in the middle years of the nineteenth century, when a student was "made to leave his cloak and cap at the door, that they may not serve to conceal his spoils. . . . [He] enters and leaves with a character hanging over him bad as that of a suspected pickpocket. . . ." In New York a critic of its libraries said in 1895 that they were completely lacking in warmth and hospitality; there was something in the tense atmosphere that made one feel that the main purpose of the custodians was "to prevent Weary Waggles and William Walker from carrying off under their waistcoats the whole set of Patent Office reports and pawning the same in the Bowery to procure beer." Brett was horrified by the prevailing opinion that a librarian was a fellow who kept people from getting the books they wished. Because a public library was founded on the principle of generosity and helpfulness, he felt that narrowing and hampering rules were foreign, repugnant, and ineffective. In that early era there was one procedure in the beautiful Boston Public Library to which Brett had never accustomed himself. Here was a magnificent reading and delivery room, a gorgeous one with the painting of the Holy Grail around it. But those entering were not trusted; they handed in slips, sat on benches for minutes or hours, and ultimately—when their names were called—received the books they had ordered. The open shelf was then unknown to the library in the Hub of the Universe.

It was also unknown in the Astor Library in New York City. In 1895 a disgruntled would-be reader there wrote as follows:

When you get safely beyond the catalogue stage of preliminaries and have made out your slip, and have handed it to the desk attendant, and have seen him read it with curling nostril and then deposit it on the corner of a table to take its chance of discovery by a sporadic boy, you can stand at attention and rest yourself until the boy appears. The interval is longer or

shorter according to the laws governing comets. The lads who
go after the books seem to have been selected with care from
among the least precipitate graduates of the District Messen-
ger service. You have started in at the catalogue when the day
was yet young, and you may be lucky enough, if it is not in
the very short days of the winter season, to procure your
books, transport them to the reading table, and settle yourself
to work before the signal for closing the library. Then the
doors are shut behind you and the treasures of Mr. Astor's
noble foundation are safe from publicity for at least another
eighteen hours.

In Brett's opinion it was not simply free access to the shelves that
needed to be justified; instead it was any restriction by a librarian.
He felt that the most important thing about the open shelf was the
appeal it made to the sense of honor. His opponents had made the
point that if temptation was put in the way of book borrowers,
thievery would be the result. Brett had no use for this argument:

> Personally I have not much use for the kind of honesty that
> depends on lack of opportunity; I think that to give a boy or
> to give a man access to the shelves is equivalent to saying, we
> believe you will take care of these books, we believe you will
> not steal them. Most people respond to this. I believe it is a
> continual training in and a strengthening of honesty. There is
> no doubt there is the temptation, they would like to carry the
> books away, and every time they don't do it they are a little
> more honest than they were before. If they are hindered or
> prevented by something outside themselves their moral fibre
> is weakened.

This was the ultimate for faith in the innate decency and honesty
of mankind in general—and Brett had it. Eighty years later there
were some who wondered. They felt that the open shelf may have
been appropriate in Brett's time, but that the increase in both population and urban crime might necessitate a re-evaluation in the
1970s.

With all of the acclaim given to Brett for initiating the open shelf
as early as 1890 for the large library, it is surprising that he went less
than half the distance toward that goal in that particular year—
belatedly completing most of the rest of the distance five years

later when he was then under some pressure to do so. An addition built at the rear of the Board of Education building made additional space available for the library in 1890, and Brett was able to persuade the board to permit free access to all circulating volumes except adult fiction and juvenile books. The volumes in the library were arranged for the first time by subject matter, the beginning of the departmental system. They were still behind glass doors but these were opened on request by the assistants in charge—except for fiction and juvenile books, which comprised about 60 percent of the total circulation of the library! This was obviously only a first step toward meaningful free access. Nonetheless, it was considered a daring experiment for a large library. Brett was pleased to state in his next annual report that circulation increased by 44 percent; that the reduced staff now required represented a saving of $1,500 (about 13 percent of a salary budget of $11,243); that fewer books had been lost; and that of those missing a large proportion were fiction—the only type of books to which free access was not allowed. The president of the Library Board was also gratified. In 1894 he reported: "This radical innovation, introduced by us, has resulted in its adoption in several of the other public libraries throughout the country, and is destined to general recognition."

There were others, including the readers of fiction and the *Cleveland Press*, who were not so happy. By the early 1890s free access had also been extended to fiction readers except during the busiest hours of the week—which then meant on Saturday. This was the day when many went to the library, so many in fact that "men with dinner buckets jostled ladies in silk, for all are on a common footing." In these busy hours, if a borrower wanted a book on history or science or travel, there was no difficulty in making the free choice—but he was not permitted to look at the well-filled bookcases in the fiction alcove. They were protected by high and forbidding counters. A few novels were placed on the counters for inspection; potential borrowers stood three-deep about these selected volumes, hastily turning over the pages. As the *Press* reported it:

> Unless one is content to crowd women and children and to act the boor, he stands little chance of being waited upon. There are instances where people have waited an hour or

more at the fiction counter. It isn't so bad in the other departments, but in the section devoted to fiction people engage in
rough and tumble scrambles for books, and then, with tem-
pers ruffled, depart, either bookless or with some undesirable
work. . . . The red tape now in vogue means literary prohibi-
tion to timid people. . . . The library might as well be limited
to 200 volumes.

Brett was an iconoclast but was imaginative and resourceful and
humble enough to accept criticism. In this case, he commended
the *Press* for its commentary and used it as a welcome excuse in
1895 for pushing aside the counters in the fiction department—
making the entire library an open-shelf operation for adults. The
juvenile department still had a closed system because of inadequate
space and supervision, but Brett promised that as soon as possible
it would be opened to the public in the same way. Beyond the
new freedom in the library, he also provided an effective means of
direct communication with the citizens of Cleveland, who owned
the library, through publication of the *Open Shelf*, which first appeared in January 1894. Now more than seventy-five years old,
this publication is probably the oldest public library bulletin in the
United States. A list of pertinent books added to the library is included in each issue. From time to time there have been special
bulletins on important persons or events, bulletins which are both
interesting and valuable as a continuing chronicle of the history of
the Cleveland Public Library. Initially the *Open Shelf* carried the
paid advertising of publishers and bookstores, and sold for one
cent a copy—as did the newspapers of that day. Later issues carried no advertising. The publication has been distributed without
charge to those who visit the library in person and with only a
modest fee for those who subscribe by mail.

CLASSIFICATION AND ORGANIZATION

The open-shelf system made it easier for borrowers to find books
suitable to their tastes; so did a new classification system, a useful
catalogue, and a divisional organization—all of which Brett soon
introduced. It will be recalled that under the system adopted by
Oviatt in 1869 books were numbered and shelved in order of their

Cleveland, general view (1853)

First site of Cleveland Public Library: Northrup and Harrington Block (1875)

The "Ark," adjacent to the Case home on Public Square,
now the site of the old Federal Building

Leonard Case, Jr.

Library deposit station at Engine House Number 2 (ca. 1900)

Library deposit station on Fireboat *Clevelander* (ca. 1900)

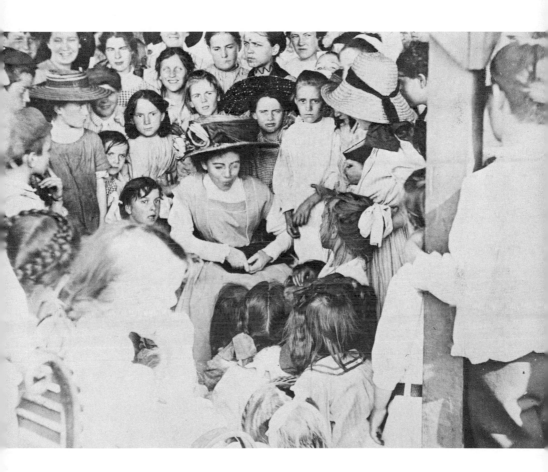

Library story hour (ca. 1900)

Circulation desk at Main Library, old Central High School building (1898)

accession without regard to class or subject matter. Because this system was based on expediency rather than logic, a person in search of books of the same type of subject—whether he was a librarian or a patron—was compelled to pursue his objective hither and yon throughout the entire library. Even after catalogues became available, either in the form of printed volumes or on cards, they were sometimes complex and inscrutable to the point of exasperation. The situation at the Astor Library in New York, as late as the 1890s, was described as follows by one scholar:

> The catalogue of the Astor Library, partly cards in cabinets, partly cards in trays, partly dog-eared and dingy volumes with countless supplements, is considered, as a whole, the most fearful and wonderful construction devised by the human mind since Daedalus built his labyrinth. You study its mysteries and practice upon its complicated mechanism for twenty years and are no further advanced than when you were a freshman. The proof of this is that the veterans of the library staff, who have spent half their lives in intimate communion with this masterpiece of muddle, seem unable to make it work much better than the first comer. In mental anguish and with an aching neck you chase a title from card to book, from book to cupboard drawer, from big volume to little supplement, from topical index to alphabetical list, from list of books previous to 1847 to list of books subsequent to 1889, and when after hot pursuit for thirty to forty-five minutes you succeed in running it down, two to one you find that the shelf and alcove numbers . . . either have been torn off the margin upon which they were faintly pencilled, or have been rendered illegible by the friction of countless eager and perspiring thumbs. I know few tests of perfect mental balance equal to an hour's wrestle with the Astor Library catalogue. I have seen men come up those gloomy steps with faces beaming; plunge smiling into the inexpressible profundity of that Awful Mystery; get red and angry after the first half hour; . . . run around dazed and aimless for half an hour more from table to table like a rat in a pit, and then stagger down stairs and out of doors with a haggard, bewildered look. . . .

Over the years a number of scholars, management impresarios, and a few frauds have devoted themselves to the difficult question of how to classify books, a problem which in special situations is sometimes insoluble, except on an ad hoc basis. Thomas Jefferson, certainly a many-sided scholar and intellectual, was one of the first to turn his active mind to the pragmatic problem of the classification of books. The War of 1812 had brought the British to Washington, with the result that the Library of Congress disappeared in flames. Jefferson was not only shocked but compared this vandalism with that at Alexandria in the early Christian Era. He also offered his own collection of books as a replacement, and after considerable congressional debate about possible subversion from the "irreligious French books" in Jefferson's collection, Congress did accept for only $23,950 the generous offer of 6,479 volumes— about twice the number burned by the British. With the collection Jefferson sent a catalogue and a scheme of classification on which he had spent a great amount of effort and study. In 1802, while he was President, he had taken the time to prepare a catalogue for the Library of Congress. It was based on subject-matter classes and was followed by the national library for nearly a century. Jefferson's system was founded on Bacon's division of knowledge into three general classes of History, Philosophy, and Fine Arts, which were in turn subdivided into subclasses. From the vantage point of hindsight, the triad of general classes was obviously too few in number; nonetheless Jefferson was the first prominent American to think of the pattern which would ultimately be improved upon by Dewey and others.

Brett also devoted himself to the problem of classification, along with those of cataloguing and a divisional structure for the library. The Dewey Relative Decimal Classification System was then new and but partially developed (there have since been sixteen revisions). Brett was impressed by its advantages and adopted—or rather adapted—it because he improved on the system in a number of ways that were beneficial to public libraries. Dewey divided knowledge into ten principal groups, rather than Jefferson's three, and each of the ten was assigned one hundred numbers. This meant, as examples, that the social sciences were in the 300s, literature in the 800s, and history in the 900s. Within each general class, principal series were denoted by tens; thus economics was found in the 330s of the social sciences, and the chronicle of North America in the 970s of history, with the history of Canada as 971, and so on. It is of interest to note that some of Brett's amendments to the Dewey theology have been recognized as accepted heresy, particularly the alphabetical (rather than the decimal) arrangement of fiction and individual biography. Some years later Brett told a colleague of his regret that he had departed from Dewey as a standard bible on classification. The colleague's response was that his own sorrow was that Melvil Dewey had not recognized the advantages of Brett's amendments. This was virtually impossible because Dewey was not noted for a flexible mind or a tendency to learn from others. Nonetheless it appears that Brett's choice of Dewey's system helped in its general adoption later—particularly because the Cleveland librarian used it in his own printed catalogue in 1889.

Neither of the first two librarians in Cleveland had succeeded in producing a catalogue of books, either by list or on cards, that was complete and functional. For this reason it is understandable that in 1885 the Library Board, after almost two decades of waiting, would request that the librarian be directed to prepare a catalogue that was so arranged and classified that "the average reader, as well as the compiler, will be able to comprehend it." It is apparent that the board classified itself among the average readers who had not understood previous lists and catalogues from the library. Brett carried out the incredible task in four years. In 1889 he saw the publication of his monumental volume, *Alphabetic Catalogue of the English Books in the Circulating Department of the Cleveland Public Library: Authors, Titles, and Subjects.* It was a dictionary catalogue for the 32,000 volumes in the Circulating Department of the library as of 1 July 1888. The object was to enable a potential borrower to find a book of which either the author, title, or subject was known—and to ascertain, from reference to this catalogue, what the library possessed that was pertinent and relevant. Brett's catalogue was obviously a very large volume; it had 1,407 pages with two columns on each page. As an example of what it offered, the synopsis on William Shakespeare was as follows—a synopsis of a full text that ran for five pages and ten columns:

Shakespeare, Wm., Eng. dramatic poet, b. 1564 d. 1616. Subdivisions: 1. Works. 2. Selections. 3. Separate plays and poems. 4. Glossaries and quotations. 5. Biographical. 6. Special subjects. 7. Authorship: Bacon, or Shakespeare. 8. Criticism, sketches, etc. 9. Tales from Shakespeare.

Such a subject heading might be general to cover classes of books such as Art, Agriculture, or Domestic Animals; it might also be more specific for such topics as Engraving, Ensilage, or Horse. Under the subject headings were given not only entire books on the topic, but also parts of books referring thereto.

All of this represented a supreme effort because it meant that Brett had to know what was in every one of the 32,000 volumes in the Circulating Department of the library. In time he did—but his long-suffering wife would observe that while the work was in progress her husband almost lived, ate, and slept with his catalogue. Proofs would be brought home; he would work on them at mealtime, so oblivious to what was going on that she cut up the food on his plate. Brett's *Catalogue of the Cleveland Public Library* turned out to be such a tour de force that two decades later it was still serving many other libraries as a prototype and a tool. The newly organized New York State Library School, among others, used it as a model dictionary catalogue. Brett was as humble as usual; he acknowledged that he got most of his ideas from a previous catalogue done in accordance with rules laid down by Charles A. Cutter, librarian of the Boston Athenaeum. In spite of this disclaimer, at that time no library had issued a catalogue so complete and so immediately useful (the one by Cutter, completed in 1882, included no books published after January 1872!). Because new books came into the library each day, it was obvious that any printed catalogue—including Brett's—would be out of date when it went to press. This situation made necessary annual or semiannual supplements. In time they would be replaced with the card catalogue now basic in every library.

Beyond a new system of classification and a usable catalogue, Brett introduced the flexible library based on divisional lines. The long-accepted plan had been to separate only circulating and reference books. Questions requiring investigation went to the Reference Department, where the same assistant might find it necessary to answer questions on metallurgy, summer resorts, or Christian theology. No one could possibly be an expert on all three, and the divisional system provided the answer. Brett began it in 1890, when some additional space permitted him to divide some books by subject matter in alcoves running like spokes from the central area. The move to the much larger Kinney and Levan Building in 1913 permitted him to complete the transformation, with all books divided by subject department in the main library. This meant that the same assistants were responsible for the same class of books day after day, developing a competence in the field that enabled them to order books with greater wisdom and to answer reference questions with more certainty of knowing, or being able to find, the answer. This organizational concept has always been associated with Brett's name, and its adoption in other cities followed in due course. In the Kinney and Levan Building, the original subject divisions were Philosophy and Religion, Sociology, Science and Technical, Literature, History, Travel and Biography, Foreign Language, Popular Library, Periodicals, Newspaper, Children's Literature, and General Reference (with coordinating functions); supporting divisions were Catalogue, Order, Maintenance, Schools, and Branches.

CUMULATIVE INDEX TO PERIODICALS

With access to books assured through the open shelf, a new system of classification, a reliable catalogue, and the divisional organization—Brett turned his attention to problems confronting scholars who placed considerable reliance on periodical literature. There was already the *Index to Periodical Literature,* first issued in 1848 and named for William Frederick Poole, the distinguished librarian who was successively associated with the Boston Athenaeum, the Newberry Library, and the public libraries in Cincinnati and Chicago. Poole's *Index* could be valuable and annoying because of the long gaps in time between editions, which varied from five to twenty-nine years! For this reason the Cleveland library found it difficult to supply information on articles in recent periodicals on various topics; frequently memory was the chief and uncertain reliance. In time, individual magazines printed their own indexes for the year just closed, and in due course a new edition of the Poole

Index might arrive—but for anyone who wanted a careful scrutiny of articles in periodicals for the recent year or years, the situation was exasperating and chaotic and time consuming.

Brett began by asking his assistants to make a slip index of the better magazines, and the usefulness of this device as a reference tool was soon proven. He realized fully that other libraries either needed this service or were already duplicating his own efforts, and as an eminently practical administrator Brett was unalterably opposed to unnecessary repetition of effort. He therefore persuaded the trustees to allow him to publish the compilation and to offer it to other libraries on a subscription basis. As a result it was the Cleveland Public Library which first distributed, in 1896 and 1897, the first quarterly issues of the *Cumulative Index to a Selected List of Periodicals*, making immediately available the contents of seventy and soon one hundred periodicals.

It was also obvious that a public library could not continue to function indefinitely as a commercial publisher. In 1898 local arrangements were made with the Helman Taylor Company, successors to the Cobb and Andrews firm, to take it over as a private publication—although for an additional period of time the guide was compiled and edited by the Cleveland library. The venture faltered under its first excursion into private management, but the second attempt in a very short time was highly successful. At the turn of the century publication of the index was moved from Cleveland to Minneapolis where it was absorbed by the H. W. Wilson Company. There Halsey W. Wilson, one of the great bibliographers of all time, merged it with his own less comprehensive *Reader's Guide to Periodical Literature*, then a minor publication which indexed only twenty of the more popular magazines and was designed for small libraries only. This new and enlarged compilation was so successful that Poole's *Index* ceased publication in 1907. *Reader's Guide*, an invaluable and familiar aid to researchers for the past seventy years, also laid the foundation for Wilson's special business of furnishing invaluable reference aids to libraries.

Brett's part in initiating this service was not one of the major contributions of his total career, but to this day he is recognized as the originator of *Reader's Guide*. This action is also an impressive example of Brett's approach to a specific problem, an approach

which was always direct and pragmatic and motivated by a desire
to give maximum service to the patrons of his library.

BRETT AND CHILDREN

On the subject of a library's obligation to children, Beardsley
and Brett were antipodal. In Puritan days children had been regarded as sinful creatures whose prime need was salvation; Beardsley too, believed that youth was essentially self-indulgent and required discipline to insure the vocational and moral training which
should be the major consideration. In the Annual Report of 1879
he worried about the subversion of both old and young. "Like older
persons," he wrote, "the imaginations of the young seek for highly
seasoned food and there is such an eager desire for sensational reading on the part of youth, that it has been deemed necessary to re-
strict drawings on the part of those attending school, to once a
week." He felt strongly that the proper business of boys and girls
should be the work of the classroom; he therefore prohibited the
"lingering" of children in the library building. It was apparent that
the concept of a children's library was hardly acceptable to a librarian who believed that the only way to improve the reading
tastes of the young was to keep them out of the library! By contrast, children and Brett were always close friends; between them,
understanding and trust was mutual. He would say that his purpose was to "give all children a cordial welcome, to make them feel
at home, to give them all possible liberty consistent with the rights
of others, and to lead them by gentle ways to the use of better
books." In the early years of his service as librarian, before the era
of extension and specialization set in, Brett himself supervised the
purchase of children's books and was acquainted with every juvenile volume on the shelves. It is little wonder that he came to be
known as "the greatest children's librarian."

He was not the first. In the early part of the nineteenth century
there were a number of individuals who donated either books or
tiny endowments, presumably in the hope that a municipality
might pick up the rest of the "tab." In 1803 Caleb Bingham, successful as a publisher and writer of textbooks, contributed 150
titles to his home town (Salisbury, Connecticut), to be made freely

available to children between the ages of nine and sixteen. He left to others the obligation to care for and distribute these books; in 1810 the citizens in town meeting did vote financial aid to the Bingham Library for Youth—perhaps the first such library in the United States to receive support from a municipality. A quarter of a century later, in 1835, there was the bequest of a physician in West Cambridge (now Arlington), Massachusetts. He left one hundred dollars for a library that would diffuse "useful knowledge and the Christian virtues" to children. This was done, at least in part, and a Jonathan Dexter was appointed librarian. Because Dexter made hats during the week, the library was open only on Saturday afternoons. After a year the town voted to appropriate forty dollars to make books free to adults as well, and this generosity marked the beginning of what is now the Arlington Public Library! In the 1850s a Colonel James Anderson of Allegheny, Pennsylvania, made his library of 400 volumes accessible to working boys. One of the urchins was Andrew Carnegie who would later erect a monument to Anderson and would contribute much of his own wealth to the building of public libraries.

In spite of these estimable individual efforts, in the waning years of the nineteenth century there had been little progress toward the goal of providing books for the children of the land. In 1876, the Centennial Year, the United States Government published a voluminous report on public libraries. The volume had an index of thirteen closely printed, double-column pages—with not a single entry under "child" or "children." Service to youth, in alcoves or rooms or other facilities of public institutions, first appeared in 1885. The initial one seems to have been a children's library established in that year by Emily Hanaway, the principal of the primary department of Grammar School No. 28 in New York City. The first public librarian to do something for children who were roaming the streets was Mrs. Minerva Sanders of Pawtucket, Rhode Island. She was something of a "radical" who believed in a people's library; she had introduced open shelves, had encouraged workingmen to come to her institution, and was most interested in children at a time when they were considered noisy nuisances. In 1887 Sanders welcomed youngsters to a corner of the reading room where she had provided four tables and chairs, lowered because she had ordered a large segment of the legs cut off; the facility seated seventy children, and there were shelves nearby stocked with books of interest to the young. The boys and girls responded by dubbing her with the affectionate sobriquet of "Auntie Sanders." In 1890 the Public Library in Brookline, Massachusetts, opened in its basement the first reading room especially for children; three years later the Minneapolis Public Library found space in a corridor for children; the next year the Denver Public Library appropriated a "ladies' reading room" and changed it into a children's library with books within easy reach on low shelves. Shortly thereafter a separate children's reading room became a part of every well-constructed and properly operated public library. No longer would children be served solely by sending collections of books to the schools. They were now being recognized as part of the public— needing their own quarters, their own book collections, and a specially trained staff to serve them. There were occasional problems which Sam Walter Foss would describe in light verse:

See the Children's gay Librarian! Oh, what boisterous
    joys are hers
As she sits upon her whirl-stool, throned amid her
    worshippers,
Guiding youngsters seeking wisdom through Thought's
    misty morning light;
Separating Tom and Bill as they clinch in deadly
    fight;
Giving lavatory treatment to the little hand that
    smears
With the soil of crusted strata laid by immemorial
    years;

In Cleveland, Brett had urged, in his first annual report, immediate attention to children and their needs. The next year, in 1885, he sent an article to the Cleveland *Plain Dealer* in which he deplored the worthless books available to the young and asked for a contribution of $5,000 from prosperous citizens, to enable the library to buy an adequate supply of better ones. The money was not forthcoming, but the article aroused favorable comment. In 1886 Brett pled for a reading room for young people, a goal that was not to be realized for more than a decade because of the lack of available space. But in 1890, more volumes were purchased in the juvenile category—almost a thousand in number—than in any other. This included sixty copies of *Little Lord Fauntleroy*, tolerated in the face of critical opinion, then and now, which has never been overly friendly to the "little-child-shall-lead-them" type of literature. In 1895 Brett placed a long table, especially for children, in the general reading room; this at least gave them some elbowroom for the perusal of illustrated books.

Three years later he proudly opened his first children's room. It was an improvised one which was made possible by partitioning with glass an alcove of the reading area (a space formerly used for fiction) and cutting a door directly into the corridor, in order to avoid annoyance and to continue the other operations of the library. The necessary changes were completed on the twenty-second of February (a holiday), and the formal opening occurred on the day following Washington's Birthday in 1898. The newly improvised room was small, thirty-five by twenty feet, but Brett found it pleasant and "for the moment adequate." In it were placed books of children's stories plus many volumes of history, travel, and science which Brett had been buying for years with children—as well as adults—in mind. There were high bookcases in close order around the walls; halfway up each case there was a broad ledge reached by a ladder on wheels, reminiscent of shoe stores and essential to reach the high shelves. In the search for books agile children were known to circumnavigate the room, one foot on the ladder and the other hopping along the ledge. In his later years one early client would testify and recall:

> I love the Cleveland libraries. What thrills have been mine as I stood perched on one leg like a stork half way up a ladder, utterly oblivious of time and space, drinking in equal parts of Jules Verne and the dust of the Central Library which Euclid Avenue knows no more.

Even so, reading and elbowroom were obviously limited in this cramped area, and in busy periods children were not encouraged to browse; the rule was "to select the book, draw it, and depart."

Brett had stated that it was his purpose to give a cordial welcome to children and present them with as much liberty as was consistent with the rights of others. This meant that they also had responsibilities, and to impress these obligations on those of tender age the Cleveland Public Library organized the Children's Library League in 1897, the first of many such organizations in the nation. The league was really the brainchild of Linda Eastman (the vice-librarian) and Effie L. Power (the children's librarian), and the appeal was for better care of borrowed books. Eastman and Power, in turn, had appropriated the basic principle from a Colonel Waring who had achieved considerable prominence through his Children's League for Clean Streets in New York City. The Colonel believed reform was most effective and far-reaching when begun with children, and to cleanse the filthy streets of Gotham he began with children who had some promise rather than adults, many of whom had none. For this reason Eastman would assert:

> The wastefulness of the American nation has become proverbial, both in private life and in public expenditure, and somewhere in the education of the rising generations there should be found a place to inculcate the principles of a true economy and a profound respect for public property.

In Cleveland the motto of the Children's Library League was: CLEAN HEARTS, CLEAN HANDS, CLEAN BOOKS. Clean hearts are sometimes a bit difficult to discern, but antiseptic hands and books are easily identifiable. For this reason each member of the league signed a pledge which had nothing to do with the physiology of the heart but had a lot to say about hands and books. The pledge affirmed that reputable books contained the living thought of good and great men and women, and for that reason were entitled to respect; the signers agreed not to treat books roughly nor mark them nor turn down pages. As is customary with crusading organizations, the Children's Library League encouraged compliance through the use of a number of devices such as red-letter honor cards and badges of white metal, for which the wearer was charged three cents. Books were widely distributed, with suggested readings *and* this admonitory statement:

Once upon a time a library book was overheard talking to a little boy who had just borrowed it. The words seemed worth recording and here they are:

"Please don't handle me with dirty hands. I should feel ashamed to be seen when the next little boy borrowed me.

"Or leave me out in the rain. Books can catch cold as well as children.

"Or make marks on me with your pen and pencil. It would spoil my looks.

. . . .

"Or put in between my leaves a pencil or anything thicker than a sheet of paper. It would strain my back.

. . . .

"Help me to keep fresh and clean, and I will help you to be happy."

In less than a year the league had a membership of more than fourteen thousand, including the entire graduating class of Central High School, which joined in a body. Beyond the advantage of greater care of books, with dirt at a discount, the league produced some unanticipated results. It increased the reading of books by members who had never used the library until they joined the league. It was not uncommon for a child to say, "Teacher, I have got clean hands. . . . Can I be joined to the Library?" The league made possible the direction of reading, through informative bookmarks, for those children who could not be reached individually. It also provided a memorable social experience for some children in Cleveland. Hitherto restricted within the narrow limits of ethnic communities, there were those for whom a league meeting downtown was a great event; some children actually saw the Public Square and Euclid Avenue for the first time. For them the league, quite apart from its fundamental purpose of protecting books, provided travel and mobility and a broadening of horizons that was most welcome.

In 1898 Brett had managed to screen off an alcove for the young. In 1901 when the library moved to temporary but new quarters, he first achieved a bona fide children's room. Although it was in the basement, the area (thirty-two by sixty-seven feet) was much larger and much more pleasant than the improvised alcove. There were six reading tables and chairs of various heights; the bookcases were calibrated on the same scale. The book collection numbered a respectable ten thousand volumes, almost evenly divided between fiction and nonfiction. Brett announced this development with pride and humility, admitting that the new facility could not compare with similar rooms in more fortunate neighboring cities—Buffalo, Toledo, Milwaukee, and Cincinnati. As a pragmatist he noted that Cleveland would do everything possible to make its quarters attractive; the room was frequently adorned with flowers or plants (the gifts of friends), and there were copies of good paintings on the walls.

This philosophy was the basis for the attractive Lewis Carroll and Robert Louis Stevenson rooms of later years. Their success is interesting in retrospect; in the early days a powerful defense had to be mounted to achieve special reading rooms for children. There was the question of what degree of noise should be tolerated, and what was proper behavior in a library. Would children's areas become playrooms, as some implied might happen? It seemed obvious that the children's rooms could not be as quiet as the other areas in the library; if they were it might represent a repression, as Professor Harriet Long has observed, "of all spontaneity and freedom, and an enforced deathly stillness. . . ." On the other hand, many of the children who patronized the library were living in noisy and crowded tenements; by comparison with their actual situation, the relative spaciousness of the children's room—and its uncluttered appearance and orderliness—were so impressive that they created an awe that was of considerable assistance in teaching many of the youthful clients their first lessons on citizenship in a democracy. One commentator described this unique atmosphere in these terms: "The minute you entered the library you knew you were in some place absolutely different from anything else. . . . It was not only the rows and rows of books, but it was the . . . soft little noises that wouldn't be sounds at all except in the library; the quiet turning of magazine pages and the rustling of a newspaper, the cautious tread of a footstep. . . ." In actual fact, the majesty of the place could affect both young and old. When the beautiful new building for the

Boston Public Library opened in 1895, the *Transcript* presented
subtle testimony to the refining influences of the environment:

> A reader, seeking the registration room, asked one of the
> stately policemen adorning the opening day, "Which way
> shall I go to the desk where we are to take out books?" He re-
> plied affably, "I ain't had no instructions yet." Then the aca-
> demic atmosphere of the place swept over his spirit and he
> stood corrected before himself. "I haven't had no instructions
> yet," he called softly after the vanishing reader, with an ac-
> cent of exquisite content.

Power had complete confidence in her claims for libraries as great
and informal educational institutions:

> Many people, young and old, go to school in our libraries
> every day. The only requirement is good behaviour. Atten-
> dance is free and students need never graduate.

In the first decade of the twentieth century children were also
being served in homes and branches and schools, and by means of
story hours in all facilities. One of the most interesting methods
of taking books to children was in homes through small collections
of books left there, quite remote from libraries, for the use of children in the neighborhood. A library visitor, usually a volunteer,
visited the home periodically to tell stories, to circulate books, and
to refresh the collection. By 1911 fifty-three of these home libraries
had been established, along with almost three hundred libraries in
schools and classrooms; by this time the distribution of books
among children was more than 40 percent of the total circulation
of the library. Storytelling was obviously an art, and the Cleveland
Public Library went to great lengths to cultivate it, because it realized that through this method youth was frequently introduced to
serious reading. In time these story hours became so popular that
when the Cleveland library found it necessary to stop them for a
while because of lack of funds in the dolorous thirties some of the
children offered to bring their own few pennies to meet the expense.

In 1908 Cleveland had the honor of opening the first branch in
the United States devoted to children only. It was Perkins House,

located in a congested neighborhood of many nationalities. Brett would note that

> immediately back of the library is a large box factory and in the vicinity are iron foundries, a cloak and casket factory and a big laundry. The saloons seem to furnish a large supply of the food in the neighborhood.

Perkins House represented an interesting collaboration of a prominent settlement organization (Goodrich House), the Day Nursery and Free Kindergarten Association, and the Cleveland Public Library—for the purpose of making assimilation of children in the community as meaningful and pleasant as possible. It was the Day Nursery and Free Kindergarten Association that offered, free of rent, a small tenement house for a children's library. Brett remodeled the structure and bought suitable furniture for a total cost of about four thousand dollars; for this small sum he changed the building into an attractive one. The story room (formerly the kitchen) seated fifty, the main room seventy; the pictures were colorful, grotesques supported the mantel, and there was a large cast of Michelangelo's *Moses* in one corner. Over the fireplace, which Brett had added for regular use during the cold months, there was a large motto from Robert Louis Stevenson:

> Where the roads on either hand
> Lead onward into fairy land.

To this branch library came foreign-born children from Germany, Russia, Italy, Austria, Hungary, Romania, England, and Poland; they were in attendance at nineteen different schools, of which thirteen were parochial. In such an environment, children's librarians worked closely with the social workers at Goodrich House and the staff of the Day Nursery. In this operation, and in branch libraries for both adults and children in sections of the cities where the foreign-born predominated, the library was performing the work of Americanization in the broadest and most liberal sense of the term. Both the child and adult foreigner found that libraries were intimate social centers in his neighborhood. A librarian asked a question of a small Polish boy: "Does your father speak English?"

Frightfully conscious of the intense nationalism of that period, the lad replied: "No, but he speaks American." The results of this training with books, story hours, and library clubs were sometimes magical in transforming a shy and bewildered little foreigner into a reasonably confident American. One girl, who had spent many hours in a children's room of a public library, would write much later: "Often I think that I did not grow up in the ghetto but in the books I read as a child in the ghetto." The same sentiment was expressed in 1922 by Christopher Morley, the American author and editor, when he wrote of his discovery of a small child seated in a doorway in the slums reading *Fifty Famous Stories Retold*:

> Is there anything on earth more touching than a child reading? The innocence and completeness with which the child's spirit is rendered up to the books, its utter absorption and forgetfulness make it a sight that moves me strangely. A child does not read to criticize and compare, but just in the unsullied joy of finding itself in a new world. To see a youngster reading in the slums is to me the most subtly heartsearching experience I know. And behind every such child is the heart and brain of some teacher or librarian who made the book possible and put it into his hand. That is the one thing librarians do, and it is the greatest thing I know of.

Almost half a century later Isaac Bashevis Singer would win the 1970 National Book Award for children's literature for his *A Day of Pleasure: Stories of a Boy Growing Up in Warsaw*. In accepting the honor he stated that there were 500 reasons why he wrote for children, and among them were the following: (1) children read books, not reviews; (2) they don't read in search for their identity; (3) they don't read to free themselves of guilt or to get rid of alienation; (4) they have no use for psychology; (5) they detest sociology; (6) they still believe in God, the family, angels, devils, witches, goblins, logic, clarity, punctuation, and other obsolete ideas and practices; (7) they love interesting stories—not commentary, guides, or footnotes; and (8) when a book is boring they yawn openly, without shame or fear of authority.

The librarian and author who was primarily responsible for the beginning stages of the work with children under Brett, and for continuing it throughout most of Eastman's years as librarian of the Cleveland Public Library, was Effie L. Power. After a brief period as school librarian at the Central High School, from which she had graduated in 1892, she began her work in the Cleveland library with such dedication that she was quite willing to serve without pay for seven months before she was put on the payroll at 12½ cents an hour. Before there was such a thing as a room or an open shelf for children, she was placed in charge of the improvised alcove under Brett's supervision and encouragement. In front of the alcove there was a forbidding counter over which the children received their books but beyond which they might not penetrate for preliminary examination of the volumes. At this counter the children flocked after school and especially on Saturday morning—so many on Saturday that adults were asked, if possible, not to come to the library in the morning hours on that day. The children were orderly in their long queues, in spite of the fact that some had walked miles for the privilege of lining up; they had sampled just enough books in their classrooms to whet their appetites for more. In those discouraging years Power did her level best to make do:

> Sometimes, on a Saturday, two lines of children formed, stretching from the second floor to the street. Often we would issue 1000 books. Each day, I would go about the library and gather up travel, biography, history and nature books either written for, or suited to, children and young people. I would arrange them on the counters of the children's alcove. Each day, they melted away like snow, exploding the theory that children wanted only fiction.

Power was well aware that literature for children did not necessarily mean books written only for children. She knew that boys and girls should be surrounded by all books that were appealing to them because they were sincere in form and content, and because they presented life imaginatively.

At the turn of the century she supervised the first children's room in Cleveland. No longer did she find it necessary to roam the entire library in search of books in the adult collection; she now had her own separate collection and subject catalogue. The result was that children seldom went beyond this room, and those who had been reading only fiction began to vary their literary interests with history, travel and science—until those categories comprised about half the books issued by the department. When a new department was created in 1903, Power became the supervisor of Children's Work. The next year she left the Cleveland Public Library for more than fifteen years, earning her degree in the Carnegie Library School, performing as a member of the faculty at the Cleveland Normal School where she lectured on children's literature and library practice, and serving as the head of the children's department in the public libraries of both Pittsburgh and St. Louis. By the time she returned to the Cleveland Public Library, to serve again as supervisor of Children's Work from 1920 to 1937, she was one of eight Cleveland women honored by inclusion in *Who's Who in America.*

In the 1920s, in cooperation with the School of Library Science at Western Reserve University, Power transformed the Cleveland Public Library Training Class in Work with Children into a graduate program leading to a master's degree. During the summer of 1926 in Cleveland she introduced the first Book Caravan. This was accomplished by commandeering a delivery truck that could be spared during the summertime and fitting it with a card table painted green, four collapsible chairs rejuvenated in the same color. Huge blue and yellow beach umbrellas provided a colorful and protective covering for children and books in parks, orphanages, and playgrounds. The Book Caravan had a capacity of about six hundred books and was designed for areas where library facilities were not available. Power was careful to make certain, as she always did, that all preliminary arrangements had been made. She obtained a permit from the police department because, bureaucratically, this educational operation was classified as peddling! She advertised in advance the places where stops would be made; the result was that crowds of children were waiting when the "library on wheels" arrived. Some registered for library cards; some looked for books on the spot and finding a volume they liked dropped down on the curb, blanket, or some other resting place where they were soon oblivious to what was going on around them. Power's idea was the forerunner of the modern bookmobile; her name of

"Caravan," an appealing one, may have been in her mind when she titled one of her own compilations *Blue Caravan Tales: Stories to Shorten the Road.*

Because of her eminence in the field, in 1928 the American Library Association requested her to write a textbook for children's librarians. She completed this chef d'oeuvre in seven months while on leave of absence at the University of Chicago. It was the first authoritative work on the subject and was widely used as a text both in the United States and Europe. When she retired from the Cleveland Public Library in 1937, it was hardly for the purpose of rest and relaxation. For two years she taught at the Columbia School of Library Service. Later as the librarian for almost a decade at Pompano Beach in Florida, she inspired its citizens to raise funds for a new library to replace the one destroyed by a hurricane twenty years earlier. Among her many books was *Osceola Buddy: A Florida Farm Mule*, written after she began a new career in that region. It is no wonder that a tableau, presented in her honor at Pompano Beach in 1949, had the title "An Orchid for Miss Effie." She felt that the flowers should go to others. It was her humble judgment that any claim to distinction she might have was based on the fact that she was the first children's librarian in the Cleveland Public Library under William Howard Brett.

SCHOOL LIBRARIES

There was a great difference between the old and the new philosophies about what a library should do. The change from one concept to the other occurred in the nineteenth century. Originally a library was considered to be something of a reservoir, a museum, or a warehouse where the records of human knowledge were preserved inviolate for posterity; a library was then the exclusive servant of the priest, the scholar, and the ruler. It was once said of the reading room at the British Museum that decorum was inviolable and silence was sacred: "If you should sneeze, you'd wish you'd never been born." In early times a patron would never have thought of taking a painting out of an art gallery or a book out of a library; the latter was then governed under the assumption that books would not be loaned under any circumstances. Later, when it was observed that such book reservoirs were becoming stagnant intellectual pools, the "cistern was made a fountain." Libraries became sources of human knowledge for all; their dominating purpose was now to put books into circulation by finding a reader for every volume—and a volume for every reader. Under the new dispensation a library was obviously an active rather than a passive force in the community. This meant that it did not wait for those who came voluntarily; it searched for potential clients as actively as a merchant looks for possible customers. Arthur E. Bostwick, the progressive librarian in St. Louis, once stated that the modern librarian "regards inactive readers and inactive books as reflections on his administrative ability and . . . endeavors to reduce both groups to a minimum."

The modern concept encountered considerable opposition, particularly in the late nineteenth century in aristocratic England where some members of the library profession heatedly condemned the new ideas as extravagant tomfoolery. Brett did not agree with his English forebears; because of his commercial experience and his overpowering desire to help people, he had no intention of sitting down and waiting for customers. He looked upon the whole community as a source for possible clients and wanted to create a demand for books where it was currently nonexistent. Furthermore, Brett found it difficult to entice marginal readers into a main library that was cramped and inconvenient, located on the second and third floors of the old Central High School building. He therefore brought the library directly to borrowers through a variety of extensions: branches, school and classroom libraries, deposit and delivery stations (including those in industrial and commercial establishments), and home libraries for children. By the time of his death in 1918 there were 25 branches ranging from large to small, 17 libraries in high and grade schools, one library in a normal school, 487 classroom libraries, 42 deposit stations, 66 delivery stations, 7 children's stations, one municipal reference library, and one library for the blind. All of this brought the total number of book outposts, quite beyond the main library, to the impressive figure of 648. By that time Brett had increased the number of volumes in the library from less than 40,000 in 1884 to

650,000 in 1918. In circulation per capita Cleveland had an impressive lead over every other metropolitan library in the nation.

Libraries owned by schools are not new in the United States, but any systematic effort on the part of public libraries to work closely with teachers is a reasonably recent phenomenon. It appears that the Worcester (Massachusetts) Public Library was the first to do so in 1879, with Cleveland second in 1884, and Detroit in third place in 1887. As soon as Brett became librarian he permitted any school-teacher to draw six additional books, for use in schoolwork, beyond the maximum of one then permitted an individual borrower. This liberalization of the rules was not as effective as anticipated, largely because of an insufficient supply of good books for school children. Brett therefore stepped up the purchase of juvenile books until they numbered more than the acquisitions in other classes. By 1890 it was possible to deposit from thirty to fifty books in seven grammar schools, where they were issued by the teachers to their pupils. The volumes had been carefully selected in history, travel, biography, popular science, and fiction—and the results were eminently satisfactory. By 1891 more than three thousand volumes had been placed in sixty-one schools; two years later there were four thousand volumes in more than one hundred schools. These deposits really constituted small branch libraries because the teachers retained the books throughout the school year, using them freely as loaning libraries for pupils—and their families. This experiment turned out to be a most useful adjunct to schoolwork, and a remarkable extension of the library. By the mid-1890s the only limitation was the lack of sufficient books to supply the demand. By this time Brett had caught the gleam; he noted that the avidity with which the books had been sought emphasized convincingly the pressing need for a system of branch libraries and delivery stations, in a city so widely extended that many residents were practically out of reach of the main library.

SAINT ANDREW AND THE BRANCHES

Brett therefore proceeded to increase the clientele of the library through deposit stations and branches. The former represented caches of books in a variety of establishments, from firehouses (even

one fireboat on the Cuyahoga River) to business establishments to
social organizations. There the main library deposited a small collection as requested by the organization, which was responsible for
its circulation during limited hours on specified days in the week.
The first one was established in 1890 when the Cleveland Hardware Company made arrangements to draw books for one hundred
of its employees. It sent for the books and was responsible for their
ultimate return. Brett was pleased with the arrangement largely
because new readers were being found; of the hundred names registered, only three had previously drawn books from the library.
Ultimately such deposits would be made in dozens of establishments, from the prominent to the obscure; among them were Halle
Brothers department store, the Bell Telephone Company, Warner
and Swasey manufacturing company, Ernst and Ernst, American
Steel and Wire, the Girl's Friendly Club, and Saint Stephen's Sodal-
ity. It was claimed that librarians with sensitive noses could determine, by the odors which clung to books, the identity of some of the
factories at which borrowers were to be found.

During the 1890s Brett also managed to establish four branch
libraries directly under the control of the main library and each
equipped with circulating, reference, periodical, and reading facilities. For the first two decades of its existence all of the circulation
had been from the inconvenient main library, except for a few
school collections and the one station at the Cleveland Hardware
Company. In 1891 the Library Board noted that, in a widely extended city without adequate public transportation, a large part
of the population was out of touch with the main library and could
be reached only by branch libraries, a method which had been successful in other cities ever since Boston Public Library established
the first one in 1870. In 1892 the first branch of the Cleveland Public
Library, known as the West Side Branch, was established in a
rented room (ninety-eight by thirty-eight feet in size) which comprised the entire second floor of a building at 562 Pearl Street (now
West Twenty-fifth). By the end of the decade three other branches
had been established on Miles Avenue, on the south side, and on
Woodland Avenue. Significantly, by 1897 half of the total circulation of the library was drawn from the four branches, without les-
sening the use of the main library which also increased its circula-

tion. This indicated conclusively that the value of the branches lay in the fact that they served citizens who otherwise would have been deprived of the convenience and privilege of library facilities.

Welcome as they were, the four branches were make-do affairs. All were in rented buildings no more than marginally adequate; the Cleveland Public Library did not own any of its branches, nor indeed (outside the main library), any property but its books, furniture, and fixtures. Expenditures for the branches had to be absorbed in the main library's meager budget. Every year, in the annual reports of the Library Board, the well-to-do of Cleveland would be implored to remember the library with generous gifts, to enable it to perform the additional community service that was so obviously necessary. In 1893 John C. Hutchins, a prominent lawyer and jurist who was president of the Library Board, noted that it was a "singular and deplorable fact that, of all the money so lavishly expended by the many rich men and women of Cleveland in various benevolent and charitable enterprises, not one cent has ever been given, either toward the erection of a library building or to help support the library." Thirty years later President John Griswold White would echo the same refrain: "These reports have so often emphasized the necessity . . . of an endowment . . . that our prayer must be beginning to be tiresome, yet we cannot refrain from the repetition." He would have agreed with the Baltimore editor and critic, H. L. Mencken, who once observed sadly that "when the library passed the hat among its patrons . . . it barely got its hat back." Brett would note with envy the New York Public Library's endowment which ran into the millions of dollars, would state that the immediate problem in Cleveland was "making one dollar do the work of three," and would assert that if Cleveland regarded the library as an indispensable part of the educational equipment of the city it must be sufficiently endowed for its work. These perennial entreaties fell on deaf ears. Of necessity, therefore, Brett turned to the possibility of "foreign aid."

This would come from the "good Saint Andrew," a philanthropist named Carnegie. Brett made the first approach in 1891 only to be turned down, curtly and completely. Perhaps Carnegie was thinking of the Rockefellers and the Hannas and Mathers; in any case he wrote:

> Your favor of the 7th instant at hand. I should like to help you,
> but until I get through spending money at Pittsburgh, I shall
> have no surplus to dispose of. Surely, there is enough public
> spirit in the prosperous city of Cleveland to give you all the
> money needed to meet the demand for books.

Brett did not give up easily; a little more than a decade later
Carnegie did succumb to his entreaties. On 4 April 1903 he wrote
Brett as follows:

> In reply to your communications, it will give me great plea-
> sure to do for Cleveland what I have done for Philadelphia,
> Cincinnati and other cities.
>
> Your statement shows that the seven needed Branch Libraries
> might be erected satisfactorily for One Hundred and Eighty
> Thousand Dollars, and that for an expenditure of Two Hun-
> dred and Fifty Thousand Dollars upon them you would have
> everything desired, even looking to the future. If the pledge
> of the City be given that it will maintain these Seven Branch
> Libraries at a cost of not less than Twenty-Five Thousand
> Dollars a year, and in addition provide sites for the buildings,
> I shall gladly give the sum of Two Hundred and Fifty Thou-
> sand Dollars as needed to pay for the erection of these Branch
> Buildings.

Cleveland was happy to accept these conditions and in time would
receive $590,000 from Carnegie for the establishment of fifteen
branch libraries. By 1907 Carnegie would be congratulating Brett
"upon exceeding even Pittsburgh in proportion to the amount of
population in Library appropriation, placing Cleveland first of all."
    Brett had his problems; so, as it turned out, did Carnegie. This
financier supported the building of selected libraries in those communities that would guarantee 10 percent of the building cost for
annual maintenance. Carnegie had begun his benefactions in 1881
with the gift of a library to his native town of Dunfermline in Scot-
land; this was followed with another to Allegheny, Pennsylvania,
his American home by adoption. By 1898 he had added fourteen
additional cities to the list. After that he went into library philanthropy on a wholesale basis. In the United States alone he would

build almost seventeen hundred library buildings at a cost of more than $41 million. There were critics who charged that these libraries were the expression of an exalted ego and that it was Carnegie's desire to scatter over the face of the earth a succession of "monuments" erected as a type of purchased glory. The sun never set on Carnegie libraries which were built in English-speaking nations all over the world, including New Zealand and Tasmania. The Irish Mr. Dooley, a journalistic creation of Finley Peter Dunne, would observe about Carnegie that "ivry time he dhrops a dollar it makes a noise like a waither fallin' downstairs with a tray iv dishes. . . ." On the other hand, Carnegie gave his money without any stipulation that his name be inscribed on the building or commemorated in any way, and it appears that his benefactions were based largely on a conviction—founded on his own experience— that the true university was a collection of books which would elevate the mass of the people. He had no quarrel with higher education for the elite, but he did not propose to subsidize it; even an appeal in the trembling hand of a nonagenarian, written by none other than William Ewart Gladstone, was rejected as Carnegie denied his petition for financial support of the famed Bodleian Library at Oxford.

Nonetheless, Carnegie was to suffer disappointment because of the fulminous reaction of labor to his donations *and* the failure of many smaller communities to live up to their promises. From 1892 labor was bitterly against Carnegie because of the deaths in the tragic strike at his Steel Works at Homestead, Pennsylvania, which had been known for its long seven-day week and low wages. One union leader said that he would "sooner enter a building built with the dirty silver Judas received for betraying Christ than enter the Carnegie library"; he accused Carnegie of building libraries and then reducing wages to pay for them. It was also apparent that some small towns accepted Carnegie money because they thought they were getting something for nothing. They were more interested in civic monuments than in functional libraries. Few such institutions had been constructed in the United States before 1898, and there were no architects experienced in the field. The result was that too many buildings had expensive pillared exteriors and were nonfunctional inside. In time, visitors to small towns in America could easily identify the two standard architectural piles, the library and the Methodist church—one known as Carnegie Classical and the other as Wesley Romanesque. As far as the libraries were concerned, money was expended on Greek temples, some of which did little more than provide a "mausoleum for a ghostly caretaker." In 1917 the Carnegie Corporation, which now managed these transactions, found it advisable to terminate its building program; from that point on, it concentrated its efforts in the library field on the training of librarians.

Carnegie had difficulties with labor unions and small towns but there was no opposition to him in library circles, and Brett became the expert who was most heavily consulted. From 1911 the Carnegie Corporation began to send all plans for library buildings to Brett for his criticism and suggestions, and also conferred with him on the grievous problem of delinquencies on the part of those local communities which failed to live up to their agreement for local maintenance—once Carnegie had supplied the building. In Ohio twenty-three out of seventy-seven communities were delinquent. The prosperous town of Benton, Texas, with a population of 6,000 and a new library that cost Carnegie $10,000, was appropriating only $15 a month from municipal funds for its maintenance! On the other hand, Carnegie libraries were well maintained in states with strong library laws, and it occurred to the Carnegie Corporation that a compilation of such laws might encourage the delinquent states to emulate the stronger ones. Brett had an unusual knowledge of the library laws of all states. Although he was more than fully occupied in his own institution, at Carnegie's request he completed a compilation of them. His *Abstract of Laws Relating to Libraries in Force in the States and Territories of the United States*, published in 1916, was typical of the self-effacing author; he completed it in non-office hours, and the title page does not bear his name! Because of signal service in every respect, it is not surprising that Carnegie—using the simplified and variable spelling in which he came to believe—would pay Brett this striking tribute:

> Cordial congratulations on your noble work. You giv me the value of the libraries, but if I were going to assess your value to Cleveland, I should hav to add a cypher or two. . . .

I thot library work was to be your certain passport into heaven, and I hope you hav no reason to be disconcerted in regard to your future prospects in the next field.

Remember what Franklin says, "the highest worship of God is service to man."

Long life to you who hav done so much to make it a heaven.

TRAINING AND LIBRARY SCHOOLS

By modern personnel standards Brett was not qualified to be a librarian; he had no college degree or professional experience at the time of his appointment as librarian of the Cleveland Public Library. To provide the initial training which he had not enjoyed, he first organized classes at the library. Later he participated in the organization and became the first dean, from 1904 until his death in 1918, of the Library School of Western Reserve University—a superlative dean although he possessed no college diploma.

He looked upon the library as an integral part of the educational system of the city and nation, and was convinced that the work of a good library assistant required no less ability or preparation than that of a teacher, and sometimes more. The problem was that the typical librarian in the post–Civil War period was incompetent. In southern towns she was usually a "decayed gentlewoman with the virtues and foibles of her class." Elsewhere the office was apt to be bestowed upon a local poet, a prominent representative of the Grand Army of the Republic, a retired minister or teacher who was short of funds, or anyone who was known to like books— whether he read them or not. The ultimate was found in Chatfield, Minnesota, where the matron of a rest room doubled as librarian. Because communities, and library boards, did not know what to expect of their librarian, the shortcomings of those who occupied the offices were not recognized for many years. Brett perceived these deficiencies and proposed to do something about them through study and training. Such a program would provide—at the very minimum—a sound knowledge of books and their selection, an understanding of reference work and its importance, a comprehension of the social and economic aspects and needs of the community to be served, and sufficient education to achieve respect and standing in the community. There was still the evil of under-payment; unfortunately many librarians deserved no more but dragged the entire salary scale to their level. It was obvious that training and quality of service, as in the medical profession, were prerequisites to prestige and adequate compensation.

Brett began his training program in 1893 when the first competi-tive examinations were given to applicants for assistant positions in the library. Fifty candidates presented themselves and nine were recommended for appointment. Brett hoped that the time would come when it could be stated that *all* assistants were high school graduates! Soon, when a few normal school and college graduates were appointed to the staff, he met with them voluntarily each week for a discussion of books and their use. The time was seven o'clock in the morning, because the library opened at eight and there was no other hour when working schedules made meetings possible. Obviously, in the gray dawn of winter mornings in Cleve-land a considerable amount of preliminary zeal and dedication was required from all participants, not only by reason of the early hour but because the following workday went on to six or even nine o'clock in the evening—a total of eleven to fourteen hours in the library. By 1912 Brett could boast that of two hundred assistants on the staff, fifty-five were college graduates—five of whom had master's degrees; in addition, twenty-six had also earned a diploma in a reputable library school.

He was well aware that few assistants had the money to leave Cleveland to attend library school; he therefore began his training program with classes at the library. In 1896 when the University of Chicago announced an extension course in library work, he or-ganized a class at the main library which heard a series of lectures in the two weeks just prior to Christmas. Thirty-nine students, al-most the entire staff of the library, were enrolled. In addition nine pages were permitted to listen if they wished, and the same privi-lege was extended to a few visitors. Each lecture was two hours in length. Brett believed the instruction enhanced appreciation of the value of library work and increased enthusiasm for it. In 1898 he developed the first of a series of six-week summer sessions, with mornings devoted to lectures and afternoons to five hours of prac-tice work. Brett, Eastman, and Power gave some of the lectures without remuneration; the principal instructor was the head cataloguer of the Dayton Public Library who gave 59 of the 104 lectures. For a class of twenty-five there were fifty applications, some of them from as far away as Brooklyn and Utah; ultimately its membership included eighteen from the Cleveland Public Library, four others from Cuyahoga County, and one each from Dayton, Wooster, and Fowlersville (New York). The fee for the course was $15. Brett collected $533.66 from tuition, the sale of supplies, and a contribution of $13.80 from a friend. Because the expenditures were also exactly $533.66 (for nonresident lecturers, supplies, printing, and a janitor), the budget was balanced with luck and the beneficence of that providential friend!

The first library school in the United States was established at Columbia University in 1887; it soon moved to Albany where it was known as the New York State Library School. In the following two decades a number of similar institutions became affiliated with libraries or universities. As early as 1897 Brett contemplated the establishment of a library school at Western Reserve University, with literary instruction from academic professors and technical instruction by staff members of the Cleveland Public Library, which would also provide the laboratory for practical work. Such a school, he was convinced, would serve not only Cleveland but the entire state of Ohio.

Seven years later Brett, now doubling as librarian of the Cleveland Public Library and dean of the Library School of Western Reserve University, was proud to report the opening of the new facility in September 1904. He noted that while the school was "not a part of the history of the Library, it is so closely connected with it and so important a step in the educational history of Cleveland, that it deserves record." This it did. In the first year, three members of the library staff were on the faculty, and fifteen more were taking partial courses of instruction. By the close of 1916, when the school had been in operation for a little more than a decade, fifty-two of its graduates (almost one-quarter of the total number) had taken positions on the staff of the library, where they received comparatively high salaries ranging from $600 to $2,400. By 1968 more than thirty members of the staff of the library had been members of the school's faculty, almost ninety had served as lecturers and consultants, and the first four deans had been associated with the Cleveland Public Library in some capacity.

In 1903 President Charles Franklin Thwing of Western Reserve University received an endowment of $100,000 for the Library School from Andrew Carnegie; it yielded an annual income of $5,000. With this stimulus the school was launched. The first class of thirty-one students entered in September 1904—an encouraging number because there had been no special advertising, the school had neither alumni nor a national reputation, and its tuition ($100 a year) was almost double that of similar schools. It was soon apparent that the total annual income of approximately $8,000 (from the Carnegie endowment plus tuition) was insufficient in spite of low salaries for the full-time staff; as late as 1917 the director was paid $2,000, the head instructor $1,320, a secretary $780, and a page $200. By 1905 Brett was imploring Carnegie to triple the endowment to insure a basic annual income of $15,000. His supplications were unsuccessful until 1917 when Carnegie contributed $5,000—an addition to the endowed fund that was both welcome and disappointing. Carnegie's total philanthropy was grand; his individual contributions were sometimes minuscule by contrast.

By 1907 the Library School was running a deficit. At this point Brett and the Cleveland Public Library came to its support in a variety of ways, large and small. It maintained a small branch library in the school, for its sole benefit. It supervised the practice work of students without compensation. The library automobile and driver were made available to the school for lecturers and visitors, and the library lantern and operator were furnished for illustrated lectures. The library contributed staff members to teach courses at less than adequate compensation (the dean received none). It advanced tuition for its own staff members, who "worked off" the loan on their return to the library. In a particularly critical period from 1907 to 1911 it managed an outright subvention of almost five thousand dollars. With the help of Carnegie *and* the Cleveland Public Library, the Library School managed to survive while Brett was its dean—although it was a close thing. In succeeding years it would establish an estimable national reputation.

A "PERMANENT" HOME?

In the late nineteenth and early twentieth centuries there was desperate need for new library buildings. Few public libraries enjoyed the luxury of structures of their own; many had undesirable and cramped headquarters in the local city hall or adjacent to the board of education or in former residences converted for library uses. Some small libraries occupied space which was hardly suitable for the reading and lending of books, for example, in a millinery shop, a hospital, a building which housed horses in a fire department, a physician's reception room, or space over a meat market. Although the situation in Cleveland was considerably better than these examples of what not to do with a library, in the thirty-four years he was librarian Brett suffered the misfortune of never having a main library building that was either adequate or permanent.

When he became librarian in 1884 the library was housed with the Board of Education in the old Central High School building at 850 Euclid Avenue. It occupied rooms on the second and third floors which were small and dark; what illumination there was came through dingy windows and gas lights. Brett managed to get more space in 1890 when an addition was constructed at the rear of the Board of Education building. He also brightened the rooms by the introduction of electric lights. In presenting a successful recommendation to the board in 1891 he cited the enthusiastic report from the librarian of the Cincinnati Public Library, which had just installed electric illumination. The librarian there not only applauded the superiority of the new source of light but believed the improvement in the temperature and quality of the air was sufficient to help in the preservation of book bindings. He was convinced that the main cause of deterioration was carbon in the atmosphere that came from the consumption of gas; this would be obviated by the introduction of incandescent light. His was an early and unique denunciation of air pollution.

In 1901 Brett supervised the first of two moves during his tenure of office; it was from one unsatisfactory place to another inadequate one. The Board of Education sold its building on Euclid Avenue in which it had housed the library rent-free for twenty-two years. At that point, the library moved to its own building, the first in its history, on part of the old City Hall lot which it leased at the southeast corner of Rockwell and East Third streets. The brick-and-stone structure, which had two stories and a basement, cost $32,500 and was erected as an alternative to the expense of leasing rooms.

It was estimated that within five or six years the rental for comparable space in the same area would exceed the cost of the new building. The library expected to stay in the new quarters for a brief period only; for that reason the original lease on the lot was for five years. The structure was designated inaccurately as the "Temporary Main Building." In this instance "temporary" meant a longish twelve years from 1901 to 1913. Ironically, the present and permanent main building, occupied in 1925, would be established at the same location. But the Library Board had no inkling in 1901 that this would be the case, and a move to still another location on Euclid Avenue would occur before a permanent home was found at long last.

Although the floor space in the temporary main building was double that of the previous quarters, it was unsatisfactory from the time of occupancy—and even before! The old Board of Education building was demolished early in 1901, and it was expected that the new building would be ready for the library not later than March of that year. Alas! the construction of the temporary main library was behind schedule, and the building was not ready for occupancy until August. The result was that Cleveland had no functional main library from the middle of March to early August 1901. The immediate problem was what could be done with 115,000 books that had no home. All adult borrowers were given the privilege of taking 5 books (instead of the usual 2) "for the duration"; through this stratagem 25,000 were withdrawn in early March (by the end of the year only 32 of them had not been returned). The balance, more than 90,000 books, was temporarily stored in whatever vacant spaces the City Hall could offer while the staff was kept reasonably busy at transitory tasks such as revising records, cleaning and repairing books, and catching up on the everlasting backlog of cataloguing. Rats occasionally wandered, from the rooms in City Hall where meat scales were inspected, into the low and ill-ventilated and dark basement of the new building when the library was finally able to occupy it; nonetheless, to utilize all available space, the Order Department and the Children's Library were there initially. If the basement was less than satisfactory, the upper floors turned out to be hopelessly inadequate for the rapidly expanding library. Within a short time the institution was forced to

William Howard Brett, Librarian, Cleveland Public Library (1884-1918)

John Griswold White

Brett with special training class (1900)

Children's Room, West Side Branch (1897)

Main Library on second and third floors of old
Central High School building (1879–1901)

Story hour at Perkins Branch (1898)

Elizabethan Club at Woodland Branch (1909)

Normal school class at work, Cleveland Public Library (ca. 1900)

rent additional quarters, at an annual cost of around $3,000, in the Society for Savings Building (for the White Collection, the Department for the Blind, and the Accounting Department) and in the Watterson Building on Second and St. Clair (for the Bindery and Stations departments). The White Collection, numbering 8,000 volumes by 1908, was uncatalogued and unavailable for use. The Newspaper Room moved from pillar to post—from the basement on East Third to the City Hall to the Old Case Homestead on Public Square and back to East Third. All of these quarters were old, inconvenient, and unsuitable.

Newspaper rooms, even when attractive and modern, are traditionally alluring to wanderers who seek refuge from cold or boredom; with a newspaper propped in front of them they can while or sleep away the long hours in an atmosphere where the aromas of the unwashed and liquorish can be intensified by central heating. Although the Newspaper Reading Room of the Cleveland Public Library in the early 1900s would have provided a promising laboratory for anyone involved in the extensive field of character study, it was often repulsive to the serious readers who were among the hundred thousand who visited it every year. It was also unpleasant for the staff member in charge, who bemoaned the fact that visitors could leave while he was required to spend eight hours daily in this environment. At that time the disreputable Union Station for railroads, at the foot of Water Street, was hardly a good advertisement for the city of Cleveland. Brett found it unfortunate that most of the guests of the city received their initial impressions from the Union Station when they arrived and from the Newspaper Reading Room where they perused their hometown newspapers. Both were incredibly shabby and undesirable.

By 1910 the temporary main building had regressed from the barely adequate to the impossible. A long search followed, in the absence of funds to build a permanent and new edifice, to find rented quarters that would be reasonably suitable. By this time, one of the structural problems was to find a building with floors strong enough to sustain the weight of books which were doubling in number every ten years. The library was fortunate in finding the new Kinney and Levan Building at 1375–85 Euclid Avenue, the site of the current Stouffer's Restaurant on what was soon to be called Playhouse Square. Interestingly, when the Halle Brothers department store had moved to a nearby ten-story building in 1910 pessimists said it would fail because of a venture into what was then a residential area of Euclid Avenue.

When the Cleveland Public Library had made the move to the temporary main building in 1901 it had been necessary to close the institution for almost half a year; this time the transition was made skillfully without the loss of even one day. The move was completed in scheduled stages, in order to inconvenience the smallest number of readers, with the books in greatest demand left till last. These numbered 40,000 in the Circulating Department, and all of them were moved in one night. Their transfer was a logistic achievement. At 6:00 P.M. on Tuesday (19 August 1913) the doors of the Circulating Department on East Third Street were closed. In the next fourteen hours the 40,000 volumes with all the records of that department were transferred and placed in proper order at the Kinney and Levan Building. At 8:00 A.M. on the following day the doors of the new library were opened to the public. This tour de force, which some regarded as an Arabian Night's performance, elicited the warm approval of library patrons.

The new quarters suffered from the handicap of being on the fifth and sixth floors (although reached by elevator), and were considerably removed from Public Square—then the center of activity in Cleveland. On the other hand, the new well-lighted structure was fireproof and triple the space previously available to the library. Most of the divisions and departments of the library were once again under a single roof. For the first time the White Collection, now numbering 25,000 volumes, was made available. The great loft on the sixth floor, a room nearly 450 feet long designed originally as a warehouse for a commercial building, enabled Brett to complete the divisional system which he had tentatively inaugurated in 1890. The juxtaposition of circulation divisions on a single floor, with bookshelves as the only dividing partitions, made the new organizational concept functional because intercommunication was so easy.

Brett was confident that this arrangement, representing the library's sixth headquarters, would serve for only a very few years until the next removal would bring the collection "into a spacious and dignified building which would be its permanent home." Actually the library would spend very close to a quarter of a century (1901–25) in the temporary main building on East Third and the make-do quarters in the Kinney and Levan Building (twelve years in each), and an adequate solution would not be achieved until seven years after Brett's tragic death. He had been dreaming of that permanent home from the time he became librarian, but progress toward it would be both tantalizing and ineffectual in his lifetime.

In 1896 the Ohio legislature (there was no such thing as home rule for cities in those days) authorized the first bond issue with which to purchase a site and construct a new building for the Cleveland Public Library. It was for $250,000. Because of the condition of the market, the bonds were not offered immediately, but they brought $295,250 in 1898—the largest amount ever paid in the state for bonds of this class. Unfortunately, no satisfactory site could be found for the permanent home, so the temporary structure was erected on East Third in 1901. In subsequent years Mayor Tom Johnson envisioned the plan of a beautiful mall, a spacious development with buildings around trees and grass, designed originally by a commission that included Daniel H. Burnham, the prominent architect and city planner who had been responsible for the general plan of the promenade at the Columbia Exposition at Chicago in 1893. The buildings in this Group Plan were to be traditional in architecture and similar in height and arch; they would ultimately include the Cleveland Public Library, the Federal Building, the Board of Education, the Federal Reserve, the *Plain Dealer*, the County Court House, the new City Hall, and the Public Auditorium. In time, they would eliminate the city's most notorious tenderloin district from Ontario to East Sixth Street—between the high bluffs on the lakefront to Superior Avenue on the south—replacing the disreputable hovels, saloons, and houses of prostitution that had prevailed in that area. The result was that in due course it would be possible to look from the north windows of the literature and history and White collections of the Cleveland Public Library across fountains and greensward to the glittering waters, blue or not so blue, of Lake Erie. Actually the French Renaissance building of gray marble, five stories high, now the permanent home of the Cleveland Public Library, would epitomize on the south the stately tone of the entire Mall group.

Because of these lofty requirements in beauty and design, it was obvious that the library could no longer rely on the quarter of a million dollars from the bond issue of 1896, if it expected to be a part of the Group Plan for the Mall. As a result it was successful in getting the citizens of Cleveland to approve an additional bond issue of two million dollars in 1912. The city of Cleveland agreed to furnish the site, without charge, in return for a pledge from the library that it would construct a suitable building which would become an integral part of the Group Plan. The deed was delivered to the library in November 1916; the area included both the space occupied by the old City Hall (where the library had been located from 1875 to 1879) and the site of the temporary main library which had adjoined the City Hall on its East Third Street side. In the same year plans for a dignified and attractive building—to stand on Superior Avenue in line with the Federal Building—were competed for, awarded, and approved. Before ground was broken the United States had entered World War I and civilian construction came to a halt. By the early 1920s construction costs had increased so much that another bond issue was necessary before the building was finally completed in 1925. In Brett's time, unfortunately, the library was never to enjoy a "permanent home."

BRETT AND CENSORSHIP

Brett was forward-looking and progressive in relation to so many philosophies and practices of his era that it is surprising to find him in a traditional—even a conservative—role on the question of the selection of books. He was on the right wing in the case of novels and what is sometimes designated as "light literature," and on the additional questions of what constitutes loyal reading in wartime.

The piously inclined have usually noted (as they did in Brett's time) that too many bad books were making their stealthy advance and needed to "be tracked to their dens, even as the pestilence that walketh needs to be hunted to its hiding place." In 1889 John

Crerar, a wealthy manufacturer and prominent Presbyterian and generous philanthropist, died in Chicago. He left upwards of three million dollars, a very considerable sum in those days, to found a library. There were restrictions; in his will he noted:

> I desire that the books and periodicals be selected with a view to create and sustain a healthy moral and Christian sentiment in the community and that all nastiness and immorality be excluded. I do not mean by this that there shall be nothing but hymn books and sermons, but I mean that dirty French novels and all skeptical trash and works of a questionable moral tone shall never be found in this library. I want its atmosphere that of Christian refinement, and its aim and object the building up of character, and I rest content that the friends I have named will carry out my wishes in these particulars.

His friends did so, in a most astute way; they established the John Crerar Library which was primarily a place for scientific and technical reference. Beyond the devout there have always been a number of intellectual aristocrats who have argued that it was folly to cater to the masses; the editor and critic H. L. Mencken, who represented the elitist point of view in the first half of the twentieth century, recommended ignoring the "boobs" who fell on the momentarily popular literature of the day with "gloats and gurgles of literary passion, and [kept] it going incessantly until suddenly its day [was] done."

On the other hand, quite beyond the fact that much popular fiction is by no means escape literature but makes a serious contribution both to knowledge of the past and to the serious consideration of present and future social problems, there is the omnipresent problem of determining *what* books are worthy or unworthy. Arthur E. Bostwick, the eminent librarian in St. Louis, would observe that if the selector of children's books were to exclude all to which objection had been made, only a very few titles would remain; he noted that some adversaries would exclude such books as *Tom Sawyer* and *Huckleberry Finn*, that others would object to favorite folk tales that showed a primitive callousness to human suffering or were told in coarse language, that still others would decry war stories. On the same point Edmund L. Pearson, who wrote many provocative essays about libraries, would state:

> I have indicated a belief that certain improvements are yet to be made in the treatment of boys in libraries. One of these is a frank acknowledgment of the fact that books for entertainment are books for entertainment, and need not be sugar-coated pills covering the medicine of "instruction" or "morals." The Puritan idea is long-lived, but there is no more reason for insisting that books read for fun shall have a "moral" wrapped up in them than in compelling boys before going in swimming to listen to a lecture on the theory of the displacement of fluids.

In 1901 Charles Ammi Cutter, for many years the librarian at the Athenaeum in Boston, would reply to the argument of elitists. He said that a perfect people could afford to have only perfect books, if such things existed. It was obvious, on the contrary, that people were far from perfect—that there was a public of great diversity in mental ability, education, taste, and ideals—and for this obvious reason a great diversity of books must be provided to suit their tastes. There was no escape, Cutter believed, from this fundamental and exasperating difficulty:

> The poor in intellect, the poor in taste, the poor in association are always with us. The strong in intellect, the daring in thought, the flexible in spirit, the exquisite are only sometimes with us. We must manage somehow to provide for them both. There are no "bewt books."

On the contrary, Brett believed it was quite possible to select "bewt" books. In his first year as librarian he was worried about the worthless and "corrupt" literature for the young which was so plentiful; this was the dime-novel type—in Brett's judgment "vicious reading" which would "lower the tone of the whole body social." Much of it, he stated, recounted the daring deeds of "courageous and magnanimous cutthroats, or the wondrous exploits of shrewd and brilliant boy detectives, scarcely more desirable company than the criminals whom they pursue." The impression on the mind of a romantic boy was inevitable; he would conclude that "a quiet life of honest labor is contemptible and that a career of adventure is the only thing worth while." Brett thought the Society for the Suppression of Vice was doing good work; unfortunately it could only advertise a small part of the evil. This was a reference to Anthony Comstock, a self-appointed "roundsman of the Lord" who in 1873 lobbied through Congress an austere postal law against obscene literature and, as a special agent of the U. S. Post Office Department, gave personal supervision to the enforcement of the statute. Comstock also organized the New York Society for the Suppression of Vice in 1873, and three years later inspired the formation of the Boston Watch and Ward Society. In 1905 George Bernard Shaw was to coin a new word when he referred to "comstockery" as the "world's standing joke at the expense of the United States." A few weeks after this pronouncement Comstock created a sensation in New York by proceeding against the Irish bard's play, *Mrs. Warren's Profession.*

In 1887 Brett was happy to inform the Library Board that the greater portion of the additions in fiction had been from the works of writers who had a well-recognized place in literature, for example, Scott, Dickens, Thackeray, and George Eliot. In more recent fiction he had added twenty-three copies of Helen Hunt Jackson's *Ramona* (a romance about the plight of American Indians which appeared in 1884) and fifty copies of Lew Wallace's *Ben Hur* (which had been published in 1880), while only one or two copies of the "lighter novels" (such as *Malaeska, the Indian Wife of the White Hunter*) had been purchased. Brett asked the board to ponder whether the purpose of the public library "might not be better fulfilled by still further curtailing the purchase of the lighter fiction." Such a policy would sacrifice the circulation and popularity of the library; in this case Brett was able to convince himself that a large circulation was not always a sure indication of success, although in every respect he was trying to increase the loan of books. He told the board that the "quality rather than the quantity of books furnished, is the truest measure of a library's usefulness."

It was a noble but losing effort. It was soon apparent, in Cleveland and in every other public library, that "lighter fiction" and juvenile books circulated far more frequently than the classics—and infinitely more so than volumes dealing with European history, biography, social science, and essays. A few years later Edmund L. Pearson would comment with amusement on this entire phenomenon:

> Led on by the necessity of appeasing "practical" trustees, we admit that we do have novels in our libraries, yes, and we are not ashamed of it either; but then, we have plenty of really valuable books that tell how to dig post holes, and shingle roofs. A magazine editor, in a moment of idleness, writes a space-filler alleging that libraries haven't as many books about potato bugs and traction engines as they should have, and a chill goes down the spine of the entire American Library Association. Of course, grown-ups do not read novels any longer for the mere pleasure of it. They do it because they are taking a course in English prose fiction, or they do it for "general culture" or "education," or some other noble purpose. And librarians read them to see if they are all right for other people to read.

Interestingly, this issue was the only one on which Brett and John Griswold White did not see eye to eye. White's range of reading extended all the way from the Bible and the Koran to Diamond Dick, and he was disturbed by the number of volumes secreted in what he called the "oubliettes" in the librarian's office, where they were seen by no one. He was concerned by Brett's statement, in the Annual Report of 1900, that Henry Fielding's *Tom Jones* "probably" should not be in the library, although Brett had found a place for it; in White's judgment "the book ought necessarily to be there." White noted that, like many books written at the time George IV was regent, *Tom Jones* was grossly improper—but it and the others nonetheless belonged in the library. The same was true of the dramatists of the Restoration whose works contained

> more unadulterated filth than even the modern French novel; they are hardly entitled to a place in the library on account of their merits as literature; yet we must consider them to be an essential part of English literature, and matter which must be accessible for study by every serious student of English literature.

Among White's gifts to the library was the sixteen-volume edition of *The Arabian Nights*, translated with commentary by Sir Richard Francis Burton. He found some of it gross and obscene, ". . . representing the daily life and . . . the stories of people who were warm-blooded, and who called a spade a spade, as they did in England until, say seventy-five years ago." White observed that there were three methods of dealing with this problem: to bowdlerize, to disguise in some language unknown to most of the readers, or to translate the whole. Of the three, White had no doubt that the third was by far the best. He agreed that Burton's translation was certainly not suitable for general reading by half-grown boys and girls, but it was most certainly a book that belonged in the library. In time, the Cleveland library would solve this problem in an eminently practical way; it issued both children's and adult's cards, entitling the holder to partial or complete use of the library's resources on the basis of age and maturity.

Brett also believed it was a library's obligation to practice a rigid censorship in wartime, and he did so after the United States entered World War I. Before that happened he was exercised by the administration's delay in entering the conflict, noting that "from the beginning, our indignation was stirred by Germany's shameless and unscrupulous disregard of treaty obligations and by her brutal and deliberate atrocities in the invaded countries." As long as the nation was neutral, however, the library as a public institution was obliged to provide books which presented the German view as well as that of the Allies. Brett admitted that he found it difficult to do so after the sinking of the *Lusitania*, which occurred almost two years before the United States entered the war. He was fearful "that a nation which failed to protect its citizens and to uphold national honor, might forfeit its right to freedom and national independence; that 'too proud to fight' might come to mean, too late to fight. . . ." For him it was a crusade, a holy war.

Early in 1917 he rejoiced when the United States finally joined the Allies in the conflict against the Central Powers, and he turned the library into an active instrument of propaganda. In doing so he placed on the shelves those books and magazines which promoted "a wholesome public sentiment in support of the government and in favor of a vigorous prosecution of the war." At the same time he eliminated all publications which tended "to divide public sentiment in its support of the government and favor giving aid and comfort to those nations with which we are at war." Among the censored volumes were those presenting the utterances of all well-meaning but blind pacifists who cried "peace! peace!" where, Brett felt, there was no peace. He was of the opinion that, for the most part, such volumes were patent camouflages for pro-German arguments. In his judgment, among the worst was *War, Peace, and the Future* by Ellen Key, a prominent Swedish feminist and author. Brett was certain that this innocent volume, published in 1916 as an argument for universal peace and an appeal to all women to oppose all wars, was in reality enemy propaganda of the worst kind.

It is interesting to compare Brett's enthusiastic censorship in 1917–18 with the attitude of the library twenty-odd years later as the United States prepared to enter the Second World War. By 1940 the nation recognized that it might be necessary to enter another conflict in order to check the rampaging fascists in Berlin and Rome and Tokyo, but it had no illusions about the matter; it had lost its faith in the credibility of propaganda and the possibility of fighting wars to end war. Charles Rush, who was then librarian, suggested to the Library Board that it adopt a "bill of rights" which had already been endorsed by many other libraries in the nation. This document, which was adopted unanimously by the Cleveland Library Board, was a far cry from Brett's narrow nationalism. It stated:

> Today indications in many parts of the world point to growing intolerance, suppression of free speech, and censorship, affecting the rights of minorities and individuals. Mindful of this, the Council of the American Library Association publicly affirms its belief in the following basic policies which should govern the service of free public libraries:
>
> 1. Books and other reading matter selected for purchase from public funds should be chosen because of value and interest to people of the community, and in no case should the selection be influenced by the race or nationality or the political or religious views of the writers.

2. As far as available material permits, all sides of questions on which differences of opinion exist should be represented fairly and adequately in the books and other reading matter purchased for public use.

Brett's support for wartime censorship can be explained if one recalls the unique attitude of the United States toward World War I, and if one understands the allure which the military provided for Brett. The First World War was a crusade for high ideals, unfortunately not realized; it was an apocalyptic mobilization to make the world safe for democracy. In such a conflict for holy objectives, any opposition—direct or oblique—was heresy. For that reason Brett, for whom all right was on the Allied side and all wrong a monopoly of the enemy, could justify an *Index Librorum Prohibitorum*.

There was also the paradox that Brett, a quiet and self-effacing individual who could not bring himself to kill a fly or a caterpillar, found wars both necessary and fascinating; he believed that armed conflicts were frequently inescapable, and that when they occurred must be fought to the hilt. During the Civil War his mother was sympathetic with the Confederacy. One can only speculate what influence this may have had on the sensitive son, living in Ohio, who was an ardent supporter of the Union. He made several abortive attempts to enter the army, once rationalizing a falsehood by placing in the bottom of his shoe a slip of paper on which he had written the number 18, so that he could say that he "was over eighteen"—a claim which was logistically true and chronologically inaccurate. These early efforts were unavailing; each time he was either refused by the military as too young or was reclaimed by an aggravated father. Finally, in the last year of the war he did reach eighteen years of age. After learning to play the fife and drum he succeeded in enlisting with the "hundred-day men" as a musician! His commanding officer was so impressed with Brett's zeal for battle that, when the first engagement occurred, he permitted the young recruit to exchange his musical instruments for a musket and to participate in the skirmish. Alas! the denouement was inglorious; Brett was captured by Morgan's Raiders and taken as a prisoner to Kentucky. This unsatisfactory experience did not diminish Brett's infatuation for military life. In 1918, when he was seventy-two, he hoped against hope that he might be permitted to go overseas with the American Expeditionary Force—this time as librarian rather than musician.

BRETT AS ADMINISTRATOR

Brett was a remarkable administrator, in part because he had both the knowledge and the courage to manage well. John Griswold White would testify eloquently to this extraordinary talent: first came careful study, then decision and action that sometimes seemed revolutionary. White remembered well his own doubts about the introduction of the open-shelf system, and the reluctance with which the board had yielded to Brett's assurance that the privileges afforded the public would not be misused; time would vindicate Brett's studied confidence. Another example of Brett's administrative skill was a new charging system for books, one that economized labor while maintaining an accurate account of transactions. In White's judgment there was no bank in the city in which an equal amount of bookkeeping was done with so little loss of time or expenditure of labor.

But Brett was an extraordinary administrator largely because he was so sensitive to the fact that successful management is more than a method of operation. He possessed an uncanny ability, as did Eastman after him, to inspire an enviable spirit of service and self-sacrifice among the personnel of the library. In retrospect this seems surprising because he ran a reasonably "tight ship"; there were many regulations in regard to procedures and conduct. Every day, just before the library opened at 8:00 A.M., it was the custom of Brett and Eastman (then the vice-librarian) to make the rounds—to satisfy themselves that the staff was on hand and that the building was in shipshape order. From time to time Brett sent notices on dress considered appropriate for librarians, with counsel against low-cut dresses (whalebone collars were in favor), short-sleeved dresses (long sleeves preferred but those to the elbow sanctioned), skirts that were more than four inches above the shoe tops ("if slit, the underskirt should be sufficiently long and appropriate"), hats that "exceed the locker space in size," and cosmetics and perfumes represented as having "no connection with business attire." Once on their inspection at the Kinney and Levan Building, Brett and Eastman took special note of the multigraph girls who were stationed behind a railing on a landing adjacent to the stairs. One of the young ladies was exposing five or six inches of leg above her buttoned shoes. Not more than fifteen minutes later a maintenance man was nailing heavy cardboard inside the railing to cut off the view.

No one seemed to resent the regulations, and Brett was able to establish among the staff a remarkable pride of belonging to, and participating in, a joint effort that was meaningful and worthwhile. This is the ultimate in the art of management, an art which many administrators never master although some of them become skillful organizers. After his death, this note was found among Brett's papers:

> Librarianship is like art; it is a jealous mistress and demands all. It is a vocation which one should not enter without a clear calling to it. If, however, one cannot help being a librarian, if one can pay the price and give the service, the reward is great.

How did Brett master this art? It was in part because he set an example. He had less interest in salary than any member of the staff and was notorious in failing to ask for travel expenses or to take vacations. Charles Kennedy, long an editor of the Cleveland *Plain Dealer* and a member of the Library Board for seventeen years, would note that Brett

> had no thought of compensation beyond the mere means of living. Painstaking in the expenditure of money entrusted to him for the work, he personally cared less for a dollar than any man I ever knew.

> This trait was brought forcefully to me when during my first term on the board the members discovered that out of his meager salary Brett was footing all the bills for the entertainment of visiting library managers, and people from other

countries who came frequently to Cleveland to investigate the library system, even then attracting worldwide attention.

He frequently turned honoraria for speeches over to some worthy cause, particularly to the children's departments of libraries. He was so generous in his dealings with others that he left little for himself. At his death in 1918 he left an estate of $1,100 and a considerable amount of indebtedness. On the question of working habits Kennedy observed that there was no schedule of hours; Brett "lived and breathed the library all the time." Because of this Spartan schedule, the blunt White once wrote Brett: "I have at sundry times hinted to you, not obscurely, that in some respects you are a damned fool."

But his success with personnel was due largely to his own personality: the simplicity and directness of his manner, his deference to the opinions of others, his consideration for their comfort and welfare, his boundless optimism about and faith in humankind. He had what the Elizabethans called "nature"—the quality of feeling for humanity. Eastman thought Brett's outstanding quality was interest in people, something that cannot be faked; in her judgment Brett's interest was "so single-minded and intense that he radiated friendliness in greater measure than most men do or can." White believed that the zeal which Brett had created in the staff of the library was the greatest asset it possessed. On the occasion of his thirtieth anniversary with the library, in 1914, there were dozens of moving testimonials. White wrote Brett that he could not "forbear to speak of your uniform kindliness, consideration and gentleness, unaccompanied by any weakness, and your strong sense of justice which has attached to you a loyal staff. . . ." Annie Spencer Cutter, for many years the able director of the Schools Department, was grateful for his liberality of spirit and "a generosity of heart and hand, . . . particularly that generosity of appreciation which always puts the finest and kindest interpretation on people's motives." Rose L. Vormelker, who was later to achieve national prominence as the director of the library's Business Information Bureau and as assistant librarian, put it in verse:

> There's a spirit so rare, in the C.P.L.,
> Whoever comes near it, marks it well,

'Tis the spirit of kindness, that day after day
Thinks only of others,—'tis Mr. Brett's way.

A TRAGIC DEATH

Brett died in triumph and in tragedy. The triumph was the magnificence of his lifework. The tragedy was the manner of his dying, which was none of his choosing.

In December 1916, when Brett was seventy, the board recognized his "long, faithful, intelligent, energetic and efficient service" by re-electing him librarian for a term of five years. This action was obviously taken in an era when retirement age was not arbitrary; it meant, in the normal course of events, that Brett would have finished his service at the close of 1922 when he would have been seventy-five years of age. The board needed him for a number of reasons, chiefly because it felt that his long service would be invaluable in planning the new library building.

By early 1918 Brett was wearing a small service pin with four stars; he had three sons and a son-in-law in the military, two of them in France. Brett himself was on part-time duty as a civilian, serving the American Library Association in the Dispatch Office in Newport News, Virginia. This was an installation for overseas shipment of books; it also served nearby military encampments holding one hundred thousand men. By the summer of 1918 he was traveling to Virginia twice a month, performing two jobs—one in Cleveland, and another on the East Coast. He hoped in time to be sent to France; his dream was to work there with soldiers in the furlough region of the AEF. Brett had no difficulty in establishing analogies between service in libraries and in the armed forces. He noted that "just as our fleets have their naval bases in which they refit and from which they sail, so our little argosies of books . . . in camp and field and fleet, look to the libraries at home as their base of supplies.

Such war service was understandable for the younger members of the staff of the Cleveland Public Library, and all of them who were professionally trained served in the armed forces or were loaned for war duty as civilians in libraries. It was completely unsuitable for Brett, beyond his own undeniable feeling of obligation. His duties at Newport News were routine and far below the talents of the distinguished librarian of the Cleveland Public Library. White would note that it made no sense for Brett to use his vacation time, which was what he was doing, to serve in a minor capacity in Virginia. One of his feminine colleagues, who was also at Newport News, speculated on what could be done to get Brett out of the place. She wrote Eastman that the entire situation was impossible and hoped White could exert some influence:

> It is too hot for him and the building is most uncomfortable. He was sick almost the whole time he was here . . . and I am worried about him. . . . there is no way of getting suitable food and often it is very bad indeed. And I doubt if he can sleep in the little hot room in the library which is right over the railroad. . . . he now fears a "conspiracy of women," so you will have to move warily to do anything to prevent his plans. . . . Perhaps Mr. White could be induced to aid and abet us until cooler weather comes. You know Mr. Brett is not accustomed to move about in the slow southern fashion and that is almost a necessity in the middle of the day at least.

Neither White nor the feminine contingent was able to deter Brett from his duty in Newport News.

In late August 1918 he did return to Cleveland for a brief consultation on the plans for the new building. On the evening of the twenty-fourth, Eastman and Brett left the Kinney and Levan Building shortly after 6:00; Brett was carrying the package of revised plans and instructions for the New York architects who had been retained to design the new library. The two librarians crossed Euclid Avenue to a safety zone, from which Eastman intended to board an eastbound streetcar. An automobile, with a driver at the wheel who had been drinking, came down Fourteenth Street at a high rate of speed, failed to make the turn into the Euclid Avenue lane for automobiles, crashed through the safety zone, narrowly missing Eastman but striking Brett. This irresponsible tippler almost succeeded in wiping out the two greatest librarians in the history of the Cleveland Public Library. The out-of-control vehicle carried Brett in front of it as it careened diagonally across the avenue to the north side where it collided with a lamp post and finally came to a stop. As Eastman saw the accident, "Mr. Brett was buffeted about as the machine pushed him ahead of it, rolled over and over, crumpled up like a ball, and finally was run over by the front wheels of the car as it was checked at the curb." He died less than an hour later at the nearby Huron Road Hospital—the victim of a fractured skull and internal injuries.

A WARRIOR'S BURIAL

Brett's body lay in state in Trinity Cathedral for several hours before the public services. The eulogies were legion, all testimonials to the charismatic quality of his personality. The "Memorial Minute" from the American Library Association, whose president Brett had been in 1896–97 and whose servant he was in war service, testified to the "heart and soul" which he put into efforts of every kind. Dr. Edwin H. Anderson, the director of the New York Public Library, wrote that

> he was one of the biggest men in the profession and certainly the one with the finest spirit. . . . He was the youngest man of his age I ever knew. Although he was seventy-two at the time of his death, I should say he died in his prime; for I knew nobody with a more flexible mind more open to new ideas.

John Griswold White, who knew Brett as well as anyone and had not hesitated to speak frankly on some of his foibles, commented that he could state in all truth that the librarian was one of the most valuable citizens Cleveland had ever had. He went on to observe that "from a nonentity, in thirty-four years of skill and devotion, he made the Cleveland Public Library one of the great libraries of the world, one of the most useful institutions of the kind in the United States, and one of the most useful institutions of any kind in the city." Newton D. Baker, the prominent Cleveland lawyer who was then secretary of war, said that Brett must be ranked as one of America's great educators. The Library Board echoed the same theme—the role of the librarian as a Professor of Books in a People's University. The board noted that

> his vision saw it as every man's library, every woman's library, even every little child's library, holding in its rich stores of

printed wealth the wisdom of the world with its special mes-
sages for each. . . . He was a great educational leader in his
clear, broad conception of the library as the institution which
informally supplements and continues through life the educational work begun by the public schools.

There were many of the opinion that Brett had actually delivered
his own high-hearted valedictory, two months before his death, in
his commencement address to the Class of 1918 of the Library
School at Western Reserve University. He had closed his address
by quoting the last words of Sir Richard Grenville, the English
naval hero and cousin of Sir Walter Raleigh, whom Brett greatly
admired. Grenville, who died courageously in the course of a naval
battle, had said:

Here die I, Richard Grenville, with a joyful and quiet mind,
for that I have ended my life as a true soldier ought to do,
that hath fought for his country, queen, religion and honor.
Whereby my soul most joyfully departeth out of this body and
shall always leave behind it an everlasting fame as a valiant
and true soldier that hath done his duty as he was bound to do.

CHAPTER FOUR

JOHN GRISWOLD WHITE

FAMILY AND EDUCATION

THE SECOND of the Cleveland Public Library's founding triumvirate was John Griswold White—brilliant lawyer, philosopher, library patron, nature lover, book collector, and a most authentic character.

He was pure Cleveland, born in 1845 on Lakeside Avenue near the present site of City Hall. As with most of the early settlers of the Western Reserve, his well-educated parents came from New England. His father, Bushnell White, was originally from Massachusetts and was a graduate of Williams College; until his death in 1885 he was a prominent and cultured attorney in Cleveland who also served, inter alia, as U.S. commissioner and as U.S. district attorney. His mother was born in Connecticut and was a graduate of the Troy Female Seminary in New York. It was founded by a lively and dynamic lady named Emma Willard who became famous as an educator (the first to prove the value of collegiate education for women) and as an author of textbooks and poems, including "Rocked in the Cradle of the Deep."

In his early days John Griswold took long walks with his erudite father; on one stroll they spoke nothing but Latin, on another Greek —on "Chess Day" they played from memory as they walked, without board or men. The youth developed an uncanny ability to read with great rapidity and to retain what he had read. This was true in spite of the handicap of poor vision. He was born nearsighted, but the myopia was not discovered until the youngster was in his teens. His companions had been referring to birds and flowers and distant

105

kites which they saw; such phenomena did not appear in White's restricted vision and he was convinced that his friends were deceiving him. Not to be outdone he described imaginary objects which amazed his colleagues because they were equally invisible. Ultimately came an oculist and glasses, and the outside world revealed marvels not dreamed of or seen before. As far as reading was concerned White preferred to do it without glasses, holding the book close to his eyes. One of his law partners claimed that White had developed the ability to read and to retain in a hard and extraordinary school. In early childhood he returned to Connecticut with his mother during the summer months; there they lived on a farm where books were scarce. Once a week on the trip to town for shopping, the young White made the acquaintance of the bookseller, who gave him permission to stand in an inconspicuous corner and read any book on the shelf until his mother returned. A story begun must be finished; to stop in the middle and wait a week to ascertain how it ended was a hardship difficult to endure. White therefore began his reading "on the run" with short stories and, as his facility increased, extended the length of the literary challenge. It was at least in part due to this unusual early training that later in life he would read several novels in a day and remember long afterward what had been read.

When asked about his education White would list the "little red school house," home, an academy at Canandaigua in New York, Central High School in Cleveland, and Western Reserve College in Hudson. He performed well as a college student, was elected to Phi Beta Kappa, and as the salutatorian at graduation delivered a commencement address in Latin. He would have been valedictorian had he not manifested some of the rugged individualism that marked his entire career. In college this appeared in his use of the library, his disdain for textbooks, his dislike of fraternities, and his affection for literary societies.

When White attended Western Reserve College, aside from a few young men from Cleveland, the body of students was composed largely of the sons of farmers. In White's judgment they had no idea of culture or of the real purpose of higher education, except as a means of getting a degree. They certainly had no intention of using the library if they could avoid it, and in this resolve were encouraged by the college itself—which placed primary emphasis on textbooks rather than collateral reading. This was not unique to Western Reserve College. At Columbia in the mid-1850s the library was open only ten hours a week, and the librarian boasted that although the trustees appropriated $1,500 a year for books, he returned nearly half the sum at the end of the year quite unused. Until 1877 the catalogue of Columbia carried a statement that no freshman could use the library unless he received special permission from the president to do so! In this era, none of the Columbia College librarians considered making books easily available an important part of their jobs, nor did they believe that libraries played a vital part in the educational program. The result of this philosophy, at Columbia, Western Reserve, and elsewhere, was that the average student relied on the textbook, which he memorized with great care.

White had no use for this educational philosophy and proceeded to read through the college library—the first manifestation of a love for book collections that continued and grew throughout his life. His commentary on the undergraduate program, as he recalled it later, was both expressive and convincing:

> I read a great deal of Latin and Greek outside of the curriculum, partly from interest, partly for information,—probably more Latin and Greek outside of the curriculum than within. I did a great deal in mathematics outside our textbooks, a great deal in science outside our textbooks. My classmates were continually telling me that I was a past participle fool to do all this work which did not at all affect my standing in the college. I was salutatorian with second honor. The man who took the first honor, the valedictorian, was a very good friend of mine, and he once set himself down to reason with me on the folly of my course. He said, "You are a much better classical scholar than I am. You have read a great many classical books, of which I only know the names, and it all don't get you nowhere. By concentrating on the books in the course, I get better marks than you do, whereas, you ought to stand higher than I, and you are a damned fool." I intimated that I

thought college was for something else than getting a sheep-skin, and that I was more interested in what I made of myself than in the marks I got.

I read a great deal of general literature. That too was pro-nounced to be folly. When we graduated I do not think any of my classmates had acquired any knowledge beyond that contained in the textbooks which they studied.

White had particularly high regard for two of his professors who actually encouraged him on the unorthodox path toward higher learning; they were Nathan Perkins Seymour in classics and Charles Augustus Young in mathematics and science. Young (who later moved to Princeton) made White a favorite, in large part because the young student's knowledge was so extensive that he discovered some mistakes in the textbooks. White played chess with Young every Wednesday night after the session of the literary society, often into the small hours of the morning.

White did not join a fraternity although at the time this was the thing to do; his father was a member of Delta Kappa Epsilon and wanted the son to affiliate with the same fraternity. He was asked to join but did not accept because he disapproved of frater-nity leadership in Hudson. He went further and organized the in-dependents until, to his father's consternation, they controlled the politics of the campus. White's real interest was in the literary so-cieties which then adorned the college scene, with their own li-braries and programs specializing in debates on subjects varying from the advisability of a congress of nations, the vote for women, to whether it is better or worse to let go of a bear's tail. His concern for literary societies was in part due to his own frank recognition of his inability to memorize verbatim. Once he had mastered a subject he could paraphrase it with brilliance, but he could not memorize the material word for word. Because of the training in extempo-raneous speech which his own society, the Philozetian, gave him, White found these societies extremely valuable—and he was furi-ous when his alma mater ultimately let them wither away. In later years he recalled:

I got as much out of the literary society as I did from anything else in college. . . . When I went to college I knew that I was going to be a lawyer; knew I would have to think on my feet, to speak extemporaneously, and, at that time I was diffident; as soon as I got on my feet I blushed, my knees began to shake, I trembled all over, and, if I had any ideas beforehand, they all vanished. I forced myself to get up every Wednesday night and tried to say something whether I had anything to say or not. The result was that before I got through college I could think better upon my feet than I could with pen in hand. Even to this day, in preparing a brief, much to the discomfiture of my stenographers, I pace up and down the room. I think I got some reputation as a fluent, extemporaneous speaker. . . . I believe today, from my experience, that a literary society is a very important thing.

LAWYER

As a lawyer White was brilliant, combative, and contentious. His presentation was always frank, straightforward, and without dissimulation; for that reason he was an enigma to some members of his profession. He was admitted to the Ohio State bar on the basis of *one* candid answer in an oral examination. After graduation from Western Reserve College in 1865 he read law for three years in his father's office, taking his examination in 1868. By this time his law training was patently superior to other applicants, many of whose curricula vitae boasted a grade school education at best. In those days admission to the bar was not based on a written examination; decisions were made by a traveling court, including a representative of the Ohio Supreme Court, who orally queried candidates. The number of questions, and the time involved, varied on the basis of the board's preliminary judgment of the candidate's qualifications as they reviewed the record before them. It was apparent that White's qualifications were superlative, and for that reason his examination established a record for brevity. The sole question was: "What is the first duty of a lawyer?" White's reply: "To collect his fees."

He thoroughly enjoyed a scrap as a trial lawyer, prepared his cases with dedication and care, and finished a long court session fresher and happier than when the case began. Actually, White played as intensively as he worked. If he was preparing a case for trial, or trying it, he did not want to think of anything else; when he went to the woods for recreation he forgot the past so that he could live in and enjoy the present. He read the same way. White was modest enough to say that he did not know law but knew where to find it. He certainly did; veteran lawyers knew when he was going to try a case because an aide appeared with a great stack of books from which references were to be cited. Once a prominent judge kept interrupting; White was annoyed and finally said, "Judge, if you will only listen until I complete my argument, you will know more about this case than you do now." Any other lawyer would have been reprimanded or cited for contempt. White went right on. There was one particularly wearing and exhausting case in which he was a prime participant, after which all the other lawyers went to a spa to recuperate; White could hardly wait to get on with the next case.

Because one of his best-known cases was that in which he acted as special counsel for the private Cleveland Railway Company against the famous Tom L. Johnson and the municipal system, White established a reputation as a lawyer who specialized in municipal law. He denied it, with his usual vehemence. In time he would become the dean of the Cleveland bar, and this reputation was based on his general virtuosity rather than any specialized competence. Actually he tried all kinds of cases; among other things he was well read in church history and church law, and he was attorney for the Catholic Diocese of Northern Ohio—although he belonged to no church. He also participated in a long litigation between two factions of the Evangelical church. For this reason no one was particularly surprised at an incident that occurred at one of the great cathedrals in England. On a tour of the edifice White displayed such extensive knowledge of the church that the guide assumed that he was of high ecclesiastical rank, and subsequently showed the party through those parts of the structure where only royalty and church dignitaries had previously been admitted. After this episode, White's legal friends began to call him "Bishop"—to the amusement of everyone.

Although White had no preference for one field of law over another, he was confident that whenever he met a specialist he had a distinct advantage over him, "in that I know much he does not—much that is outside his field. . . ." White was convinced that the competent and knowledgeable lawyer could only come from training that was broadly based in the liberal arts. For that reason he favored a collegiate requirement for admission to law schools; he hoped that law might become like medicine, requiring more and more learning. He was convinced that proper training for the profession required

> knowledge of the history and development of the law, and knowledge not only of the law, but of modern society, modern institutions, their relations to humanity, and to what must be the directions and the progress of the law. No longer should the bar have men who were mere pettifoggers.

White was well aware of the attraction of politics for lawyers, but he stoutly resisted the tendency. Asked whether he thought beginners in the practice of law should enter politics he replied: "No, I do not. But try to keep them out." Although offered many opportunities of holding important public offices, he refused them all, and his only activity in public life was his long-time membership on the board of the Cleveland Public Library. He refused membership in the American Bar Association because he could not subscribe to one provision in its code of ethics. This was the restriction on criticism of the conduct of a judge on the basis of his record. White felt that the exact opposite was the fundamental duty of every American lawyer. He observed that he was authorized to practice before every court in the land, including the Supreme Court of the United States. On the basis of his experience he had always regarded it as one of his first duties to oppose a bad judge and to support a good one. He added: "I have criticized judges and opposed judges for re-election, because of incompetence, ignorance, bad habits, unfairness and misconduct as judge, and I shall continue to do so."

INDIVIDUALIST AND "CHARACTER"

White was a stalwart individualist who respected the rights of others but brooked no tyranny over himself. He was frightened by no man or woman and always spoke what was on his mind, sometimes with a gruffness that could not quite hide an underlying chuckle. He had been a devoted son of a family in which he was the last survivor; he was also unswervingly loyal to his friends and to the Cleveland Public Library.

In appearance he was short, stocky, and bearded. There was such an impression of physical vigor that the discovery of his forceful and aggressive personality occasioned no surprise. He wore unpressed blue-serge suits, gaiter shoes specially made for him, and a slouch hat. He always put on a "boiled shirt" but occasionally neglected to put the stiff collar on it before coming downtown. When he remembered the collar he attached a black string tie, but occasionally forgot to tie it. For years he appeared on Cleveland streets walking on zero days to the courthouse on the lakefront without an overcoat. Actually there was no need for one because he wore heavy red-flannel underwear that sometimes protruded in colorful fashion around his sleeves and pants cuffs. It could also be amusing in other ways. One of his close friends recalled that

> one year White went to Idaho for a vacation—to a place called Chamberlain's Basement. The country was rugged. White told Paul Kehoe, who was with him that he was going to rest quietly—at the end of the day—because he had a swelling in his left knee. The next morning the swelling was no better, and White said he would remain there. It was no better in another day; White said they must do something about it, he could hardly move his leg. Kehoe looked at it. He found that his red underwear was tied around his back as a spare and got down into his pant leg and wadded in above his boot tops so tight he couldn't move his leg.

He avoided all entangling alliances, including marriage. This was in part due to great devotion to his mother. There had been a younger sister who died at the age of nine, leaving John Griswold the pride of his father and the idol of his mother. Once, when asked why he never married, the reply was: "It would break Mother's heart." In the middle years of his life he was offered strong support for a judgeship on the circuit court, a high honor; he declined because the court was required to spend part of its time away from the city which would leave his widowed mother alone.

In his will White remembered several women with bequests: a faithful servant of the family for many years, his housekeeper, and the widow and two daughters of "my late friend, Captain Ed. Kelley." During his lifetime he was generous with presents to the wives of friends and to the stenographers in the law office: white kid gloves, lace handkerchiefs, candy (never less than ten-pound boxes), white china with gold for wedding presents. Nonetheless he was never comfortable in the presence of the other sex. He wrote from Jackson Hole, the isolated spot where he vacationed in Wyoming, that he had seen two women there; he claimed that he was not certain he would ever return.

In 1925 he was asked to comment on the changes he had seen in the city. He began by saying that when he first knew Cleveland it was an overgrown village; in his judgment it still was—the only thing "citified" about it was the traffic congestion. There were some differences in the hair and the dress of women, but underneath, the ladies remained the same. He had seen them go from long hair and hoop skirts to much shorter ones—from the Victorians of the post–Civil War era to the flappers who appeared after World War I. In the mid-1920s he wrote:

> Sunday night, I was at the corner of Euclid and 105th and a group of "more or less" young women crossed the street toward me, and I observed that their dress was the precise reverse of crinoline, and as far as possible suppressed all the secondary feminine characteristics. In those days the women wore their hair long . . . now they bob it, . . . But notwithstanding all this my impression is that the "nature of the critter" is still just the same. There is no essential difference.

Stubbornly attached to a daily routine and schedule, he was more than annoyed by any interruption or change in it. He moved his office and his residence but once in the entire course of his life, and then reluctantly. In the late years of his professional career the law firm (then White, Cannon, and Spieth) decided to move from the Williamson Building on Public Square to the Union Commerce Building at Euclid and Ninth, where both the building and the office furniture would be brand-new. At first White absolutely refused to move; finally his partners convinced him that the new building was desirable, whereupon he said he would accompany them but would have no part of the new furniture. Ultimately there was another compromise on this point; it was agreed that he could take his rolltop desk. It was an ancient one with pigeonholes stuffed with yellowing newspapers and letters, and with books everywhere about—but White never had the slightest trouble in finding what he wanted.

After his mother's death some of his friends persuaded him to move from the downtown home on Lakeside Avenue where he was born to the residential district on East Eighty-ninth Street. The new house was large and commodious, with five bathrooms; White moved there with two Irish maids and two dogs of uncertain lineage. Every October he had all windows and doors doubly sealed for the winter months; from that time until spring, fresh air was unknown in the establishment. He had little interest in food and either ate rapidly or concentrated on the book in front of him. Because of his inattention to the feeding process, a portion of his meal was frequently deposited on his waistcoat. The children of legal friends, who were aware of his aversion to a topcoat, sometimes chanted a verse about his fortitude:

> Here's to old John G. White,
> Who loves to break
> The winds from out the West,
> With nothing to protect him
> But the breakfast on his vest.

From his new residence on Eighty-ninth Street he took the street-car downtown to his office. He never owned an overcoat or an automobile. His technique in crossing the street, bad eyes and all, was to duck his head and go full speed ahead; in his judgment, if there was traffic ahead it had better consider its future. After he was knocked down, while waiting for public transportation at Eighty-ninth and Euclid, his partners decided it best to pick him up in the morning and to deposit him at home in the evening. This was done by taxi, and the firm was more than happy to pay for it.

Except for a few close friends he was basically a loner; he certainly was not socially minded. He never joined a church. He was a charter member of the Union Club but went there so seldom that he had to be identified at the door. He also belonged to the University and Rowfant clubs, but attended rarely. He was resolved to wear no harness applied by outsiders; in one of his last letters he wrote:

> I am getting as impatient of temperance tyranny as I was at the tyrannical saloon keepers some years back. I believe in liberty, and I do not like unreasoning domination no matter who it is that imposes the collar. It may be doctors, it may be divines, it may be prohibitionists, it may be saloon keepers, it may be in a good cause, it may be in a bad cause—it makes no difference, I am not willing to be tyrannized over.

Once when the present building was being constructed for the Cleveland Public Library (he was then president of the Library Board), labor unions came to his office and said: "Mr. White, what's it worth to you if you don't have strikes?" The reply was: "It is worth nothing. Leave my office." In politics his father had been an ardent Whig, and in his early days the son had inclined toward the Democratic party. As one conservative friend described it, "seeing the error," he became and remained a staunch Republican. This was not altogether true. By 1928 he had come out for birth control and Al Smith—both unpopular causes. He said that he had once voted for a Democrat (Wilson in 1912), and now "couldn't stand Hoover."

Nothing could better illustrate White's stalwart individualism than his procedure on 23 October 1923 when the eminent Lloyd George of Great Britain was scheduled to dedicate, at 2:00 P.M., the cornerstone of the Cleveland Public Library at its present location. There was a special luncheon beforehand at the Chamber of Commerce not far away. Because of long-winded introductions and interminable speeches Lloyd George was delayed in his appearance at the speaker's platform at the library, which was his only purpose in appearing in Cleveland. Characteristically, White had not attended the luncheon. Promptly at 2:00 P.M., as the president of the Library Board, White pulled out his watch and began the program. Fortunately Lloyd George finally arrived, somewhat out of breath, in time to deliver his major address. From White's own personal philosophy the entire episode was important; he did not intend to be "overdid" by anyone—including the prestigious ex-prime minister of England.

SERVICES AS BOARD MEMBER

White was the greatest benefactor the Cleveland Public Library has ever had. From 1884, when he was elected to its board for the first time, until his death in 1928 the library was foremost in his thoughts. He was responsible for the great White Collection of Orientalia, Folklore, and Chess which has fully justified the inclusion of his name in the list of American book collectors, along with the Huntingtons, Folgers, Morgans, and Newberrys. But beyond his extensive contribution as a bibliophile, he served the library in many other ways. He was a member of the board for more than twenty years (1884–86 and 1910–28), and during seventeen of them was its president. In his first year on the board, a most critical one, he played a vital role in presiding over the hearing on Beardsley and in the selection of Brett as his successor. In another decisive year, that of 1918 when Brett was killed, White was again president of the board and was instrumental in seeing to it that Eastman was selected to succeed Brett. In the mid-1920s when the new building was being erected he gave freely of his time in lengthy consultations with architects and engineers.

During all of this time his money and his ability were at the librarian's disposal to the utmost. Although he had a large law practice he offered his legal counsel, without thought of compensation, to the library itself and to many of its staff members, from the pages in the stacks to the librarian. He was particularly helpful, again without recompense, in shaping tax legislation that would secure more dependable income for libraries and provide safeguards against political influence. In Eastman's judgment Brett and White were jointly responsible for great improvement in the laws relating to city school-district libraries—over the opposition of rural members of the Ohio legislature who were "agin" proposed benefits for cities. In his final years White set for himself a new goal: the establishment of a staff pension system. He made arrangements for the program with the Prudential Insurance Company, and his last objective was actually achieved within three weeks after his death. Under the plan, the employees of the library contributed 4 percent of their salaries, and this was matched by the library itself; on retirement—if they had served enough years—they were to receive a pension equivalent to 50 percent of their average salary over the previous thirty-five years, together with a paid-up life insurance policy of $1,000. Although the details of the library's pension systems have been a source of controversy since the years of the Great Depression, at the time White introduced the first one, it was more generous than any contemporary plan that was actuarially sound.

CHESS AND CHECKERS

White believed strongly that every man should have hobbies. In his younger days he had taken a great interest in yachting, to the point where he was able to design and build his own craft; at that time he had cruised the Great Lakes in his cabin yacht *Camilla*. In this case he thought the hobby also gave him certain advantages in his profession; he learned enough to understand and handle admiralty and maritime cases at law. After that, he developed a fascination for old maps and began to collect them as a means of studying world conditions and historic changes. Soon he came to the conclusion that chess was more educational, with the result that his collection on chess and checkers, still by far the largest in the world, was on its way. White was himself an able chess player in his early years. In the 1880s he played a series with the current world's champion; he lost more games than he won, but his performance was a creditable one.

White's collection of chess memorabilia was all-inclusive. For printed books his aim was to buy every edition of every book and as many manuscripts as possible—ultimately nearly one thousand manuscripts. One of the latter, purchased by White in 1909, was published in 1480 and contained Jean de Vignay's translation of a manuscript by Jacobus de Cessolis, *De Ludo Scacchorum* (On the game of chess). Sometimes there are collateral benefits from such purchases, and there was with this acquisition. The Cessolis manuscript happened to be bound with several political treatises in

Latin, one of which was *Oculis pastoralis pascens officia.* This later turned out to be unique and famous and is now known among Italian scholars as *Il Codice de Cleveland.*

In addition to the materials primarily concerned with chess, White collected important literary works that make significant reference to the game. Castiglione's *The Courtier,* a well-known treatise on etiquette, social problems, and intellectual accomplishments which was published in 1518, is represented in the White Collection by 57 editions from the sixteenth century alone. The *Gesta Romanorum,* actually a collection of medieval Latin stories that has little to do with Roman history, is found in the chess collection in 46 editions, including 9 printed in the fifteenth century. There is the *Rubaiyat of Omar Khayyam* in the priceless Fitzgerald edition of 1859. Another valuable by-product of White's interest is the collection of Rabelais. Because Rabelais wrote of chess, White brought together as complete a collection of editions of *Gargantua and Pantagruel* as exists anywhere; there are at least 120 editions comprising 304 volumes.

There is *Through the Looking Glass,* an Alice in Wonderland volume in which chess is mentioned. It is a first-edition published in 1872 and illustrated by Sir John Tenniel, the English caricaturist famous for his good-humored political cartoons in *Punch.* The collection has a copy of this original edition, containing a charming note in the script of Tenniel.

One of the most interesting items White secured for the collection is a replica of a manuscript of the *Shah Namah* (The book of kings) by the Persian poet Firdausi, whom the Persians themselves rank higher than Omar Khayyam, although the latter is better known in English-speaking countries. The copy of Firdausi was made for White in Constantinople, and both the book and the binding are of Turkish workmanship. Because the greatest Persian poet mentioned chess, the collection happens to be enriched by this prized work.

When White died in 1928 he gave to the Cleveland Public Library all of his Chess and Checkers Collection, which he had retained in his possession during his lifetime. His will confirmed the gift on chess and added:

Home library of Children's Department (1903)

Home library on Hill Street (ca. 1900)

Juvenile alcove at Main Library (1898)

Temporary Main Library at Rockwell and East Third streets (1901-1913)

Circulating Department, temporary Main Library

Order Department, temporary Main Library (1912)

Book Caravan at Sowinski School (1920)

Lloyd George speaking at the laying of the cornerstone of new Main Library (October 23, 1923)

A list of this collection is formed by the entries in my interleaved copy of v. d. Linde's *Jartausend,* which are marked with a red star or dagger, also it is enumerated in his *Geschichte und Literatur des Schachspiels,* . . . I desire said trustees do not hastily decide that books, photographs, or engravings are mere duplicates.

No trustee did; years of scholarly study were required to decide the merit of the White Collection, and no decision could be made "hastily" by trustees—as White, possibly grinning sardonically when he wrote the will, was well aware. Actually, White had gone far beyond Dr. Van der Linde and his bibliography of chess lore entitled *Das erste Jartausend der Schachlitteratur* (the first thousand years of literature on chess), which covered the period from 850 to 1880. It was published in Berlin in 1881. White, with his assiduous scholarship, added more titles than were found in Van der Linde's original work! Beyond books and manuscripts he also gave the library hundreds of chessmen of great value. These curios which White had purchased ranged from a Chinese walrus ivory set, attributed to the twelfth century, to elaborately carved modern Chinese ivory and modern Chelsea chessmen in bright colors.

The Chess and Checkers Collection—numbering 12,000 volumes plus the chessmen—was appraised when White died at $300,000. Beyond the intrinsic worth of the texts, exquisite bindings adorned many of the volumes, particularly those by modern French and English masters. The collection was given in its entirety to the Cleveland Public Library and was so extensive that it had more than twice the number of items listed in the largest chess catalogue then available, that of the Royal Library in The Hague. Beyond this benefaction, for more than a quarter of a century (from 1899 to 1928) White had been annually giving the library volumes on orientalia and folklore, (as will be noted in the next section of this chapter). In addition he left the library the bulk of his liquid assets, worth in cash about a quarter of a million dollars, to provide an endowment for additional purchases. Thus, at White's death the total value of the Chess and Checkers Collection, that of the Orientalia and Folklore Collection plus the endowment for future purchases in those areas was well over a million dollars.

ORIENTALIA AND FOLKLORE

The John G. White Collection of Orientalia and Folklore began in 1899, accidentally. The United States had just acquired the Philippines, but the library had practically nothing on that archipelago or any other part of the Orient. White believed that Americans ought to equip themselves with some knowledge of the East. In addition, at this particular moment Mayor Robert McKisson cut the library appropriation. In the judgment of a *Plain Dealer* reporter the reason was that "Hizzoner" needed street cleaners rather than books simply because the former could vote in elections. As a result of this political action the library was compelled to discharge a number of employees, to reduce its hours, and to curtail the purchase of books. White wondered what he might do to supplement the library's meager income; he concluded that he would buy some of the books it should have. Brett's first Annual Report of 1885 had noted a donation from White of 122 maps and 4 books; in the next fourteen years White's contributions averaged only 35 titles a year.

A great increase began in 1899, after which White's annual gifts averaged more than two thousand. From this point White's Collection of Folklore and Orientalia was a logically planned and gradually perfected library of special resources—almost without rival. In February 1899 White wrote Brett about the new collection, with an aside on the librarian's puritanical attitude toward "naughty" books:

> Herewith I send you for the library four volumes, two of which are a translation of a Collection of Neapolitan Folk Stories. May I suggest to you, if you have not already done so, the formation of a division of "Folk Lore." My immediate reason for making the suggestion is that I purchased lately Burton's Translation of the Arabian Nights, which I propose giving to the Library as soon as I have finished with it. This would very properly go into a shelf of Folk Lore. There they will be removed from the general crowd and at the same time not consigned to the oubliette of the librarian's office, a place quite unworthy of them. The translation which I send here-

with is occasionally too plain spoken for general reading, yet there is nothing improper about it.

In his Annual Report of 1899 Brett would record that the most important and valuable gift from an individual was a collection of Arabic folklore (eighty-five volumes bound and unbound), the gift of Mr. White. By 1928 these gifts in orientalia and folklore would number more than sixty thousand volumes and would have an estimated value approaching one million dollars. If White had given several hundred thousand dollars in a lump sum to the library it would have been featured in every newspaper in the nation. Instead, he gave, annually, hundreds of valuable books and manuscripts. Ultimately, when it was no longer news, Cleveland would awaken to the fact that it had the finest collection of orientalia and folklore in the nation. This was a part of the modest White's design. He once wrote: "I hope you will not think I am affecting modesty when I say that I would prefer not to have so much ado about the books which I may give to the Library."

As a lawyer White was preeminent because of his emphasis on factual information ably presented. As a book collector he was preeminent because of his fascination with the esoteric, the mysterious, the unknown, and the foreign—all of which he would have avoided in a court of law. He never had any intention of providing a collection which would have popular appeal; his purpose was to "furnish scholars and students who wish to seek original sources with such works as the funds at the disposal of the library authorities would not otherwise permit." By this he certainly did not mean the publications of the day—no matter how valuable—but works, chronicles, histories, memoirs, and letters which formed the original sources from which knowledge could be obtained.

His selections were chosen with care and by plan. He told Brett that when the mayor had reduced the library's budget in 1899, he had prepared a list of folklore and orientalia which he was determined to give to the library. Some of it he wanted to read himself; other selections, he felt, ought not to be absent from any "well regulated Library." As far as books on the Orient were concerned he did not intend to give books *about* Eastern peoples but to let Ori-

entals speak for themselves. He bought only translations, prefer-
ably editions that had both the translation and the original text.
He wanted all the different translations that he could find, so one
could be compared with another and, where there was sufficient
knowledge, with the original. He was realistic:

> Of course people cannot be made to read these Oriental
> books, but at any rate the library gives them an opportunity,
> and if they read with their brain, as well as with their eyes,
> they will certainly begin to appreciate that Orientals have
> different manners, different thoughts, as well as different cus-
> toms from ours, and that what would be the best government
> for us, would be the most oppressive tyranny for them; that
> it would be the greatest abuse of power, to attempt to impose
> our feelings, our customs, or law on people so alien in every
> respect. At the same time they will have a chance to form
> some idea of Hindoo and Arabic religion and thought, and
> will not have to take it all second-hand. . . .

He defined "folklore" in his own special and meticulous way, a
definition that was broad in some respects and restrictive in others.
On the one hand, he gave the subject a broad interpretation; he
wanted not only folk tales or stories, but manners, customs, music,
and superstitions as well. In the case of superstitions, however,
there were limitations. He wanted no organized religions once they
had become established and conventional—whether they appeared
as Mohammedan or Christian theological works—or any other controversial books of a religious nature. He was interested in the
"superstition" found in all unsystematic religious beliefs, for example, fetishism, animism, totemism, ancestral worship, magic from
India and Africa and Oceania, legends of the saints, and "all other
unorganized debris of religion." The plan for the collection continues, as White requested, to provide source material for scholars
who are interested in the history of thought and the development
of human imagination.

Among the many items in the folklore collection, medieval romances constitute a strong feature and include the tales of King
Arthur, Charlemagne, and Alexander the Great among the many
other heroes of the writers in the Middle Ages. There are more

than sixteen hundred volumes of proverbs, the largest such collection in the United States. Noteworthy among materials on fables are many editions of the Sanskrit *Hitopadesa* and other compilations of animal tales, along with many editions of the epic of Reynard the Fox. The collection on Robin Hood is surpassed only by the materials in England at the Library of Nottingham. Altogether, the White Collection on Folklore is one of the world's largest. Its universal importance was indicated by the publication, in 1965 by G. K. Hall and Company of Boston (which specializes in reference works), of catalogues of the folklore-folk song and chess collections. The two volumes, in quarto size, contained 25,000 entries, and were originally priced at $105 a set.

This collection is also enriched by a variety of "by-products," simply because White could not resist the purchase of valuable books, regardless of field, if he thought they were needed in Cleveland. Early travels had a particular fascination for him: "where people are pushing out into the unknown, finding everything wonderful, misunderstanding much, but preserving to us ... knowledge of customs, modes of thought and faiths that advancing civilization has destroyed." The material on gypsies ranks second only to that in the Gypsy Lore Society of London. Other special fields which are well rounded include early literature in Icelandic, Old Irish, and Middle Dutch. There are many grammars and dictionaries, including 400 African, 250 Arabic, and 175 Chinese.

There is much on the theory of law and comparative law. In this and other professional fields White had believed that only books dealing with principles, rather than with cases or statutes, should be bought; this was because "principles endure," but "their concrete application is out of date before the book leaves the printer." In 1908 he told Brett that he was purchasing for the library Pethier's *Traités des Successions*, a classic two-volume work on civil law published in 1812. White noted that law libraries in Cleveland had not reached the position where they believed books on foreign systems of law to be either of value or interesting; for that reason he felt that those interested in the theory of the law should be able to read about it in the Cleveland Public Library. The same reasoning applied to the English Chronicles by the Master of the Rolls, of which some 250 bulky volumes had been published by the time White commented on them in 1905. He told Brett that he must have this collection of medieval British and Irish sources in the library because it was not equalled by those of any other country; the *Monumenta Germaniae historica* on Teutonic medieval history could not rival it. Even the American Revolution is represented in the White Collection with volumes from the libraries of Lord North and General Gage.

Beyond special subject-matter fields it is possible to cite numerous examples of specific works and languages which so interested White that he collected enough editions to make them invaluable to a scholar. Of the *Arabian Nights* there are editions in fifty-three languages; the Koran is present in thirty-eight languages (the British Museum has it in twenty). There are more than 250 Singhalese works, making the collection the best outside of the British Museum or Ceylon. The Sanskrit collection has long been the largest and most complete in the United States, and the same is true of the holdings in Arabic and Syriac. The Buddhist canonical books, or *Tripitaka* (literally "triple basket"), are available in Pali, in a 750-volume Chinese set, and in a 39-volume edition presented by the King of Siam; that nation's grand patriarch also presented 27 volumes of Siamese commentaries to accompany the gift. The sacred writings known as the *Avesta*, attributed to Zoroaster, are present in various editions and languages along with commentaries.

BOOK COLLECTOR

Along with the ardor and excitement of collecting, White had something which collectors often lack—a love of reading for its own sake. Furthermore, he not only read the books he was collecting but almost anything else he could lay his hands on. Charles E. Kennedy, long prominent on both the *Plain Dealer* and the Library Board, would comment that White, a classicist and philosopher, also reveled in what were known as "thrust and parry" novels—red-blooded duelling romances of land and sea, dealing with buccaneers and stagecoach robbers. Every week specified members of the staff of the library would send books to White, carefully selected by those who knew his tastes to be catholic. In time, there was little in the field of philosophy, law, religion, history, folklore, ethnology, ethics, and popular literature that his mind did not encompass; for this reason he was sometimes called "a living encyclopedia." One could cite Goldsmith: "And still they gaz'd, and still the wonder grew, how one small head could carry all he knew."

White did not read every word of the more than sixty thousand volumes on orientalia and folklore that he gave the library; he did read some in their entirety, and enough of the balance to know exactly what they were about. A few examples, from his many written commentaries, are indicative of his thoughtful analyses of these volumes. He would send Brett a note, asking him to dispatch an assistant to collect the current volumes he was presenting to the library; this message would frequently be accompanied by a commentary on the books, in considerable detail and with great discernment. Within two months in 1899 he sent editions of Valmiki's great Sanskrit epic of India, the *Ramayana*, in which Rama (to recover his abducted wife) allied himself with the king of the monkeys and fought a mighty battle in Ceylon. The first translation, in five volumes, was in poetry; White didn't think much of the poetry although he found it easy reading, but was disturbed that it was considerably abridged. The second translation was in prose; he found it "frightfully prosy"—all the poetry had evaporated. There was a *History of India As Told by Its Native Historians*, in eight volumes. White thought the schema was fine, but the execution was not equal to the design. He had read the *Makamat* (Assemblies) of Abu Mohammed al-Kasim al-Hariri in two volumes, a presentation in euphuistic style of fifty episodes in which an old rogue of the twelfth century goes from place to place earning his living by clever talk. As far as the first volume was concerned, White found the notes more interesting than the text; both volumes had made him think more highly of Burton's *Arabian Nights*, simply because there was much in the *Makamat* that he would never have understood had it not been for a prior reading of Burton.

When he sent Brett the *Cabinet des Fées* in forty-one volumes (published in Geneva and Paris in 1785 and 1789), he asked the librarian to pay close attention to Volume 37, because of the bibliography and biography found there on various French authors or translators of fairy tales. There was the *Baharistan*, a collection of pithy short stories written by Jami, a fifteenth-century Persian poet. White found him strangely modern: "I found in it the old story of the Irishman who looked over the shoulder of a gentleman writing in the coffee house." This was a stock tale out of American vaudeville, indicative of the fact that there is little new under the sun. He sent a volume with a forbidding title, *Minhāj-i-Sarāj, Tabākat-i-Nāsiri*, translated by a Major H. G. Rafferty in the last part of the nineteenth century. White believed it to be especially interesting because it was one of only two existing accounts, written by contemporaries, of the conquests of Genghis Khan and the fall of the Abbasside Caliphate in the thirteenth century. He found that the pious Mohammedan spoke of the infidel Mongols in much the same manner "in which our Christian European historians speak of their Hunnish conquerors." He thought *The Book of Black Magic*, by Arthur E. Waite (London, 1898), fascinating because it was the only one he had seen which told how to "work the oracle."

White could be critical, even hypercritical, of authors and editors and dealers. There were Volumes 14 and 15 of *Documents from the Temple Archives of Nippur*, edited by Albert T. Clay. In White's judgment:

> Two more utterly worthless books published under the guise of learning, I never saw. They are nothing but a series of tablets used in the book-keeping of the Temple; not being complete, they don't tell us what it took to run a first-class provincial temple. They don't inform us as to prices nor as to rents. All that the editor seems to see that they furnish is a list of names of private persons, uninteresting themselves, which can only serve to date other tables equally uninteresting, and perhaps to fix the chronological order of obscure kings, who never did anything of interest nowadays.

He had grave doubts about a volume on *Folk Tales from Tibet*: "The preface sounds honest, but the stories are old acquaintances, and the similarity of the hare and Brer Rabbit looks suspicious." There was a volume titled *Dan au Derig*, published in Edinburgh in 1874, purporting to be folk verses from Ireland. White wrote Brett: "These poems seem to me exceedingly fishy, comparing them with other translations from the Irish which I sent to you." He thought little of the *Code of Hammurabi* in the edition associated with the name of William Rainey Harper, the biblical scholar who was president of the University of Chicago. He informed Brett that he distrusted anything emanating from the University of Chicago because "its professors are constantly playing to the gallery, and I very much distrust their scholarship for that reason." He wrote what he called a "useless letter" to Messrs. Kegan, Paul, Trench, Trubner and Company in London—but told these dealers that he was sending it anyway. They had just informed him that *Serendia*, originally published for twelve guineas, was now seventy-five pounds. This was outrageous; their prices had increased to the point where he told them frankly, "I buy one book in England, where I used to buy thirty to fifty." White was a shrewd bargainer and found the market much better in Germany and France and the Slavic nations.

It is apparent that a considerable knowledge of, and a total appreciation for, all foreign languages is essential for anyone connected with or using the White Collection—as donor, administrator, or scholar. White set the example. In college he had been a classicist with a solid knowledge of Latin and Greek. He considered the study of languages excellent training for the thinking man; in his later years he would deplore the fact that undergraduates were given considerable option in the selection of their courses and regretted that Latin and Greek were no longer as widely studied as they once had been. Beyond his college training, completely on his own he taught himself to read German, French, Italian, and Spanish. Because he was self-taught and was interested primarily in a reading knowledge, he always pronounced these modern languages on the basis of what he saw in English, which was not usually what a native would have said. No matter; he developed an unusual linguistic virtuosity, and in his time was probably the only lawyer in the United States who had some acquaintance with Arabic, Persian, and Sanskrit. He originally acquired some facility in these languages as a by-product of his chess collection; many of its books were in Oriental languages, untranslated. White said modestly that his achievement was not really so great, because chess books had a limited vocabulary, perhaps only fifty to a hundred words. Nonetheless, every strange language was a challenge, and it was most unusual for him to admit as he did in 1914 in a commentary on a large number of recent and esoteric titles he had just contributed to the library:

> For good measure I will throw in one I cannot read. If anyone at the library can make it out, advise me.

By the time the Cleveland Public Library celebrated its centennial in 1969 the White Collection had more than 115,000 volumes in more than seven thousand languages and dialects, including over fifty incunabula, that is, books printed before 1501. Included in this vast array were most of the varied materials which have been used to make books over the centuries, for example, clay tablets, bark strips, parchment, and various types of paper.

For more than a quarter of a century after White's death the administrator and the translator who deserve major credit for building and interpreting the White Collection were Gordon W. Thayer and Francis E. Sommer. Thayer was curator from 1916 to 1956 and won acclaim for building the collection from the solid foundation which its founder had established. He had earned baccalaureate and master's degrees from Harvard in English, had served the library of his alma mater, during World War I spent his apprenticeship in the trenches through the Saint-Mihiel offensive and then became chief librarian for General John J. Pershing. With his profound knowledge of history and a wry sense of humor he came to the conclusion that war had changed considerably since the time when a man could buckle on his shield and sword and say to his lady: "Wife, me-thinks I shall sally forth and slay me five hundred Saracens before breakfast"; it was now an impersonal, push-button affair with poison gas and machine guns—Thayer said he could be recorded as "agin" it. As curator of the White Collection he was a bibliophile who combined an enviable knowledge of books with an uncanny sense of what and when to buy. He was a worthy successor to White, augmenting the value of the collection in every respect.

Sommer was a linguist par excellence. Born in Speyer on the German Rhine, raised in Belgium, he went to college in Antwerp—a language crossroads—where he learned Italian, French, Flemish,

Latin, English, and Spanish as well as his native German. Before he was sixteen he had started the study of Persian, Turkish, Arabic, and Hebrew. He picked up a knowledge of Sanskrit during vacations and learned Romanian from a friend. He served in the Swedish and American diplomatic corps in Russia, and during World War I worked for the International Red Cross. In these capacities he added Swedish, Russian, Chinese, Polish, Ukrainian, and Tatar to his repertoire. During World War II his grammars of Pacific Ocean languages were used by the United States Armed Forces in that area; these were in Eskimo, Russian, Chinese, Arabic, Korean, and Japanese. A Boston newspaper, usually noted for its conservatism, once credited him with knowing 3,125 languages! Sommer's comment on the allegation was as follows: "This was no slight exaggeration. It was preposterous." It would have been more accurate to state that no one knew more languages than Sommer and that only a handful knew as many. He admitted to speaking 14 fluently, but confessed he was a bit rusty in Turkish; he read 22 easily and had a limited vocabulary but some working knowledge of 45 others. By this time he was making no attempt to learn any new ones. As he explained it:

> I am afraid to cram any more words into my head. Either the top will come off, or some morning I will wake up speaking Babel.

Sommer considered Russian and Polish the most difficult of the major Western languages to learn, with Japanese the most perplexing of the prominent Oriental ones. Of the Romance languages Romanian was the easiest, in his judgment, and Persian was the least demanding of the Oriental languages. There was a legend that, if the Sphinx ever decided to talk, Egypt would find it mandatory to import Sommer by plane—before that enigmatic monument once again lapsed into silence! In addition to his linguistic skill Sommer was also an accomplished musician. He had studied cello and the theory of music at the Conservatory at Antwerp; in Cleveland he was heard on the radio both as soloist and in ensembles.

In 1939 Thayer, Sommer, Fern Long (who became head of the Adult Education Department and later acting director of the library), and Margaret Fergusson (the director of the International Institute) decided to commemorate the filing of the five-thousandth entry in the index of languages contained in the White Collection. It was Koko from the Congo area. This they did with a unique affair called the Omnicibal Banquet (Omnicibal was a specially coined word based on the Latin word for food—*cibus*). They would have no part of the better-known dishes such as Hungarian goulash, Italian spaghetti, French fried potatoes, Swiss steak, Polish ham, Irish stew, Russian caviar, Scotch broth, and Welsh rarebit. Their menu was exotic. For that alleged reason, invitations were sent only to those with perfect stomachs, and all of those who agreed to come were supposed to sign a waiver for possible consequences.

The banquet gave the library staff and their friends a grand opportunity to indulge in erudite persiflage and high humor. The program indicated that the dinner would be held in B.E. 2482, First Moon, Tenth Sun—which just happened to be the year of the Buddhist era corresponding to 10 January A.D. 1939. The motto for the occasion was *Mumesechecocco vexio egussa cagua*, from the language of the Saliva Indians of the Orinoco basin. Freely translated as "Mud is your best food, eat more of it," this was a hilarious fabrication for the occasion only; actually the words meant "One, two, three, four." The guests, forty in number, were given two menus—one for the purpose of exhibition and the other for guidance in eating. The first was titled *Woyute Sni* which means "Cold Food" in the Dakota language. In this case the offerings were for reading only; some of them were:

CHOPPED STRAW SAUSAGE

(*Moroccan style*)

TROPICAL RAINWORM JELLY FROM SUMATRA

SMOKED DEVIL FISH

(*Harmless to angels*)

PICKLED ELECTRIC EEL

(*Very shocking!*)

CHEESE FROM EVERYWHERE

(*except Limburg*)

OCEAN ALGAE FROM IRAQ

(*Dip spoon in water first*)

SPICED FLYING FISH
(*Keep your feet on the ground!*)

There was another list of alleged foods that could be sampled by permission only! Theoretically they included:

GOAT MILK CHEESE
(*Milk from the goat of Mahatma Ghandi;*
too rare to be devoured)
RANCID BUTTER FROM TIBET
(*Held in high esteem, by Tibetans of all classes.*
To appreciate flavor, please step outside)
GEOPHAGOUS DELICACY
(*Favorite dish of the mudeaters of the Orinoco basin.*
Sample brought by an explorer at the risk of his life)
PITCHEREE BALL
(*Mild Australian narcotic made of weeds mixed with the*
ashes of gum-tree leaves. Not recommended to non-natives!)

The "eating" bill of fare was entitled *Khadyadrabyer Talika*, which is the pure Bengali term for "menu." It read as follows:

KHADYADRABYER TALIKA

SOUP
Hung-Shui with emulsified kumiss

ENTREE
Sliced kangaroo with boomerang sauce

VEGETABLES
Zanzibar coral plant à la Nirvana
Bengal millet   Lotus salad
Chopped aconite
Whipped seaweed from the Red Sea

BREAD & BUTTER

Cozonac   Kuskusu

Tibetan yak butter preserved with

grass juice

DESSERT

Zebra cake

Sour Himalaya snow

Black mutton wine à la Mongole

ONLY THE LESS ATTRACTIVE TYPES OF BEVERAGES WILL BE SERVED

The Cleveland *Plain Dealer* noted that the sliced kangaroo with boomerang sauce looked and tasted quite like roast beef, that the Zanzibar coral plant à la Nirvana was remarkably like cauliflower, and that no one could have told sour Himalaya snow from lemon ice. The *Plain Dealer* was absolutely right. The Thayer-Sommer-Long-Fergusson quadrumvirate had devised an esoteric menu which disguised well-known comestibles as much as possible. The use of Russian borscht with sour cream was suggested by Long and immediately accepted by the committee; Sommer gave it the Chinese name of *Hung-Shui* ("Red Water") because it was made with red beets. The gravy was called boomerang sauce because the effect would be felt later. Rice was described as Bengal millet; lotus salad was simply a euphonious name for lettuce. Garden parsley passed for poisonous aconite; whipped seaweed from the Red Sea was successfully colored horseradish mixed with chopped red beets. Foreign names for cereals, the Romanian cozonac and the African kuskusu, were employed to disguise plain American bread, while the butter was dyed green in order to suggest Tibetan yak butter preserved in grass juice. Hungarian layer cake was re-titled zebra cake. The black mutton wine à la Mongole was just simply hot coffee.

Everyone enjoyed the occasion to its end, certainly one which exposed more than a few of the myriad offerings of the White Collection. The guests parted with a lusty rendition of the tune *Klosh polakely t'sladie!* In Chinook this means "Goodnight, ladies."

NATURE LOVER

White liked to spend his summers in Wyoming where he could
fish to his heart's content. It was there that he ended his days, looking up at the Grand Tetons he loved. He lived in nature and in
books with equal relish, and knew the ways of the field, the forest,
and the waters as well as he did the paths and the highways of
literature. Before departing on his vacations he was known to go
into a famous Cleveland bookstore, Korner and Wood, and ask for
volumes "dripping with gore on every page." In those days it was a
three-day trip by railroad from Cleveland to Jackson Hole; White
would put nine novels in his suitcase and nine more in the trunk.
On the trip out he would read three novels a day from the suitcase;
on arrival in Wyoming he would switch the literary contents of
trunk and suitcase for the return journey.

White's party usually included some of his law partners, and they
went into rough country. Jackson Hole is a fertile mountain valley,
almost fifty miles long and six to eight miles wide; among its salient
features is Jackson Lake, eighteen by four miles, through which the
Snake River flows. White could rhapsodize about the area. In 1905
he would write about sleeping:

> Out upon the beach with our feet within a foot or two of the
> water's edge, the shale accomodating itself to every inequal-
> ity of the human frame, the lapping of the waves made a
> sweet lullaby and we all slept soundly. . . . At that time Jack-
> son Lake was a most beautiful lake, blue as a colleen's eye.
> Surrounded for the most part by a forest, with here and there
> beautiful beaches and meadows above the lake, the inlet run-
> ning for some time through a forest, until it reaches the mead-
> ows above, the lake near enough to the Teton Mountains
> to reflect their shape, filled with fish, it was a most beautiful
> mountain lake.

He would philosophize about the doves who aroused them in the
morning:

> Wakened by the mournful music of the mourning doves, who
> through our stay have tried to persuade us that true love is
> sadness, that the path of true love is never smooth, and that

fruition ends in sorrow; after summer comes winter; that those that love must part. Whence have they such sorrowful earthly wisdom?

At times he could be boastful. In his diary for 16 July 1919 there was a notation: ". . . warmish night. 3 blankets just right." It was no exaggeration; Jackson Hole had enough altitude that during the early morning hours ice in the water pail was not infrequent.

To be sure, there were physical hardships and discomforts. Once the pack train attempted to ford Pilgrim Creek and had "a h—— of a time." White did not think that any of his group manifested much sense in the episode. A horse carrying the sugar and flour became mired in the creek and "it took the united strength—not the brains, for they had none—of the party to get it out." For centuries travelers have expatiated, and sometimes exaggerated, on the size and lethal characteristics of mosquitoes in the West, and White was no exception. On one occasion he noted:

> We camped at Lewis Falls, where the king of the mosquitoes holds court even in mid-winter. Among the sports of the court are skiing, snowballing and the like. Occasional forest rangers who venture there in winter say it is a fearsome sight to see the mosquitoes engaged in snowballing.

White was there in summer, and mosquitoes were a fearsome sight in this season as well. He was trying to write in the evening:

> They sail between me and the page. They light on the page. They buzz in the ear. They attack the ears and neck. They entangle themselves in the hair. They bite foreheads, cheeks, and noses. They bore for blood on the backs of the hand. They hold enquiry meetings on the sleeves. In short, they are a damned, miserable nuisance.

In actuality White was invigorated by the challenge and the demands of this exciting environment. In 1923, when he was almost eighty, he would write: "Ye Gods, what more could the heart of man desire,—fine camp, beautiful scenery, pleasant weather, and flapjacks?"

After White reached the age of seventy his law partners began to worry about the advisability of his going alone to Jackson Hole; from this point on they made certain that someone from the firm accompanied him. In his early seventies this was an unnecessary precaution. A younger partner would go West with White and would return so exhausted that he had to take another vacation to recuperate. White would come back so invigorated that he would tie up a stenographer for a month while he dictated a play-by-play report of the trip. These chronicles are available, year by year and in great detail, at the Cleveland Public Library. But when White reached the age of eighty, everyone had cause to be concerned, including White. He began to note that the last twenty years had made a great difference in his legs and wind and climbing power. There was further proof of "vanished youth and strength"; it took him forty minutes to walk a mile on the road. He noted, as realistically as ever:

> Hate lying in the shade while others are at work. Miss my former pep and snap. While idleness is as distasteful as ever, I haven't the energy to do things. . . . My right eye, long poor, is getting much worse. My knees are stiffer. My elk-hide boots always heavy now seem to make my feet belong to someone else. What a pity to be writing these sad confessions this beautiful morning lying in the shade while packing is going on.

In his youth, vis-a-vis his parents and college authorities, White never did what he had been forbidden to do—but sometimes he failed to ask permission! This might involve a visit to the lake or the "old swimming hole" or engagement in a prank of one kind or another. This practice carried over to the end of his days. In 1928 he did not ask a physician whether he could go to Jackson Hole because he was certain that his request would be denied. As a result he was so ill on his last trip West that he was taken across the Chicago Terminal in a wheelchair and was carried in a bed to Jackson Lake. At the beginning of his last illness he refused to have a nearby physician come to the mountains because, as he said, "The doctor might order me out of camp, and that order I would not obey." At Jackson Hole two trained nurses boiled water over a wood fire and performed whatever else was necessary for his comfort. It was there in late August 1928 that he died, close to the lake and the mountains that had been his intimate companions for many years. At the time of his passing he was so far removed from civilization that it took eight hours for the word to reach the outside world. White had always preferred isolation—in a variety of ways.

CONTRIBUTION

In his will White directed the trustees to care for the lot in Lake View Cemetery "where my father, mother, and sister are buried, and where I wish to be interred, and of the monument thereon. . . ." The funeral was held at the First Unitarian Church at Euclid and East Eighty-second Street, where the Reverend Dilworth Lupton conducted a simple service for the "grand old man of the Cleveland Bar." Lupton said, inter alia: "Mr. White was a man rich in deeds, a man who shunned the limelight and publicity."

In reflecting on White one is inclined to think of Sir Thomas Bodley, and of the immortality that inheres in books. Few libraries exceed in fame the Bodleian at Oxford, founded about 1600 by Bodley who was an Elizabethan diplomat. Many had implored him to establish almshouses, to found a hospital, to devote his money to various charitable and worthy causes. To all these entreaties he turned a deaf ear. Others might heal broken bodies; he intended to do something for men's minds. Because of his decision, the Bodleian Library has helped in the development of the minds of generations of Oxford men, and the name of Bodley is known wherever men of culture gather to talk a common language of learning and wisdom.

The late John Love, long a contemplative columnist for the *Cleveland Press*, once said that five hundred years from now the best known Clevelander of his era was likely to be John Griswold White—rather than the fabricators of products in wood and metal and stone whose valuable work is inevitably overcome by the devastation of time and obsolescence. White knew that all the constructions of man, whether of granite or brass, in due course pass away, and that only thought is eternal. One of the last books he purchased for the library contained these lines, which apply to him as perfectly as if they had been written in his honor:

> These are our works, the works our souls display,
> Behold our works when we have passed away.

CHAPTER FIVE

LINDA ANNE EASTMAN

EARLY YEARS

LINDA ANNE EASTMAN served the Cleveland Public Library for almost half a century, three years in relatively minor capacities, twenty-two years as vice-librarian under Brett, and twenty years as librarian. She began her service in 1892 as a lowly apprentice at 12½ cents an hour, and was receiving an annual salary of $9,000 when she retired in 1938 during a depression-ridden decade. In her first year in the early 1890s the library had all of eighteen employees, if one counted the pages, and a few less than fifty-eight thousand books. When she left the institution—the only woman librarian to have assumed so much responsibility in a city as large as Cleveland—there were twelve hundred employees and more than two million volumes in the library. She would continue in the illustrious footsteps of Brett, and would blaze a few new trails of her own.

The Eastman family came to New England in 1636 and appeared in Ohio in 1828; on the paternal side it descended from Miles Standish. Linda Eastman was born in Oberlin two years after the close of the Civil War. When she was seven the family moved to Cleveland where she resided during most of the ninety-five years of her life. Five of the six children in her family were engaged in public service or in occupations associated with the fine arts. Of the three sisters, two were librarians and one was a teacher. One brother was an artist, and another was a music publisher and dealer in violins.

Linda Eastman attended the public schools of Cleveland, graduating from West High with honors. She then took a course at Cleveland Normal School and entered the teaching profession, which she was to follow for six years. Her first job was in a small frame school in west Cleveland where she began to borrow books from the public library. She soon found the books more influential than the oral lessons and came to feel that the library was the real center of the educative process. In her student days she had enjoyed a chance meeting with Brett, an encounter so impressive that it probably had an influence in changing the direction of her life. As a small girl she had gone to the library and was told that a volume needed in her schoolwork was not available. Brett happened to overhear the conversation and told her to wait, saying he would see to it that someone hurried out and bought a copy for her. The emotional impact of this friendly and totally unexpected concern on Brett's part may very well have influenced her choice of library work as an ultimate career—a prime example of the effect small but genuine acts can have.

By 1892 she had made up her mind; in the school there was too much indifference on the part of many students and too little opportunity to show the interested ones what the world of books had to offer. She wrote Brett:

> I love books, and the part of teaching which is so uncongenial to me is the forcing of knowledge into those pupils who have no taste at all for books or reading—and they, in our public schools, are legion. The library worker is constantly helping people to the books they want, and also bringing to their notice those of which they knew nothing, and it seems to me the field is as broad, in an educational way, as that of the schools. I am willing to begin at the bottom and run my risk in working up, for the sake of engaging in an occupation toward which I have long felt an inclination.

Brett was impressed but talked to her candidly about the hazards of the decision and asked her to give serious thought to the pros and cons. He pointed out that as a teacher she was already well up the professional ladder; as a librarian she must start on the lowest rung and would receive half of what she had been getting in salary. She was not deterred and scored 98 percent on the demanding written examination which Brett had initiated for applicants. It was on seven fields—literature, history, arithmetic, geography, grammar, spelling, and penmanship. She began library work as an apprentice at one dollar for an eight-hour day and soon received appointment as assistant in the West Side Branch on Pearl Street (West Twenty-fifth) at $900 a year. It was the first branch established by the Cleveland Public Library and was situated near the market in a barren room over a store. While working there she took an extension course from the New York State Library School at Albany; by special arrangement she was sent the full notes for the complete two-year program. In 1894 the library opened its second branch, the one at Miles Park, and Eastman was made its librarian. In the same year she began the publication of the *Open Shelf*—a selected, annotated list of new books—as its first editor. The following year she was offered the position of head cataloguer and vice-librarian at the Dayton Public Library; it paid $100 more a year, that is, $1,000, and Cleveland had no position which was comparable in responsibility and appeal. Eastman accepted the assignment, remained in Dayton for one year, and returned to Cleveland to the newly created position of vice-librarian in 1896. When Brett was killed in 1918 the Library Board did not hesitate; there were numerous male applicants for the top post but Eastman was selected unanimously. Charles E. Kennedy, the prominent journalist and veteran member of the Library Board, was convinced that in the choice of Eastman "the trustees paid a debt to one whose creative, intelligent work along library lines has never been surpassed." Actually, she had neither applied for the position as librarian nor indicated in any way that she wanted consideration. John Quincy Adams once said that the job should seek the person, not vice versa. Eastman was in complete agreement with the New England Puritan.

A PERMANENT HOME

Two events dominated the twenty years of Eastman's tenure as librarian: the construction and occupancy of the new and permanent library building in the 1920s, and the frightful impact of the Great Depression in the next decade. When the library moved to the Kinney and Levan Building in 1913, it calculated that those quarters would be adequate for not more than seven years, that is, until 1920, with books and use increasing at a normal rate. Actually both increased at an abnormal tempo with the result that the situation was harrowing and depressing by 1921. The large room on the sixth floor, once intended as a warehouse, had seemed both commodious and conducive to the departmentalization of the library in 1913. With the rapid growth in the library's activities, the one-room accommodation turned out to be less than satisfactory. The accessibility of books and the compactness of the arrangement, which had once seemed to be desirable, had now degenerated into a clutter of inanimate objects and a complete lack of elbowroom for human beings. All pretension to aesthetic effect, either in ornamentation or spaciousness, had to be abandoned. As the number of books increased, a second story of book stacks was built on top of the first one; book shelves were also built at the ends of aisles, around doorways, and behind bulletin boards. As the White Collection increased, there was no place to either shelve or exhibit it. The library had been made the depository of the book collection of the Cleveland Engineering Society, but there was no space available to house it, either in the Division of Technology or indeed anywhere in the library. Reading rooms were so crowded that they no longer provided the peace and tranquility that was essential for browsing, reference, study, or use by groups for club or society meetings. Office space for the staff of the main library was so lacking that heads of departments who wished to write articles or reports had to do so in the already overcrowded main reading room.

It will be recalled that a bond issue of $250,000 had been authorized in 1896—not enough to purchase a suitable site. To this had been added $2 million from another bond authorization in 1912. In 1916 the city of Cleveland donated the present site of the main library, with the understanding that the new library building would conform in architecture with other structures in the Group Plan. Dr. A. D. F. Hamlin, who later became president of the Administrative Board of the School of Architecture of Columbia University, was retained as advisor for the building program. He planned a contest for the selection of the architect for the new structure. Two juries of architectural authorities were chosen, one in New York and one in Cleveland. Eight architectural firms entered the nationwide competition. With all of the plans before them, the two juries—acting independently—selected Walker and Weeks of Cleveland (this firm also served later as the architects of the Federal Reserve and Board of Education buildings nearby, Severance Hall in University Circle, and the U.S. Post Office Building in the Terminal Group).

Shortly after this award was made the United States entered World War I and the government asked for a postponement of all public building. By 1921, when construction was again possible, prices had doubled. So had the need for library space. In 1918 the average daily attendance in the Kinney and Levan Building was 2,000; Eastman was convinced this would rise to 5,000 in the new building and that it would be a waste of the taxpayer's money to build for a smaller number. On the day before Brett's death in 1918 she managed to convince him, and he instructed the architect to plan a building that would accommodate an eventual daily attendance of 5,000, considered by some to be adequate for fifty years. Actually, Eastman's guess of 5,000 a day, to be reached sometime in the future, turned out to be one of her few mistakes. In the first year of occupancy the daily average of persons entering the building on weekdays was 5,057; by 1929 Eastman was wishing there was some way to expand the walls (she did rent space in nearby buildings); by the year of her retirement in 1938 the average daily attendance was 7,000. In the darkest days of the depression it had sometimes run as high as 12,000.

With $2.5 million available from previous bond issues, another authorization of $2 million was required to finance a building that would cost more than $4,600,000. A major campaign was mounted by the library. Eastman and members of her staff made speech after speech before audiences large and small. Churches read supporting statements from the pulpit; businesses were reached through bulletins; slides and films were shown in moving-picture houses; newspapers were deluged with copy; more than a quarter of a million leaflets and dodgers were distributed; windshield stickers were offered to motorists. During the final week someone donated a truck; it was decorated as a float which toured the city displaying an immense book covered with slogans in giant type which all could read. In the library bond issue for $2 million in 1912 the total number of votes cast was a few more than 34,000, and the majority in favor was 1,477. In 1921 more than 140,000 votes were cast on the library bond issue, and it carried by a majority of over 20,000. Except for the campaign for mayor, the vote on the library issue exceeded that for any other issue or candidate. Another bond issue in the same election, that for a criminal courts building, was defeated. Eastman and her staff had every reason to be proud of their accomplishment.

With money in hand Eastman proceeded with the laying of the cornerstone for the new building in October 1923, and with the dedication of the completed building in May 1925. The laying of the cornerstone was a gala affair with international overtones. The main address was given by David Lloyd George, the statesman from Wales who had been prime minister of Great Britain during World War I and a member of the "Big Four" at the Versailles Peace Conference in 1919. Lloyd George appeared in Cleveland with Dame Margaret and Miss Megan, a daughter. He was met with appropriate ceremony by Mayor Fred Kohler and Newton D. Baker, the Cleveland lawyer who had been secretary of war during the critical years of World War I. Downtown hotels and stores and office buildings were festooned with Stars and Stripes hung beside the Union Jack—a proximity reminiscent of the close association during World War I but one which did not reflect accurately the differences which had developed by 1923. The Welsh in Cleveland were delighted by the appearance of their countryman and entertained him at tea. The Irish in Cleveland were outraged that a politician who had tried to shore up the hated British Empire would be invited by anyone for any occasion. They requested a permit for a counterparade on Superior Avenue; this was denied by Mayor Kohler. They sent a protest to John G. White, the president of the Library Board. This was a mistake. White replied:

> The public library of the city of Cleveland and its board is an American organization and institution. It is neither British nor Irish. It is not a hyphenated American. It entertains no fear, such as you may seem to have, of the United States ever becoming a part of the British Empire.

The new Cleveland Public Library building was opened to the public on 6 May 1925. On the previous day it had been inspected by more than three thousand guests, with eight hundred proud members of the staff serving as guides and escorts. Again Eastman managed to move, this time from the Kinney and Levan Building, with a minimum of inconvenience for readers, a repetition of her performance in 1913. The planning for this move had gone on for two years; 2,500 special boxes were built, each one just large enough to hold a shelf of books. Properly marked, it was a relatively simple operation to move the volumes from their resting place in the old structure and to place them on the corresponding shelf in the new. Maintaining service in the old building as its books were removed was another matter, but it was carried on until 30 April. On the last night about thirty regular patrons were still maintaining a vigil in the periodical section. For weeks workmen had been closing in; this was the last stronghold. Finally the remaining tables and chairs were removed, and at closing time a tired librarian took books from the last three readers, who were perched on boxes, and told them they were no longer in a library. A "temporary" sojourn of twelve years in the Kinney and Levan Building, originally designed as a warehouse, had finally come to an end.

The new and "permanent" home, constructed with care as a library, presented a striking and welcome contrast. Only two library buildings in the nation, the New York Public Library and the Library of Congress, were larger, and both of these were inferior in plan and equipment. The new Cleveland library had six floors, including a purely functional half-basement, or thirteen floors if supplementary mezzanines were counted. In all, there were forty-seven miles of shelf space. The conventional plan of a central stack room, rising from basement to roof, was abandoned in favor of one that gave each of the sixteen large reading rooms its own belt of stacks. Ample daylight had to be provided for all reading rooms, and the architects, Walker and Weeks of Cleveland, increased the amount of available daylight 40 percent beyond that afforded to the older Federal Building next door. A Spanish-style courtyard provided some of this ample light.

The exterior was in eighteenth-century French style and imitated the Federal Building in general appearance, though not in detail. The interior made lavish use of marble and hand-wrought metalwork, while some major spaces, the main entrance hall included, had delicately ornamented vaulting. Brett Memorial Hall, the main reading room, seated two hundred comfortably; its walls were lined with Botticino marble up to the coffered vaults that were painted in rose, blue, and gold. Its furniture was executed in old English oak. The White Collection, adequately housed at last, was given its own room on the third floor, designed and furnished, according to White's wishes, with pink marble wainscotting and doorframes, iron grillework, and a coffered Renaissance ceiling. Other departments of the library benefitted from the new space that now became available; for children, there were the Lewis Carroll and Robert Louis Stevenson rooms. The Newspaper Room, having been an isolated wanderer in and around Public Square for a quarter of a century, was now able to join the other departments under the same roof. While many of the furnishings for the new building were of wood the architects, to minimize the fire hazard, eliminated timber entirely from the construction with the exception of the exterior flagpoles.

Occupying the entire west side and part of the south side of the main floor, handy to the main entrance, was the division often called "the first point of contact and the court of last appeal." This was General Reference. It now contained the public catalogue and all cyclopedic and other material too general in nature to belong to the subject divisions. Add to this the yearbooks, city and trade directories, gazeteers, pamphlet and clipping files, government reports and indexes, magazine and newspaper files, and it became apparent that this division could at last perform a major portion of the immediate reference work of the library and attend to a major share of requests for information. "If You Don't Know Ask the Library" became the central rule, with a barrage of questions both overwhelming and bewildering. One reference librarian, also a bard, broke into this verse after a distracting day:

> At times behind a desk he sits,
> At times about the room he flits.
> Folks interrupt his perfect ease
> By asking questions such as these:
> "How tall was prehistoric Man?"
> "How old, I pray, was Sister Ann?"

"What must you do if cats have fits?"
"What woman first invented mitts?"
"Who said 'To labor is to pray'?"
"How much did Daniel Lambert weigh?"
"Should you spell it 'wo' or 'woe'?"
"What is the fare to Kokomo?"
"Is Clark's name really, truly, Champ?"
"Can you lend me a postage stamp?"
"Have you the rimes of Edward Lear?"
"What wages do they give you here?"
"What dictionary is the best?"
"Did Brummel wear a satin vest?"
"How do you spell 'anaemic' please?"
"What is a Gorgonzola cheese?"
"Who ferried souls across the Styx?"
"What is the square of ninety-six?"
"Are oysters good to eat in March?"
"Are green bananas full of starch?"
"Where is that book I used to see?"
"I guess you don't remember me?"
"Haf you der Hohenzollernspiel?"
"Where shall I put this apple peel?"
"Où est, m'sieu, la grande Larousse?"
"Did you say 'two-spot' or the 'deuce'?"
"Say mister, where's the telephone?"
"Now which is right, to 'lend' or 'loan'?"
"How do you use this catalogue?"
"Oh hear that noise! Is that my dog?"
"Have you a book called 'Shapes of Fear'?"
"You mind if I leave baby here?"

By 1970 the General Reference Division of the Cleveland Public Library had more than 160,000 items in its collection, which qualified it as a major library in itself. Before the First World War people had been accustomed to *go to* the library; now many of them *call* it. In recent years the United States has become a nation of telephoniacs—with the result that by 1970 the Cleveland Public Library was receiving 200,000 telephone calls a year, half of them in General Reference and Public Catalogue, with upwards of half a dozen staff members manning the phones during busy hours of the day. Edmund Lester Pearson, who was always acute in his observations on libraries, noted the transition from the old days, when the chief function of the librarian was to "hand out books over a counter," to the modern era when it became his or her responsibility "to hold the cup of knowledge itself to the lips of the thirsty, and to discharge the functions of high priest of the Pierian Spring." This demanding task was done well enough that one admirer, struggling with an especially difficult problem, wrote that "only God and the library know" the answer. Another devotee, even more confident, claimed that "If I lost my little dog Towser, I should go straight to the Public Library, for I know the Library could and would find him." The expectation and hope for such service is now general and universal; today all librarians, wherever found in the building, are expected to know the answers. Sam Walter Foss in his *The Song of the Library Staff*, a collection of poems both perceptive and amusing, would versify in this manner:

> See the Reference Librarian and the joys that appertain
> to her;
>
> . . . .
>
> See this flower of perfect knowledge, blooming like a
> lush geranium,
> All converging rays of wisdom focussed just beneath
> her cranium;
> She is stuffed with erudition as you'd stuff a leather
> cushion,
> And her wisdom is her speciality—its marketing her
> mission.
> How they throng *to* her, all empty, grovelling in
> their insufficience;
> How they come *from* her, o'erflooded by the sea of her
> omniscience!
> And they knew she knows she knows things—while she
> drips her learned theses
> The percentage of illiteracy perceptibly decreases.
> Ah, they knew she knows she knows things, and her look
> is education;
> And to look at her is culture, and to know her is
> salvation.

MARILLA FREEMAN

The individual librarian who had the important responsibility of administering a main building that was both new and impressive was a staff member who was equally impressive and relatively new to Cleveland. She was Marilla Waite Freeman, a complete foil to her superior, Linda Eastman, who was in charge of the entire system. Both were highly competent, commanding respect and loyalty, although they were quite different in manner and personality. Eastman was quiet, soft-spoken, indifferent about dress and plain in appearance, prim and precise as an administrator, prudish about manners and morals and books, her whole life dedicated to and in large part lived in Cleveland and the Cleveland Public Library. Freeman was outspoken in a voice that could always be heard, attractive in features and bearing, sometimes unorthodox in administration, catholic in attitudes and literary tastes, cosmopolitan in experience, many-sided in interests that extended from library work to poetry to training in the law. Far removed from the popular image of a librarian in her day, she was so vivid and dramatic in personality that critics sometimes called her a prima donna. A reporter once likened Eastman's office to a cool and dignified sanctuary. "There is," he wrote, "a tendency to tiptoe as you go in; it is like walking into a church." Freeman's office reflected neither sanctity nor placidity. There was considerable activity and bustle in and around it—so much that the head of the adjacent literature department, who craved peace and tranquility, moved her desk as far away as the limit of the room would permit. "Am I talking too loud?" Freeman once inquired of a visitor. She added: "You know, I haven't a library voice."

Freeman was born in Honeoye Falls (in western New York) on 21 February 1871. This can be ascertained only from personnel and pension records at the Cleveland Public Library. She was reticent about her age, kept it a secret, and gave no date of birth in the many biographical sketches that were published, for example, in *Who's Who in Library Service*. Because of this quirk in personality, which could be amusing, she was once characterized—quite accurately— as a "woman of undetermined age but very determined character." When she died in 1961 the *Cleveland Press*, lacking complete evidence, could only state that death had come to Miss Freeman "who was well past 90"; actually she had just reached that milestone. Her family stemmed from the Pilgrims at Plymouth, particularly John Alden; for this reason her father, who was a Presbyterian clergyman, was named Samuel Alden Freeman. The daughter received the baccalaureate degree from the University of Chicago in 1897 and to this accomplishment added a summer course in library work at the New York State Library School at Albany. There followed a variety of solid experiences in all phases of library work: in research under the famous librarian and historian William Frederick Poole at the Newberry in Chicago; as head librarian at Michigan City (Indiana), a library which she organized and developed from its beginning, at Davenport (Iowa), and at the Goodwyn Library in Memphis (Tennessee); as reference librarian in Louisville (Kentucky) and Newark (New Jersey). During World War I she was in charge of the Base Hospital Library at Camp Dix in New Jersey. After this conflict was over, Freeman, always ready to accept a challenge, earned a degree from the Law School of the University of Memphis and was admitted to the practice of law in the state of Tennessee. This she never did; she once said that she had studied law to discipline her mind. This legal training, however, resulted in her appointment in 1921 as librarian of the Foreign Law Department of the Harvard Law Library. It was from this specialized and prestigious institution that she came to Cleveland in 1922 as librarian of the main library—a position she occupied until her retirement in 1940.

By the time of her retirement she was around seventy years of age, give or take a little, depending on who was doing the figuring and from what records, if any. During World War II she moved to New York City where she served with distinction as a special representative of the Cleveland Public Library; her function was to aid in the accumulation of "underground documents" which would become the nucleus of a special collection in the Midwest concerning World War II. New York, as the first port of call for many European refugees, was also the place to which clandestine publications from all warring nations first found their way. Later she served as director of the library of Saint Joseph Hospital in New York, a logical sequel to her wartime position as librarian of the base hospital at Camp Dix in 1918. From 1949 to 1951 she served as the chairman of the Motion Picture Preview Committee of the American Library Association, an assignment for which she was particularly qualified because of her pioneer work in that field in Cleveland. Her first contribution to the *Library Journal* had appeared in July 1899; until the late summer of 1959, when Freeman was eighty-eight, she was still editing the department titled "New Films from Books" in that magazine, contributing to it her own perceptive reviews of motion pictures.

It was a long and remarkable professional record; she was a stimulating contributor to the *Library Journal* for sixty years, an active member of the American Library Association for almost seven decades. She had a vision of what libraries should become, and through these professional channels was able to inspire many younger librarians with a desire to bring these ideals into being. She also had the rare gift of breathing life into everything that deeply interested her. When she left one of her early posts, a disappointed trustee of the library thrust a remarkable tribute into her hand as she boarded the train. "Oh, yes," he had written, "someone else can be found to do the work—but who will breathe upon the clay?"

Beginning in 1924 Freeman increased the use of the library enormously by the use of posters and displays, but particularly through bookmarks built around motion pictures, plays, and symphonies which were about to be performed in the city. The bookmarks listed pertinent reading which would contribute to greater understanding and appreciation of the performance, with the cost of printing borne by the theatres. The experiment began with a small bookmark of fifteen titles on the French Revolution in connection with the film *Scaramouche* which was about to appear in Cleveland. It expanded, in its cinematic phase, to dozens of others which were carefully selected because of the excellence of the production and a close relationship with literature or history. In time, the bookmarks published for a single performance would run as high as 45,000, distributed at the library, at women's clubs, and at theatres and halls where pictures, plays, and musical performances were presented. Freeman found this a most effective device to introduce the library to a public, particularly in the case of films, which did not have a bowing—let alone a borrowing—acquaintance with it. This brought in hundreds of readers, not only for the book or play on which the production was based, but for biography and history and social background associated with it. The list of movies which elicited the greatest demand for books of history were *Lives of a Bengal Lancer, House of Rothschild, Rasputin, Christina of Sweden, Henry VIII, Catherine the Great, Viva Villa,* and *The Mighty Barnum.* Others were almost as successful. Biographies of Clive and Wellington had been gathering dust on the shelves; suddenly they were in great demand when *Clive of India* and *The Iron Duke* appeared on the screen. In popular literature all eighty copies of *David Copperfield* and *Of Human Bondage* were out, and there was a long waiting list for several weeks after the movies were shown; many began to read, for the first time, the works of Dickens or Maugham.

Freeman's creed was that the public library should be the most democratic institution in the community, and that it "must have no prejudices of race, religion, politics, or literature." She envisaged libraries as flexible institutions, constantly involved in adapting themselves to the needs of people. She campaigned against the intervention of censorship or the obtrusiveness of routines or the paralysis of red tape. In carrying out these ideals and principles she sponsored everything from the Business Information Bureau to the Poetry Society of America. She read and reviewed and purchased for the library all types of literature—especially drama, poetry, and novels—because she found in these literary genres an expression of the changing life of the times. She was tolerant of both the conventional and the avant-garde; as an example, she managed to bring in James Joyce's *Ulysses* while Eastman arched the conventional eyebrow. But she agreed with Stark Young, the drama critic and novelist, that "sincere badness must be treated with respect." For this reason she argued that it was as unpardonable for the mind to be as closed to Harold Bell Wright as to Theodore Dreiser; the library must buy for both exceptional and average readers. When the subject matter of novels or poetry raised problems of library censorship, she always urged other librarians to give the new writer a hearing, to accept him in what he believed to be a search for truth. For this reason she was able to take the New

Realism or the New Criticism or the New Wave in her stride. She
was also acutely aware that censorship breeds a desire for the
banned work. She enjoyed telling about the staff member who was
asked: "Can't you let me have a good restricted book?" The potential reader was frightfully disappointed to be told there were
none.

In the library itself she was kinetic and demanding, insistent that
not one minute of her time, or that of any reader, should be wasted.
Always busy, if she had to wait for Eastman in the latter's outer
office, Freeman kept Eastman's phones occupied. Once she found
it necessary to go to a hospital for minor repairs. There she exhibited none of the qualities a "patient" is supposed to represent;
she kept the phones busy and dictated to a secretary. Accustomed
to work late in the evening she thought her secretary should do the
same, even though the dictation and typing ran on until midnight.
Over the years such demands created a few morale problems. Because she expected to be perpetually busy and occupied, she assumed all readers had the same objective. Her motto was: "Never
let anyone leave the library without either the information for
which he came, or the knowledge where he may find it." This injunction could lead to extraordinary endeavor. Once Freeman went
into the reference section, saw a man at a desk doing nothing but
twiddling his thumbs. She hurried to an assistant, called her attention to the potential reader who was wasting valuable time, and
suggested that the assistant offer to be of service. The staff member
pointed out that the man wanted the New York Directory and was
waiting for it because the volume was temporarily in use by another
reader. This reply was not good enough for Freeman. Her rejoinder
was: "Give him the Chicago Directory for the time being!"

An interesting paradox in Freeman's career was her interest and
knowledge in two fields usually considered antithetical: law and
poetry. In 1920 Floyd Dell, the American poet and novelist, published an autobiographical novel entitled *Moon-Calf*. Many readers were caught by the charm of Helen Raymond, the librarian in
the midwestern town of Port Royal. Dell was happy to admit that
the librarian was Marilla Freeman and that the city was Davenport
(Iowa), where he resided as a fifteen-year-old in 1902. Much of his
spare time then was spent at the Carnegie Library and at Socialist

meetings; at the library he "lived the simple life with Robinson Crusoe, soared with Jules Verne to the moon, suffered nobly with Mark Twain's prince who was a pauper, stood with Horatio at the bridge, and scorned pomp with the Count of Monte Cristo." He was also writing poetry, and one of his poems, with Freeman's counsel and encouragement, would be accepted by *Century Magazine*—a remarkable achievement for a teen-ager. It was because of her sympathy and understanding and interest, he later testified, that he developed a genuine appreciation for and devotion to books. He also said that "very gently and very firmly and very wisely" she helped him to gain conscious control of his art. At first he had seen her only from afar,

> as she came and went about the library . . . , disappearing all too quickly into that secluded and sacred region, her private office. I knew her name and her official position; but to me she was not so much the librarian as the spirit, half familiar and half divine, which haunted this place of books. . . . Something in her light step, her serene glance, personified for me the spirit of these literary treasures; . . . made visible in radiant cool flesh. . . . But I had never thought of her as quite belonging to the world of reality. And now suddenly she appeared to me among the bookstacks, holding out her hand, saying, "You are Floyd Dell, aren't you? I am Marilla Freeman."
>
> Marilla Freeman was an extraordinarily beautiful young woman, tall and slender, wide-browed, with soft hair, grey-blue eyes, a tender whimsical mouth, and a lovely voice—an idealist, and also a practical person, who immediately took charge of my destinies. I fell in love with her deeply, and became from the first moment of our friendship involved in a battle of wills with her—a battle not mitigated by the great affection we had for one another. . . .

The conflict developed because Freeman saw in Dell a young poet who needed both encouragement and discipline. Dell rebelled, although he recognized it as a wise program:

> The fact was that for the first time I had met a person capable of bossing me; and though the bossing was done with angelic sweetness and patience, it was implacable. I resented it bitter-

ly that a goddess should stoop to these practical matters. I
wished to remain in the enchanted circle of her affection;
I wanted her to be a kind of mother-goddess.

He vowed he would never see her again, but he did, each time
bringing a new poem as an excuse. Actually Freeman was pushing
him into the world of reality. He had thought of writing as part of
an ideal world, something apart from making a living; he intended
to get a factory job and go on writing. She assumed that a writer
ought to make a living through his work. She therefore read his
poems critically and found them beautiful but with serious defects.
She saw to it that he met other writers and persons with literary
tastes in the Davenport area; this introduced him into some of the
very houses that, as a Socialist, he had vowed to pull down. Later,
after Freeman had left Davenport, her letter of introduction to the
Evening Post in Chicago helped Dell land a job as assistant editor
of Chicago's only literary supplement.

In Cleveland she was active in bringing poets to the city for readings before the Women's City Club and audiences at the library,
among them Countee Cullen, Langston Hughes, Robert Frost, and
William Butler Yeats. She once listed the things she liked to do
best; near the top was her desire to make poetry live for people.
She knew many poets, lectured frequently on their work, and was
an accomplished reader of poems. In her office two objects were
prominent: one was a framed portrait of Walt Whitman who had
been her "standard of measurement for height, breadth, and
depth"; the other was a hand-lettered and illumined copy of a
poem by Vachel Lindsay, which the poet himself had given her.
Both Floyd Dell and John Masefield, the poet laureate of England,
had been impressed by her charismatic quality. Among others, they
too, visited her in Cleveland. As with Dell, her relationship with
Masefield was one of mutual admiration; in her lectures she enjoyed
reading his poetry, and he sent her autographed copies of his books
as they were published. On 12 May 1937 Freeman, working in her
office at the library, was unaware that Masefield—in a special broadcast by short-wave radio—had mentioned her name to countless
listeners all over the world. The poet laureate was speaking in London on Coronation Day, which honored George VI. Near the close
of his speech he said:

I shall never forget going to a city library in Memphis, Tennessee, and seeing a big and beautiful room for the use of the youth of the city which had been arranged by Miss Freeman, who now directs your great library at Cleveland, Ohio.

Beyond that of the king, her name was the only one mentioned by the poet in his address.

CONCERN FOR THE BLIND

During Eastman's two decades as librarian all divisions and departments of the library expanded in their obligations and their services. Beyond this encouraging development there were three new operations that were innovative or unique—and sometimes both: the Travel Section, the Business Information Bureau, and the several new services to institutions and hospitals and the blind.

Cleveland Public Library had long been in the front rank of the libraries providing special services to those who were handicapped or restricted for one reason or another: the blind, the ill in hospitals, and the inmates of institutions. In the early years the motive force behind this progressive program was Eastman. It was her enthusiasm and untiring support that kept it going in the face of bitter disappointment and annoying delay.

Cleveland was not the first to inaugurate library service for the blind. In 1868 the Boston Public Library had begun to collect books in raised type, and in the 1880s Philadelphia was providing similar services for its blind. Shortly before the turn of the century Eastman made an effort to aid those in the community who were unable to read Braille; she did so by organizing a club of blind people who gathered weekly to listen as volunteers read aloud to them. This group met at Goodrich House, a social settlement in the congested downtown area which had been built in 1897 by Mr. and Mrs. Samuel Mather (important to Cleveland for both steel and philanthropy). In 1903 Eastman began instruction in Braille with a class that met every Wednesday at the library; volunteers brought class members to the meetings in carriages and streetcars. She also established a bureau for the distribution of free concert, lecture, and theatre tickets; again volunteers were found to act as guides and to provide transportation. In 1906 Eastman became one of the initial three trustees of the newly organized Society for the Blind which thereafter took over responsibility for instruction and recreation. This left the Cleveland Public Library with the important and expensive obligation to provide the books.

As early as 1903 the library's annual report noted that books for the blind were much too expensive for most of those who would benefit by their use, noting that one of the most important additions during the year had been seventy-four books for the blind —secured partly from gifts and partly from the library's own budget—as a start toward "providing those starving readers with . . . sorely needed intellectual and spiritual nourishment." During that first year these books circulated but a few times, chiefly because no way had been found to get the cumbersome volumes to the blind people who were so eager to receive them. In 1904 Congress solved that problem by providing free mail service. The library offerings grew steadily if not rapidly, and by 1928 the six thousand volumes in Braille at the library had circulated twelve thousand times during the year. From its beginning, Eastman had regarded the Library for the Blind as her own special project, and by the time she retired in 1938 it was serving all of northern Ohio with a circulation of some thirty thousand registered readers.

The obstacles barring needed extension of this service were the old ones of money, personnel, and storage space. Books in Braille were expensive. In the early days a local voluntary organization called the Howe Publishing Society for the Blind helped by producing books with raised type; its stereotype machine and press were in the basement of the old Court House where rent-free space was provided by the county for some years. Besides books, a juvenile magazine was issued monthly and sent to all blind children in the city; its talented editor was Annie Cutter of the Schools Department of the Cleveland Public Library, who made a careful study of the special needs and tastes of blind children. But a small local press of this kind was at best a stopgap. In 1914 the library allocated $75 to purchase embossed reading; this was .22 percent of the total book budget of $34,025. In 1930 the allocation was $1,750. But by this time the cost of making plates and printing twenty-five copies from them averaged $225 for a three-volume set and $450 for a four-volume work, in major part because of the relatively small sale and distribution. Because of limited budgets, the library's observation in its Annual Report of 1906 was just as valid in later years: "Books in raised type for the blind are so expensive and they serve so small a proportion of the population that only a small part of the book funds can go for that purpose." By this time it was apparent that a substantial endowment or support from public sources was essential.

Books in Braille are both bulky and unwieldy; *David Copperfield*, as an example, is in twenty-three volumes, each one nearly fourteen by fourteen inches in size. Just after the turn of the century the crowded condition of the Cleveland library necessitated removal of the embossed collection, small as it was, to outside quarters. Beginning in 1907 the Library for the Blind *and* the John G. White Collection were placed in Room 515 of the Society for Savings Building—both cared for by one part-time librarian. Three years later the collection in Braille, now numbering more than five hundred volumes, was transferred to Goodrich Settlement House, then the headquarters of the Cleveland Society for the Blind. There it joined the Newspaper Division of the library, which had also been farmed out. Again, books in Braille had become auxiliary to another and larger collection; previously it had been the White Collection, now it was newspapers. At long last in 1925, with the new main library building, the collection gained its first central and individual quarters along with a full-time librarian to direct its activity. In Room 47 on the basement level it had 760 feet of steel shelving and three large tables with chairs for any who wished to read. For a few years these quarters were adequate.

The large number of blind veterans returning from the First World War provided new impetus for federal aid. It came in 1931 with the Pratt-Smoot Act appropriating $100,000 to provide books in Braille. At this point the Cleveland Public Library was one of the twenty-eight libraries designated with regional status to serve the blind in the United States. Its region comprised fifty-nine counties in northern Ohio. The next year, with the help of funds from the Carnegie Corporation, experimentation began on long-playing discs which would be practical for the recording of books. These were sorely needed because less than 20 percent of the blind could make satisfactory use of raised type. An approach to the ear was therefore substituted for touch reading. The first titles in this new medium, to be known as talking books, were received by the Cleveland Public Library in 1934. Included were selections from the Bible, the Declaration of Independence and other national documents, three Shakespearean dramas, a collection of poetry, and five novels. This new departure was so successful that beginning in 1935, Congress, in its annual book appropriation for the blind, included both volumes in Braille and the phonograph records called talking books. The latter have proved a lifesaver for those who cannot read with their fingers. Originally there were not enough talking book machines, and most readers found them much too expensive for private purchase. Beginning in 1935 President Roosevelt allocated money from Emergency Relief Funds for the production of these machines, and by 1938 more than fourteen thousand were in use, distributed to each state in proportion to the number of blind residents. Since World War II a major development has been books on magnetic tape. A unique feature of the Cleveland library tape service has been the processing and duplicating assistance given to it by volunteers of the Cleveland Chapter of the Telephone Pioneers of America, most of them retired employees of the Bell Telephone Company.

SERVICE TO HOSPITALS

Before 1917 a hospital would no sooner have thought of distributing free books to its patients than it would have been inclined to give them free slippers. The First World War brought about a great change; by the close of that conflict the distribution of books to disabled soldiers in base hospitals had been endorsed by everyone. The soldiers were enthusiastic, doctors referred to the service as "bibliotherapy," and nurses were appreciative because it made their work easier. After a book cart had been through a ward there were fewer calls for extra pillows, hot-water bottles, and ice packs.

In 1924 Eastman wrote an article in the *Modern Hospital* about the therapeutic value of reading. In it she quoted, with evident approval, a statement from the author and humorist John Kendrick Bangs, who asserted that if he were a doctor he would make books a part of the materia medica and would prescribe them for his patients. He did not find this suggestion either new or revolutionary. A library at ancient Thebes had inscribed the words "Medicine for the Soul" over its door, and Diodorus, a historian who was contemporary with Christ, had described books as "the medicine of the mind." Bangs went on to say:

> A course of Mark Twain and Bernard Shaw is good for any man's liver; and I cannot even estimate the number of occasions when, afflicted by insomnia, I have wrestled sleep from the pages of books which I shall not name, as freighted with the anodyne of slumber as any poppy-field from Hindustan to Ponkapog. Literature contains the herbage of thought that cures. Whether used as anesthetic to soothe a distraught nerve, or as tonic to stir to action a sluggish circulation, books serve the purpose.

By 1924 Eastman was happy to report that the Stations Department had begun a service to hospitals. In 1926 responsibility for the program was turned over to the newly created Hospital Division. At first the service was limited to six hospitals and infirmaries. With the aid of volunteers there was a weekly distribution of books selected with great care for patients with the widest possible range of interests and reading backgrounds. The reception of this reading matter was both enthusiastic and heart-warming. "Library day" became a red-letter one for many patients, and the sincere welcome given to assistants more than compensated for the aching backs and feet incidental to pushing heavy book carts over floors that were unyielding. One of the institutions served in the early years was the Warrensville Infirmary, sometimes called—in pejorative terms—the Poorhouse (in 1952 it would become Highland View, with a much better reputation and facilities). An elderly lady at the Warrensville Infirmary wrote to Eastman about the regular visit on Friday of an assistant from the public library; no crowds greeted her but she provided

> happy hours, help in forgetting pain and suffering, the lightening of the gloomy gray lives of many who have had little to make life a pleasure and are now nearing the end of the trail. God sent us a blessing when Miss ——— came to us.

> Could you but see the smiles that greet her from every bed, see the faces . . . as they hear her quick cheery-sounding step, you might realize something of what she means to us. Personally I regret that there are not about three Fridays in the week. . . . Many thousands may enjoy and profit by the Cleveland Library, but it is readers such as we have out here who love and pray for it.

By 1928 more than eighty thousand volumes were being distributed in these hospitals. A decade later, in spite of the economic depression, the service had been almost doubled (to eleven instead of six hospitals). Those who did not read English were seldom disappointed because the circulation list included books in twenty-two languages. In 1970 the visiting librarians, although they represented an outside institution, were functioning as part of the staff in twenty-four hospitals; in type they were classified as general, tuberculosis, mental, children's, extended care, and maternity. They were also bringing opportunities for education, amusement, comfort, and sometimes inspiration to those in fifteen institutions —to both adults and juveniles in correctional facilities, to unmarried mothers in homes, to homeless and neglected children in shelters, and to the aged in denominational havens. Library work in hospitals and institutions can be rewarding and is always challenging; that in mental hospitals (whose patients occupy approximately half of all hospital space in the United States) is particularly so. This kind of individual assistance is both demanding and complex by the very diversity of the problem. Illness in mental institutions is so democratic in its occurrence that the patients may be housewives, doctors, college students, lawyers, teachers, carpenters, nurses, nuns, musicians, stevedores, engineers, mechanics, businessmen, social workers, farmers, chemists, and librarians— with backgrounds representative of many different nationalities, races, and religions.

BUSINESS INFORMATION BUREAU

In her Annual Report of 1928 Eastman announced the organization of a new service to make the library's considerable wealth of business materials, then dispersed here and there throughout the building, more quickly available. She believed that if the new bureau for this purpose accomplished half of what was planned, its bearing on the future welfare of both businessmen and the library would be far-reaching. It would effectively demonstrate the economic value of the library to businessmen; at the same time it might also convince them that the institution was worthy of more tax support than it was receiving.

The emerging Business Information Bureau (later the Business Information Department) was not the first in the United States. Service to business on a planned and organized basis was the brainchild of a pioneering librarian, John Cotton Dana, under whom Freeman was privileged to serve for two years (1910–11). She admired him greatly and said that he had become the same "guide, philosopher and friend" to her that "he must have been to so many aspiring young librarians of that day. . . ." Dana established the first business branch in 1904 at the Newark Public Library. He had a mind that was both seminal and iconoclastic—in the vanguard for such diverse innovations and institutions as open shelves, children's libraries, business bureaus, and even art museums! His service to business was ideal in concept but limited in operation, consisting of a small collection of current business books, trade and telephone directories, and periodicals. In 1911 the New York Public Library made a gesture toward the same goal by forming an economics division in its Reference Department, and five years later the public library in Minneapolis established its Business and Municipal Branch. Overseas, in 1916, Glasgow founded its Commercial Library, the first of that type in Great Britain; similar institutions were soon established in Liverpool and Manchester as well.

Cleveland was not the first, but by the 1950s its business service was among the best—very possibly the best—offered by public libraries of the United States. The major reason for this enviable reputation was the librarian selected by Eastman and Freeman to head it. She was Rose Vormelker, who held the position for more than a quarter of a century, until she became assistant director of the entire library in 1955. A graduate of East High School in Cleveland, she began her library career as a page in one of the library's branches at an income, largely psychic, of ten cents an hour. Later she attended Oberlin College and the Library School of Western Reserve University. She worked briefly in the technology departments of both the Detroit and Cleveland libraries, then organized a special industrial library for the White Motor Company in Cleveland. In 1928 she returned to the Cleveland Public Library to prepare the way for a business bureau. In this operation she began with an empty desk and no books. At first she spent her time interviewing businessmen and industrial leaders in the area about their expectations from a competent research library. After this investigation she assembled an initial collection from other departments —general reference, technology, and social science—which were understandably loath to surrender volumes then in their possession. To these were added some specialized aids and loose-leaf material. Her Bureau of Business Information bravely began its regular service on 16 December 1929, only a few weeks after the Great Crash of the stock market. In her endeavors Vormelker established a tradition of responsiveness to every request along with a rare facility for anticipating the needs of the business community. It was she who established the bulletin, *Business Information Sources*, with a slogan which became the goal of the bureau: "A man's judgment is no better than his information." The first issue, which appeared on 15 January 1930, showed remarkable courage in its attempt to assess the stock market for its readers. Now called *Business and Technology Sources*, the quarterly bulletin has been published continuously since 1930.

Although it lacked adequate funds and building space, the library had long foreseen the special importance of business information for the Cleveland area. Geographically, Cuyahoga County comprises only 1 percent of the state area; by contrast, in 1968, it had more than 23 percent of the state's industry (measured by number of companies) and more than 20 percent of its industrial employees. For this reason alone the work of the Business Information Bureau had to be extensive. It was also complex because of the great variety of industries and labor unions in the region; Cleveland was not a one-industry or a one-labor-union town.

Because of this situation the bureau had outgrown its reading space within a few weeks after it began its operations; business in the library was flourishing although it was in a shocking state of decline elsewhere. The bureau was located on the Superior Avenue side of the second floor of the main building, hemmed in between technology on one flank and philosophy-religion on the other. One sceptic noted that its connection with theology was purely accidental, despite the claims sometimes made for business and its service to mankind. Unfortunately the bureau would be confronted, and would learn to live, with inadequate quarters for thirty years. In 1934 there was some relief when the philosophy-religion department moved to the third floor, where it was more at home with fine arts and the White Collection. But within a short time the bureau was serving more than a hundred thousand readers each year, and in due course the stacks became so crowded that books were being "shelved" not only in the regular cases but on the floor that normally gave access to them. In these early years most visitors knew the Business Information Bureau as the BIB; Freeman once said that the initials really stood for "Bursting Its Bounds." Fortunately, in August 1959 it was able to move into commodious new quarters, with equally new equipment and furniture, in the library's Business and Science building which had just been acquired from the Cleveland *Plain Dealer*. By 1970 it housed a gigantic collection of some 145,000 books plus an uncounted multitude of business reports, pamphlets, clippings, corporate files, directories, manuals, periodicals, indexes, and catalogues. In the use of these resources this department, along with General Reference, has continued to witness a growing avalanche of inquiries by telephone.

Apart from the usual evidence of contracts signed and lawsuits won as a result of research in the department, its reputation in far places has been prominent enough to be impressive always, and at times amusing. There was the New York banker who went to an economic collection in London for information on inflation; there he was referred to the Cleveland Public Library as the best source for this information. There was the president of a large corporation who admitted that one of the reasons his company moved its general offices to Cleveland was "the excellence of the Cleveland Public Library and the remarkable scope of its business information service." There was the red-faced attorney in the office of the auditor of Cuyahoga County. He had spent time and money on a trip to the New York Public Library because of an urgent need for particular and specialized business information, only to be informed that the information he required was available at the Cleveland Public Library—just three blocks from his office.

TRAVEL SECTION

The Travel Section of the library was unique when it first appeared in 1926, and remains so. It was the brainchild of Donna Root, a graduate of Smith College and of the Library School at Western Reserve University, whose valuable and devoted service to the library extended over almost a half century. In time she became the head of the combined History, Biography, and Travel Division, but in the early years her chief interest was the travel field. She believed that the well-informed person would receive more enjoyment from a trip if he or she knew about the place before setting out. Her slogan was to "Read Before You Travel." She made it easy and interesting to do so, not only for actual trips but also for armchair tours.

In 1926 the inaugural of the travel service was enlivened with a poster entitled "Hampton Court." Designed as an advertisement for an English railroad, it portrayed Henry VIII as a gardener and his six wives as potted plants! Henry, with sprinkling can and rake, was tending an unusual garden—the heads of two plants had been lopped off.

The original idea for the department was to file descriptive pamphlets issued by railroad and steamship lines, and to supplement this limited collection with selected volumes on the history, geography, and society of the major countries in the world. In the early years, travelers who brought their problems to the library ranged from the woman who asked, "How much shall I tip the porter?" to the pioneer air pilot who wanted to know the physical and economic features of Honduras and "whether to follow the advice of a friend and take along two Colt 45s?"

The remarkable increase in travel after World War II, the result of abundant money and air transportation and the global operations in which the United States continued to be engaged, was matched by the travel section of the Cleveland Public Library.

By 1970 the first small file cabinet and the scattering of books available in 1926 had grown into a large travel room and abundant books, brochures, and periodicals; the room was attractively decorated with posters, maps, globes, and a model of the Eiffel Tower. Among the travel books are rare volumes including the first editions of unusual journeys, accounts of explorations, and immigrant guides—some of them dating back to the 1770s.

From the Eastman era to the present the Cleveland Public Library has offered basic travel information that cannot be duplicated in any library in the world. When she retired in 1966, Donna Root was frank to admit there was one service the Travel Section did not provide. She confessed:

> It doesn't handle space travel. That goes to the science department!

THE GREAT DEPRESSION

The progress of the Cleveland Public Library during the first ten years of Eastman's stewardship was impressive. Between 1918 and 1928 the number of books in the library almost tripled (from 600,000 to 1,800,000); their use more than doubled. Tax receipts for maintenance and the number of employees reflected the same trend in this decade of general prosperity. The maintenance budget increased from about one-half million to a bit less than two million dollars; full-time staff members rose in number from 385 in 1918 to 848 in 1928.

During the turbulent twenties the library had more than matched the growth of Cleveland. Regrettably in the next decade, during the Great Depression, the library more than equalled the area's decline—in a number of unfortunate ways. Expenditures for salaries and wages dropped from the peak of $1,371,788 in 1931 to $918,450 in 1933, a reduction of 32 percent. Some recovery had been noted by 1936, but in that year the library was still 10 percent below the figure for 1931. Salaries were cut drastically. In 1936, of 1,137 employees, 549 were receiving under $75 a month, 158 were earning between $75 and $100, and 120 were drawing between $100 and $125 per month. The library staff included a sizable number of college-trained personnel, with two to four years of experience, who were receiving less than $100 a month. It was an embarrassing but actual fact that most county and municipal offices were paying their unskilled labor as much, or more. Book acquisitions dropped in number with frightening speed. In the five-year period from 1926 to 1931 the library allocated an average of more than 18 percent of its total operating budget for books and periodicals; in the next five years the budget was about 12 percent. At times no new volumes were purchased at all. In 1932 there was something pathetically brave in the placard over the "New Books" rack at the main library:

> No New Books for Display This Week Because of
> Curtailed Funds.
>
> Have You Read These Older Titles?
>
> You'll Find Them Interesting.

Fortunately, the library's backlog of strength in its book collections permitted the retention of satisfactory service standards. When Professor Leon Carnovsky from the University of Chicago completed a study of the Cleveland Public Library in 1939, he was able to certify that its book collection was still excellent. In history, as one example, it was stronger than the famed Newberry Library in Chicago. But Carnovsky warned that the library could not *continue* to scale down its book appropriations and at the same time retain the current high quality of its collection.

The somber 1930s witnessed a serious decline in the library's income and book acquisitions and salaries for its staff. The same years also saw a marked addition to its workload as the number of users and total circulation increased by 20 percent. Cleveland was in the doldrums but the public library was experiencing an unexpected boom. In 1930 a returning traveler edged his way through a large and purposeful crowd in the lobby of the main library and exclaimed: "So this is where everybody is! Business as usual at the Public Library." Actually business was "more than usual," and that explained the library's dilemma; in the face of an increased workload and expanding services, it was faced with a serious reduction in financial support.

It is both ironic and logical that in times of drastic business decline, when people are unemployed and in a state of psychological and economic depression, they turn to the free services of the library. Some read and studied for potential future jobs as good or better than the ones they had lost; others cultivated absorbing and inexpensive hobbies. Many read because they were confronted with an overabundance of involuntary leisure and no money. In books they found satisfactory entertainment that furnished some release from worry. Eastman noted that the library provided a blessed sanity for some:

> Many of the librarians have been told by wives taking out many books, "If I didn't have these, I don't know what we'd do. They're the only things which saved my husband's reason. At least they give him something to do. He has a chance to forget himself."

In making available this "bread line of the spirit," libraries constituted one of the major relief agencies during the dark days of the depression. They performed a remarkable public welfare service in a period of deep financial stress. They also helped in supplying some antidote for the radicalism and discontent that accompanies every period of unemployment and depression. In 1930 one visitor to the library remarked:

> I may be in an ugly mood when I come, but the peace and serenity of this place have a magic effect. Before I know it I feel right with the world and myself.

In addition to the loss of income which afflicted almost every individual and institution in the Great Depression, during the early 1930s libraries in Ohio were caught in a transition from one kind of tax support to another—with the result that for a number of months *no* tax income of any kind was available. Many closed; Eastman, employing draconian measures, managed to keep the Cleveland library open. Prior to 1931 libraries received their income, as did all other political subdivisions, from the general property tax. For the library, based upon its needs, the specific levy could not exceed one and a half mills. The Great Depression produced a monumental crisis in the funding of local and state governments. To alleviate the mounting financial problems of property owners, an amendment to the state constitution imposed a tax limitation of fifteen mills—reduced to ten mills in 1934—on all real property. With this restriction, there was *nothing* left for public libraries. Some shut their doors; others managed to stay open with volunteer help or a reduced staff on lower salaries, plus some desperate borrowing at the last minute.

Between 1931 and 1933 the Ohio General Assembly adopted a series of new tax laws, among them the establishment of the classified property tax, that is, the intangible tax on interest, dividends, and certain kinds of business income. Libraries were given a first lien on the proceeds of this new tax because they had been deprived of revenues from all other sources. One problem for libraries was the critical interval between the time when the *last* income from the property tax would come in and that when the *first* intangible tax would be collected, an interval during which no income would be available. This regrettable delay was extended by taxpayers' suits against the new tax on intangibles; these further postponed the receipt of new funds. The result was that, in contrast to what it had received in 1930, the revenue of the Cleveland Public Library in 1933 decreased by nearly $750,000—more than one-third of its former income.

The year 1932 was the critical one. Eastman met the crisis with actions which were both necessary and resolute. She borrowed from collateral but available funds that had been established over the years for specific long-term projects, particularly the building fund (for branches) and a property-insurance fund available because the library was then self-insured. It will be recalled that she cut salaries and the purchase of books to a shocking level. Repairs and replacements were also deferred except where danger to life or limb was involved. She closed some school branches and stations entirely; the remaining school libraries were open only 60 percent of the time. All branches were closed part of each working day, either in the morning or evening. The main library was closed on Sundays and holidays for the first time in fifty years; it had been open 364 days in the year, including Sundays and holidays, with the one exception of the Fourth of July! Some employees were laid off. For those still on the payroll, full-time salaries were cut 10 percent. Where this reduction was accompanied by a concomitant change from a full- to a three-quarters-time schedule—as happened to many —personal income was decreased as much as 35 percent. This was not sufficient to balance the budget, so Eastman borrowed almost $200,000 from Cleveland banks, holding out as security the possible collection of new income from the intangible tax. In spite of this, a payday was missed in September 1932. A repetition of this calamity was avoided only by an extraordinary action of the county auditor; he advanced money against income expected in future months.

In its gethsemane the library received stalwart support from its readers and from the newspapers of Cleveland, along with welcome help from the federal government. The assistance from the Public Works Administraion (PWA) and the Works Progress Administration (WPA) was both unexpected and unparalleled. Between 1935 and 1939 the main library and the branches were cleaned, repaired, painted, and repointed. Thirty musicians copied scores for the music collection. The federal government's most impressive and permanent benefactions, however, were the three colorful PWA murals in the main building that several decades later still remain vivid and distinctive. In the central corridor on the main building's second floor, the mural was by Donald D. Bayard, a graduate of the School of Fine Arts at Yale. Its locale is the mouth of the Cuyahoga River; the action in the painting is indicative of lake shipping on one side and rural Ohio life and canal transportation on the other. In a lecture room on the foundation floor, where it is now seldom seen or appreciated, Olga Coltman painted a three-panelled mural. The central panel is a dramatic presentation of two bridges over the Cuyahoga River, one a high-level, the other a drawbridge. The panel on the left portrays a skyscraper, the one on the right by contrast depicts the Saint Theodosius Greek Orthodox Church rising above houses on a hill. But the major PWA mural, seen with pleasure by the greatest number of visitors to the library throughout the years, is the one in Brett Hall which provides such a chromatic addition to this principal room of the building. A presentation of Public Square, it was done by the well-known Cleveland painter William Sommer and offers an entertaining and energetic harmony with the architectural features of this exciting room. It shows the Cleveland of more than a century and a half ago—a fence still standing around Public Square, and the barnyards with magnificently painted domestic animals being crowded out of the picture by encroaching buildings. In this mural, which has a majestic sailing ship on the Great Lakes at the top, Sommer presents the Old Stone Church (religion), the Court House (law), the Academy (culture), and the Hotel (welcome abode for the weary traveler). His animals are particularly noteworthy; they represent horses and cattle sniffing, for the last time, the air from the land soon to be occupied by the great city. One can only speculate about the air over the same area in the late twentieth century. Sommer's painting is dominated by a glorious sun; as he phrased it, "Then we look at the sun stretching arms down to embrace the city and carry into eternity all past attainments."

Readers and newspapers also rallied to the support of the library. One reader suggested an "Overdue Week." He proposed that every Clevelander with funds be asked to take out one or more books and keep them a week beyond the due date; the contribution of twelve cents per book would be for "The Cause."* Newspapers prodded the state legislature and political subdivisions of Cuyahoga County to provide necessary funds. The Cleveland *Plain Dealer* hoped that the economics of the situation would not "shut out the light" to "thousands now jobless who used the main library and its branches as a means of shutting out the gloom that presses upon them. . . ." On one cold December day in 1931 it testified to the value of a newspaper reading room in the main library that afforded "shelter, warmth and comfort to men who otherwise would be forced to stand outdoors." The *Plain Dealer* told the pathetic

---

* A decade later, ironically, there was a substantial increase in income from fines, for another reason. During World War II, which followed the leisure-rich and money-poor 1930s, fines on overdue books were running $1,500 a month above the average during the depression; the library's monthly income from fines was $6,000, a rate of $72,000 a year. The reason was that borrowers now had plenty of money but no leisure time and found it more economical to keep than return books promptly. (See Eugene F. Gleason, "Library Wartime Figures Show Readers in Haste—Fines Rise," Cleveland *Plain Dealer*, 1 Apr. 1944).

story of an author, whose book was on the shelves of the library, who could not afford the price of even a magazine. The author stated:

> My library card, which costs me nothing, has been a sort of meal ticket of the spirit. I would rather give up my overcoat than lose the use of that card. An occasional hour in the Main Library itself has made many a hard day much easier. Not to extend the metaphor unduly, my card is a passport permitting me heartening visits to happier lands bordered by book covers. To find it useless would mean deportation bordering on the tragic.

In spite of these economic and psychological traumas Eastman, like Brett before her, maintained a high level of institutional morale. John G. White once claimed that the city of Cleveland got more from its library than did any other metropolis and that the reasons were Brett and Eastman. He averred that these two made the ultimate in contributions, not only by their labors but by creating a spirit among employees that was altogether admirable because of its self-sacrificing character. In White's opinion the zeal of the staff was the greatest asset that the library possessed—and so it was. Under Brett and Eastman the library had both heart and soul; the entire staff offered a sympathetic understanding that made life a little richer and human hearts a little happier.

In 1969 Polykarp Kusch, the dean of faculties at Columbia University and the recipient of the Nobel Prize in physics, would recall the privilege and the pleasure of his experience forty years earlier as a page in the Cleveland Public Library. He was born in Germany; his father was Polish and his mother Dutch. The desperately poor family moved to Cleveland, and the son helped support himself at Case Institute of Technology through his labors in the library. Both institutions influenced him greatly. He entered Case with the intention of becoming a chemist, found the subject "cookbooky," and changed to physics—then considered, by his fellow students, to be a subject for lunatics. The institute also changed him in other directions; he entered "as a well-indoctrinated Christian youth and left four years later with strong anticlerical attitudes." But it was the atmosphere of the Cleveland Public Library, at once benign and beneficial, that he remembered particularly:

That marvellous building! In 1926, when I started working there, it was a new, shiny marble building. It was a lovely thing. . . . Inside, it had an air of repose that invited reading. This is not true of all libraries. I read incessantly. The German novelists. Jakob Wasserman. French novelists. Jules Romains. Not great writers, but not trivial, either. I have great affection for the Cleveland Public Library. I worked there over a period of five years. It was an absolutely great experience. My fellow-pages were energetic, bright people, all from the submerged classes, and we worked for thirty cents an hour.

Other readers offered their praise of the library's contribution, both orally and in the columns of metropolitan newspapers. John W. Love, the learned columnist on economic matters in the *Cleveland Press*, observed that the best way to really understand the achievements of the Cleveland Public Library was to use other libraries! William F. McDermott, the drama critic of the Cleveland *Plain Dealer*, was an economic conservative who believed public institutions to be less efficient than those privately owned. In his judgment the Cleveland library was the rare exception; it had no bureaucratic red tape and none of the frigid impersonality that was typical of publicly owned organizations. Instead there was willing and eager service which gave the reader a pleasant feeling that he existed as an important individual. Cornelia Stratton Porter was a prolific author and lecturer on social, industrial, and educational problems. She had studied all over the United States; she had also spent a considerable amount of time in the libraries in London, Paris, Vienna, Rome, and Geneva. In spite of the fact that she had an attractive house in Boston, within a long stone's throw of excellent university and public libraries, she came to Cleveland in the summer and rented a hotel room. She did so because she wanted to spoil herself; she craved the privilege of "writing a book in the finest library . . . I've yet discovered on the face of the earth."

RESIGNATION AND HONORS

In 1938, when Eastman was seventy-one, she retired from the library—full of years and honors. She told the board that it had long known her "desire to turn the responsibilities . . . over to the successor whom you may select, before the passing years begin to slow up my own working powers to the possible detriment of the Library." She lived on for another quarter century before her death in 1963 when she was nearing ninety-six years of age.

The honors had come in profusion. In her own profession she had been president of the Ohio Library Association (1903–4) and of the American Library Association (1928–29). She had received honorary degrees from Oberlin, Western Reserve University, and Mount Holyoke College. There were special citations by the Cleveland Chamber of Commerce, the Citizens League of Cleveland, and the Carnegie Corporation of New York. She was a full professor in the Library School of Western Reserve University, like Brett achieving that rank in spite of the fact that she had no college degree. She enjoyed this academic distinction and observed that if Brett was the "father" of the school, she had long considered herself "the grandmother . . . a sort of doting grandmother."

She was intensely proud of her profession and of her colleagues; although they were still far from perfect, she believed "library folk . . . to quote from the Psalms, 'just a little lower than the angels.'" But her outstanding characteristic was humility and modesty. Alfred Benesch, who was a member of the Board of Education for many years, would testify:

> The test of her greatness is her deep humility—not the humility that doubts its own power, but the humility characterized by a curious feeling that greatness is not in the individual, but rather through the individual who sees something divine in all the children of men.

THE EASTMAN GARDEN

In 1937, just before Eastman retired, the city had designated the area on the Mall between the library and the *Plain Dealer* building as Eastman Park, to be beautified and maintained as such. By July of that year green benches and tables with striped umbrellas were in place. There were racks of books and magazines for patrons; they could read from 10:00 A.M. to 6:00 P.M., weather permitting. It was hoped that this outdoor reading room, with blue sky for a ceiling and shade throughout the afternoon, would provide a cool interlude in the day's heat—"a splash of color and comfort reminiscent of the left bank of the Seine or old Madrid in happier days."

Alas! it was not to be—at least for some years—because there was no control of ingress to the area. For that reason Eastman Park did not recall the Left Bank or Old Spain as much as it did an authentic American jungle for tramps. In the 1940s and 1950s reporters from the *Plain Dealer* recalled vividly what went on in the area:

> In those halcyon days when nights were hot, we could poke our heads out of the windows on the fifth floor and view any number of strange goings on in Eastman Park.
>
> We observed such things as very unkempt gentlemen tipping up bottles (which they left behind); somnolent and equally untidy gentlemen all bedded down for the night on mattresses of newspapers (which they also left behind); couples oblivious to everything except themselves—much too oblivious. . . .
>
> It was not a pretty place, and more than one observer was heard to say: "Why don't they get the drunks and bums out of here?"

In time "they" did, but it took careful planning. In 1957 the library purchased the *Plain Dealer* building (which would house business and science) and in 1959 leased Eastman Park from the city for the nominal payment of one dollar a year. Within a short time the Friends of the Library, inspired by Mrs. Robert Jamison, had transformed the place. They designed a garden that provided security because of its impressive iron fence and gates and its single entrance from the new Business and Science building of the library. The area within was beautifully planted with flowering crab and gum trees and English ivy. The Eastman Garden became a popular civic project. The ornamental iron gates came from the former Francis E. Drury home on Euclid Avenue, their elegance reminiscent of a time when that avenue was in its prime. The attractive armillary sundial, always intriguing in the out-of-doors,

was given in honor of Eva Morris Baker, a librarian and horticul-
turist. Two jardinieres, donated by the Cleveland Museum of Natural History, were formerly at the residence of the late Leonard C.
Hanna, Jr. The attractive wall fountain was the gift of Mr. and
Mrs. Robert H. Jamison, who severally had been members of the
Board of Education and the Library Board. In addition more than
twenty-five thousand dollars for the completion of the garden was
contributed by the Louis D. Beaumont Foundation, the Cleveland
Foundation, and funds associated with the Hanna and Mather families. Because of donations, it was possible to complete the attractive garden without a penny's cost to the taxpayer. The *Plain
Dealer*, which had once observed the area with both fascination
and disdain, was ecstatic about the creation of the "town's first
bum-proof shelter." It thought this was a splendid way indeed to
find and to spend money and concluded that "if so much beauty can
be created from an area where so little beauty formerly existed, it
might give Cleveland's leaders, both public and civic, ideas for the
improvement of other public land."

The Eastman Garden continues as a particularly appropriate
tribute to a remarkable librarian—a small park with ornamental
gates and jardinieres and flowers and herbs and recorded classical
music in season. There, grateful denizens of nearby buildings can
enjoy both Bach and sandwiches, if they choose to bring their lunch
along. It is a delightful environment for reading and listening and
eating alfresco. Its quiet beauty and dignity would please Eastman. In her lifetime she had moved through the library with complete dedication—almost as an abbess.

CHAPTER SIX

NADIR

CHARLES EVERETT RUSH

A FEW DAYS AFTER Eastman announced her resignation, the Library
Board designated Charles Everett Rush as her successor. His qualifications were substantial, but some did not find them the particular ones essential for appointment to the top position in a public
library with the prestige—and the continuing problems—of the one
in Cleveland. Rush was a Quaker whose ancestors first appeared in
Virginia during the early years of the seventeenth century; both
of his parents were ministers in the Society of Friends. He was
born in Indiana and earned his baccalaureate degree at Earlham
College, a Quaker institution where he paid for his education by
working in the library. His degree in library science was from the
New York State School at Albany, and the groundwork for his career was laid in a number of midwestern libraries in Wisconsin,
Michigan, Missouri, and Iowa, culminating in his tenure as librarian in Indianapolis from 1917 to 1928. During the next three decades, except for his three years in Cleveland (1938–41), he served
in the groves of academe: as librarian at Teachers College at Columbia (1928–31), as associate to the librarian at Yale (1931–38),
and finally as librarian at the University of North Carolina from
1941 until his retirement in 1954. For a number of reasons, particularly those connected with rigid administrative controls introduced by some public library boards of trustees, he was to find the
academic environment more rewarding. At the end of the 1930s,
in Cleveland, the Library Board was returning to the close supervision which had perplexed Librarians Oviatt and Beardsley in

the beginning years of the institution. Rush was to find this surveillance just as annoying and frustrating as had his early predecessors.

LIBRARY BOARDS—"OLD AND NEW"

At the time of Eastman's resignation the Library Board of Trustees, and the Board of Education which appointed it, were in the early stages of a portentous change in both membership and purpose. This development presaged trouble for any librarian in Cleveland. For decades both boards had been composed of men far removed from politics and any kind of ethnic or religious pressure. In the case of the Library Board there were the Hopkins, Mathers, Hays, Ranneys, Whites, Clarkes, Grassellis, Nortons, and Josephs who enjoyed full public confidence because of extensive backgrounds in cultural and civic pursuits. Because of this and other reasons, during the earlier period the Cleveland Public Library had become one of the outstanding institutions of its type in the world. After 1884 the board and its librarians (Brett and Eastman) enjoyed mutual interests and objectives; as a result the meetings of the board were sometimes referred to as pro forma. Phil Porter, an outspoken reporter on the Cleveland *Plain Dealer*, described the situation as follows:

> For years, the proceedings of the library board have been about as productive of news as a meeting of the committee on parliamentary law of the Hicksville Ladies' Literary Society. . . . hardly anyone knew who the members of the board were. They were usually civic minded as the result of conspicuous service in their professions . . . or they had some money or social position, and didn't mind the extra non-salaried work on the library boards.

In the "old days," if there was a charge of "politics," it meant that a party boss, Democrat or Republican, dictated appointments of faithful party workers. In the first seven decades of its history this had seldom happened in the library. Because of continuing unemployment throughout the Great Depression, by the late 1930s the library's situation changed completely. Certain pressure groups, rather than parties, exercised a new type of "political" influence. The result, as Porter described it, was that "various lightweights, labor stooges, and avowed representatives of racial and religious groups began to run on platforms of divvying up the jobs. . . . The old days vanished." Former board members were denounced as a "bunch of snobs" and as a "stuffed-shirt brigade." Their places were taken by persons chosen to represent ethnic, labor, and religious groups which were said to be more representative of cosmopolitan Cleveland than wealth, social position, and influence. One extreme Catholic averred that because 60 percent of the population of Cleveland was Catholic, that denomination should have a majority on the board. Against this development Alfred Benesch, a "minority" member of the Board of Education, later entered a vigorous dissent:

> I want to say . . . that I would not vote for a union man merely because he is a union man. I would not vote for any man simply because he is a member of a group. I would not vote for a man merely because he belonged to the Union Club, or was a Jew or a Negro.

Under the "new" policy the Board of Education chose Library Board members not by reason of their interest in and knowledge of books, but on the basis of their appeal to certain groups with substantial voting strength. As a result some of the new board members were complete unknowns, except in their small communities. Within such parochial limitations their intentions might have been the best in the world, but as Porter saw it, they did not

> know any more about library management or educational trends than your Aunt Minnie knows about Diesel engines. In fact, some of them know as little about books as some of the school board members know about education.

Some of the new members bore a strong resemblance to the small-town library board member who once insisted that all a library needed was a Bible and a dictionary. This brought from skeptics the observation that more public libraries were handicapped by unqualified trustees than by ineffective librarians. One of the new trustees in Cleveland, described as a "cigar-smoking, grammar-smashing labor leader," rose to the position of president of the board. He once boasted that he had not read a book in his life and did not intend to start now; later he qualified this assertion by the admission that he had read Diamond Dick in his youthful days. He stated boldly that he did not know what books the library had and didn't "give a damn." The *Plain Dealer* arrived at the obvious conclusion that he had been chosen, not because of any real appreciation of the worth of the library, but solely because he was a labor leader; it editorialized wistfully that "a mistake of that kind must not be made again."

In 1939 one of the new appointments raised a great hue and cry in the press and elsewhere. It was the election to the Library Board of a young attorney with a characteristic middle-European name who was the son of a former city councilman and street commissioner from the Fourteenth Ward. His designation was a prime illustration of the axiom, followed by political formula-makers in Cleveland, that "if you're going to get anywhere you have to have a Pole." This action was particularly objectionable to many because the fledgling board member was elected in the place of Frederick W. Dorn, a member of a leading law firm in the city who had long been interested in all things cultural and literary. Alfred A. Benesch, who supported the reappointment of Dorn, told his colleagues on the Board of Education that appointment to the Library Board should be a "badge of distinction" and that Dorn's graduation from Harvard "should not be held against him." Benesch noted that he himself had lived in Cleveland for sixty years and had never heard of the young man proposed as Dorn's successor until he "read the paper yesterday." When sought out by reporters, the successful candidate, who was twenty-nine and looked younger, seemed bewildered by his sudden elevation from obscurity to the distinction of membership on the Library Board. He said, "I don't know how it happened." Others did. The *Cleveland News*, noting that the new member also stated that he had every intention of learning to be a useful member of the board, asserted:

> This intention, and the fact that [he] has drawn books from the Public Library, seems to be his chief qualification. . . . In

a city which boasts about its culture, it seems a mockery that
this pleasant and unassuming young barrister with no particular aspirations to public service should be chosen to succeed as well-read and understanding a man as Frederick
Dorn, former president of the Board.

The *Cleveland Press* was both irate and outspoken; it asserted that
the appointment of an unqualified person hardly flattered the
Slavic groups in the city.

> There are scores of men in Cleveland of recent foreign origin
> whose interests in education, in literature, in civic affairs gen-
> erally would qualify them excellently. It is not a compliment
> to the nationality groups of Cleveland to imply that a good
> personal character, agreeable manners, and some dabbling in
> ward politics are the highest claims to honorable office that
> can be put forth among them. . . .

> The conclusion seems inescapable that [he] is being chosen
> partly because he is not an outstanding person. Hence the
> majority of the School Board feel they can rely on him for
> easy compliance in policies that may be developed by them
> for the Library.

A solution for this problem came after three years, for an unanticipated reason; in 1942 the young board member resigned to enter
the army. At that time the *Plain Dealer* hoped that his resignation
would give the Board of Education "its first opportunity to begin
the important job of rebuilding the library board."

JOBS FOR CLEVELANDERS

In their control of the schools and libraries of Cleveland, both
the Board of Education and the Library Board developed a policy
of restriction based on the formula of "Cleveland jobs for Clevelanders." This became so xenophobic that occasionally it worked
to the disadvantage of candidates who lived even as far away as
Rocky River and Shaker Heights. Edwin J. Bradley, an engineer-
salesman who was president of the Board of Education in 1938, was

such a protagonist of this policy that he developed something he was proud to call the "Bradley Principle" for both libraries and schools. He explained it as follows:

> For years, teachers were being imported from the four corners of the United States. Local men and women, sons and daughters of our taxpayers—people who have made Cleveland a great city—were being relegated to the ash pile in order that these carpetbaggers might come into our system to take positions that rightfully belong to our people.

To Phil Porter, in the *Plain Dealer*, this was rank nonsense simply because brains and ability are not a matter of geography or residence, but Porter was the first to admit that rank nonsense was sometimes opportunistic politics. The *Press* observed that only a "pygmy-minded administrator placed petty local patriotism above a desire to obtain the best talent available for the job." Its advice was ignored.

In the case of the library, pay was small but there were a number of jobs that could easily be handed out to nieces and nephews of friends and neighbors, rather than to those who had attained the highest grades in library school. Among other placements, the newspapers charged that Bradley had found a library job for a former secretary who was unemployed. There were also a number of major positions that excited interest and envy. Named for watchful control of all these appointments, through his chairmanship of the Employment Committee, was William J. Corrigan—who succeeded Emil Joseph on the Library Board. Joseph was a lawyer, philanthropist, bibliophile, and art collector who had been a member of the board for a quarter of a century and its president for six years. He came from an old Cleveland family which had first appeared in the city during the 1870s and had established a firm which became prominent in the manufacture of clothing. Among other honors Joseph had been cited by Columbia University in 1932 as one of its ten most distinguished living graduates. After his death in the summer of 1938 the Board of Education quickly selected Corrigan during what was described as a "tumultuous meeting"; on that occasion minority members Alfred Benesch and

Norma J. Wulff had charged the existence of a "star chamber." As Joseph's successor, Corrigan presented quite a contrast in the flamboyance of his personality and the spectacularity of his legal practice. Corrigan was a talented and aggressive Irish attorney, with the square jaw of a pugilist, who specialized in labor and criminal-defense cases. His virtuosity as a courtroom dramatist was sufficient to remind some of Clarence Darrow. He defended organized labor in an era when it was unpopular to do so, and he was ready and willing to provide the legal protection to which alleged murderers and racketeers are entitled. As a defense attorney his most famous case would be the murder trial of Dr. Sam Sheppard, the osteopath in Cleveland who was charged in the 1950s with the murder of his wife. In this trial Corrigan, looking like an indignant bulldog most of the time, fascinated everyone "as he stalked all over the courtroom with his white hair ruffled and his hard-muscled face working every minute." On the Library Board he would serve for eleven years and would be elected president on three occasions. At the time of his appointment in 1938 he was expected to keep patronage under control, and he did—so completely that in due course responsibility for personnel was taken away from the librarian.

THE INVESTIGATIONS

The new board instituted a number of investigations and appraisals, confidently expecting that the findings would discredit the previous management of the library and endorse its own actions. There were to be three of these inquiries: one by an examiner from the state auditor's office on library finances, one on business administration, and a third by a group of consultants on the professional operation of the library. One member was convinced that when the state examiner's report on finances was made public, "you'll see the need of a general house cleaning." Another claimed that for years the public schools had been the sacred cow, and the library system the sacred calf, of Cleveland; he was certain that when all of the investigatory reports were made public "the sacred calf myth will be exploded and . . . the changes . . . made will undoubtedly be fully justified." For the board these expectations became sad illusions.

PWA Mural (completed 1934) by William Sommer, Brett Hall, Main Library

Marilla Waite Freeman, Librarian of Main Library building (1922–1940)

Linda Anne Eastman, Librarian (1918–1938)

Main lobby of Cleveland Public Library

Gates to the entrance of the exhibition corridor of the John G. White Collection

Gateway to Eastman Reading Garden

Charles Everett Rush, Librarian (1938–1941)

Clarence Sheridan Metcalf, Librarian (1941–1950)

The report by State Examiner John H. Turner, which was expected to be explosive in its impact, turned out to be a dud. It questioned the wisdom of certain expenditures, for example, one involving a loss of more than thirty thousand dollars in real estate on Kinsman Road. It objected to the purchase of a portrait of John G. White and of a bust of William H. Brett. The *Cleveland Press* found the latter commentary "well advanced into absurdity" because the great contributions of White and Brett fully justified suitable memorials in their honor. But the main conclusion of the Turner Report was decidedly complimentary to the library; there was no evidence of either dishonesty or graft in the expenditure of some thirty million dollars over the past fifteen years.

The report on business and purchasing methods proved even more disappointing, not only by reason of its findings but also because it exposed to public view the board's own internal strife and struggle. At the insistence of board member Howell Wright the business appraisal was conducted by Colonel Joseph H. Alexander. This was objectionable to Librarian Rush, who fought unsuccessfully against the study. During his brief tenure Alexander bore the title of "assistant librarian" without any apparent qualifications for this professional designation (he had been president of the Cleveland Railway Company in the prosperous 1920s, and was a WPA director in the less opulent 1930s). Given $1,500 for the study, his report was a routine one. He recommended competitive bids "where practicable," the possible closing and relocations of certain branches, the discontinuance of the library's laundry and cafeteria on the fifth floor of the main building, and a unified accounting department. The recommendation for competitive bidding was particularly interesting because Wright, who was Alexander's protagonist on the board, had just been indicted on the charge of bribery in connection with bookbinding firms. The Alexander Report was so vapid that the president of the Library Board, who had hoped for a substance that wasn't there, said: "There's nothing in it. I think Joe Alexander must have needed the $1,500."

It was the appraisal of the professional operation of the library that was awaited with the greatest interest. This was the only investigation endorsed by Rush. To complete it a competent staff worked for six months under the direction of Dr. Leon Carnovsky who was from the Library School at the University of Chicago.

Rush expected the investigation to examine not only procedures and methods but also to present a "general look-ahead to see if we are headed in the right direction and emphasizing the right things." It was designed to find out what was right and wrong with the library.

The Carnovsky Report, which appeared in early August 1939, testified that there was indeed much to praise. It recommended some changes, among them the retirement of older staff members, the creation of a personnel department, a remedy for overcrowding at the main library, and merger with the County Library. But its general and confident conclusion was that "Cleveland is pre-eminent among the larger cities of the world in the amount and quality of library service which it receives." It found the book collection and the Schools Division especially noteworthy, and the community services far better than those in any other metropolitan area in the United States. Carnovsky was particularly pleased to find that the Cleveland library, by contrast with the one in Chicago, could legally engage competent personnel without regard to residence. Nonetheless he reported that the great majority of the staff were native Clevelanders, and that almost two-thirds were born in Cleveland or elsewhere in Ohio. The Library Board, however, could hardly have been pleased with his statement on the professional staff which

> shows . . . greater recruitment from beyond Cleveland. Since professional positions in a library like Cleveland's frequently require persons of rather specialized qualifications, it is fortunate that the administration has been free to attract such individuals from other sections of the country. Parenthetically it may be observed that Cleveland differs sharply from Chicago in this respect.
>
> Chicago has long been hampered in the selections of persons for important administrative positions because a civil service law imposes a one-year residence requirement.
>
> There is of course no objection to favoring local residents *unless* such favoritism results in rejecting persons of greater experience and general competence.

The newspapers of Cleveland were pleased with the findings. The *Press* noted that detractors of the library had been waiting

"with fingers in their ears and glee in their eyes" for the explosion
that would accompany the Carnovsky Report; the detonation had
now burst, but "instead of peppering the library administration
with shrapnel they have showered it with flowers." The report
served notice to the community that the Cleveland Public Library
was one of rare excellence and that the trustees should cease forth-
with their encroachment upon the administrative function of the
librarian. The *Plain Dealer* was more pointed in its remarks. It wondered why it was necessary to go to the expense of the Carnovsky
and Alexander surveys to prove what Clevelanders already knew,
that is, that their public library was outstandingly superior in public service and had been ably and economically administered; it
hoped that "even the library board knows it by now." The lesson to
be learned was obvious to Phil Porter:

> The surveys are now out, and if there is anything revolution-
> ary in them, it has been printed with invisible ink. The recom-
> mendations were such obvious ones . . . that they were hardly
> newsworthy and only by liberal treatment on the part of the
> editors were given a Page One position. . . . They were the
> exact opposite of bombshells. . . .

> So now the library board members find that they are dissatis-
> fied, that the much-vaunted excuse for a big tear-up has not
> materialized, and they are even criticizing their own surveys
> in public.

HOWELL WRIGHT

In the summer of 1938, during the metamorphosis in the membership of the Library Board of Trustees, there had been a great
clamor over the new member selected to replace Robert C. Norton,
who was a perfect example of the Establishment of Cleveland.
His family had prospered in steel and banking. It had also given
generously of its time and wealth to the cultural and educational
life of the city, particularly to Western Reserve University, the
Museum of Art, and the Western Reserve Historical Society. Norton loved art and literature; he owned fine collections of paintings,
books, and Napoleonic treasures. In spite of these cultural qualifications Edwin J. Bradley, the president of the Board of Education,

stated that Norton should not be re-elected to another term because he had violated the "Bradley Principle." Norton had voted for an "out-of-towner"—Charles Rush—as the librarian who would succeed Eastman. For Norton's place, Bradley proposed Howell Wright, once characterized by the *Cleveland Press* as a "notorious political hack, a spoils politician of the first order, . . . and . . . more recently a stooge for public utilities." Long identified with the Democratic political machine in Cuyahoga County, Wright had held a number of political jobs—as manager of the city hospital and of metropolitan utilities, and as a lobbyist for private-utilities firms. A number of civic groups, including the Citizens League and the Cleveland Engineering Society, asked the Board of Education to delay action until opposing arguments could be heard. This effort was doomed from the beginning; Bradley not only opposed delay but was quoted as saying: "My mind is made up on the appointment and if I listened until doomsday I wouldn't change it." He characterized Wright as a man who was "outstanding in engineering and a student of books." Four other members of the board supported him in this stubborn position, with the result that Wright was elected as Norton went down to defeat. The vote was five to two.

Wright was soon elevated to the positions of secretary-treasurer and chairman of the Finance Committee of the Library Board. The *Plain Dealer* was shocked at this "signal that the library system is to be thrown open to political spoilsmen"; it could find no reason to believe that Wright would become an experienced library executive overnight. Unfortunately, for Bradley and the Library Board, the *Plain Dealer* was prescient. Within a few months it was apparent that Wright was far more interested in the covers than in the contents of books.

In September 1939 officers of two binderies, with which the library had contracts, testified that they had been approached by Mr. Wright. One of them, who had been invited to lunch, reported that "after I paid for the lunch this bombshell fell in my face." Wright's surprising proposition was that, in return for a payment of $1,000 directly to him from each company, their contracts would be assured because, as Wright put it, "What I decide will be done." One of the officers was threatened; he was told that if the payment was not made immediately, within the next few days, "You may see your shingle out—'For Sale.'" This solicitation of bribes was promptly reported to law-enforcement authorities. For his flagrant dishonesty Wright was convicted and sentenced to three years in the penitentiary. His crime did not enhance the prestige of the Library Board, which belatedly announced that henceforth all bindery contracts would be let on the basis of competitive bidding.

LIBRARIAN VS. LIBRARY BOARD

By October 1939 the "new" Library Board appeared to be discredited. One of its prominent members, the chairman of the Finance Committee who was also the secretary-treasurer of the board, had gone to the penitentiary. The long-expected reports, particularly those from Turner and Carnovsky, had approved the stewardship and virtuosity of preceding boards, which the current membership had treated with contempt and disdain. At this point the *Plain Dealer* concluded:

> About all the library board really needs now is to leave the new librarian, Rush, alone to make the system operate the way he has undoubtedly planned, and to give up the idea of political patronage.

As it turned out, the board had no intention of following this advice.

William Corrigan, chairman of the Employment Committee, proposed a policy in January 1940 which would permit any employee of the library to appeal to the Board of Trustees for a reversal of any decision of the librarian affecting his employment. Samuel Kornhauser, a prominent Cleveland attorney who had become the board's minority of one, vigorously expressed his opposition to the proposal. He stated that Corrigan's policy would subvert the authority of the librarian to the point where it would degrade the dignity and effectiveness of his office. In the final vote on Corrigan's ploy, Kornhauser was outvoted by the considerable margin of six to one.

On 1 March Rush wrote a letter to the president of the board. It constituted an appeal for understanding and forbearance that was both conciliatory and pathetic. He pointed out that the recent reports commissioned by the board had indicated there was nothing seriously wrong with the library:

> This Library is a good ship. . . . Given full liberty of direction, I can lead this institution into calm waters. Yes, there are a few barnacles and some rusty spots here and there, but none of these requires dry docking for proper attention. . . . Agitation among ourselves and in the press will only delay our progress. . . .
>
> If we can settle into normal board procedure; if we can avoid agitation; if each arm of supervision can stick to its sphere of authority without encroachment; . . . if we can strengthen the hand of the administration and manage our affairs as is done in good library administration elsewhere, . . . we shall all come out of the fog before there is much danger of disaster.
>
> If the Board can concentrate on matters . . . and policies of major importance, and by formal action can clearly define the field of administrative authority, investing the Librarian with full responsibility and control in personnel matters, . . . I am confident that we can move into a new phase of public trust and approval.

It was not to be. By 1 May Rush's health was precarious enough that he asked for half-time status. On 16 May he needed additional rest and requested a leave of absence extending over several months; it was said that he was suffering from arthritis. The board granted his request on the assurance that Rush would handle vital administrative questions by mail, leaving Vice-Librarian Prouty in charge of other matters. By the time he returned from Cape Cod in early September, "with renewed energy and spirit," new problems had developed which required a full measure of both.

Shortly after he came to Cleveland in 1938 Rush had brought in Amy Winslow and Russell Munn as assistants in his own office. Both were excellent librarians who ultimately held important and responsible positions. Munn was born in Newfoundland, earned his baccalaureate degree at the University of British Columbia, his library diploma from Columbia, and came to Cleveland after service as a librarian with the Tennessee Valley Authority and the

National Youth Administration. At the close of World War II he became the librarian of the Akron Public Library, a position he held for more than two decades. Rush had known Winslow for many years; they were distantly related (Rush's mother was a Winslow), both had attended Earlham College and the New York Library School, and she had worked under his direction at Indianapolis. In the 1930s she was head of the Industry and Science Department at the Enoch Pratt Library in Baltimore. In her early months in Cleveland, before becoming a personal assistant to Rush, she had worked on the appraisal staff under the supervision of Leon Carnovsky. Later she became head librarian of the Cuyahoga County Library (from 1941 to 1945) and then returned to the Enoch Pratt Library in Baltimore, of which she became director in 1951.

In September 1940, when Rush returned from his leave of absence, two top positions in the library were vacant: Freeman (whose contribution has already been discussed, pp. 148–55) had retired as librarian of the main library in May, and in July Prouty had resigned as vice-librarian because of poor health aggravated by failing eyesight. Louise Prouty was a graduate of Wellesley who received her early training in the Boston Public Library. In Cleveland she had begun her career as a branch librarian in 1911, had gone up the ladder to assistant librarian and librarian of the main library, and then to vice-librarian of the whole system from 1922 to 1940. The replacement of Freeman and Prouty, particularly in these critical months, presented a serious problem for the library and for Rush.

Rush nominated Winslow as vice-librarian (in place of Prouty) and Munn as librarian of the main library (succeeding Freeman). The board refused to approve the appointments, with only Kornhauser in dissent. In the following weeks the Library Board took over the personnel operations of the library. On 25 October it approved the librarian's recommendations for appointments and promotions with the exception of thirteen names "upon which the Librarian was asked to submit further data substantiating their Cleveland residency." In connection with vacancies for vice-librarian and librarian of the main library, the board requested Rush to present to its Employment Committee "the records of the 66 people who now occupy the positions of heads of departments and divisions, and any others who in the opinion of the Librarian may be qualified for these positions." At this point Kornhauser's prediction had become a reality; the dignity and effectiveness of the librarian's position had been eroded to an alarming degree.

RESIGNATION OF RUSH

On 7 February 1941 the lead editorial in the *Cleveland News* was entitled "They Asked for It!"; the next day its counterpart in the *Plain Dealer* read "Congratulations, Mr. Rush." These ironic expressions of pleasure and good wishes concerned the resignation of the librarian, which had been submitted to the board on 6 February. In it he announced his acceptance of the position of librarian at the University of North Carolina and said:

> In every personal way, I deeply regret I must leave the City of Cleveland, its library and its staff, and the many hundreds of loyal friendships I shall always treasure, but even more important than these are harmony and professional opportunity. The latter, I know and am assured, I shall find in genuine and high degree in North Carolina.

The newspaper commentaries were acrid. All noted that Rush had resigned a $9,000-a-year job for one paying $4,908, the difference of $4,092 representing the sacrifice he was willing to make for "harmony and professional opportunity." In the *Plain Dealer*, Porter noted that Rush had insisted on bringing in out-of-town assistants, including a highly competent distant relative, giving the board an opportunity to counter with the "standard old political wheeze of 'Cleveland jobs for Clevelanders.'" In general, however, Porter felt that if Rush had any fault it was a lack of aggressiveness in restraining a board—primarily interested in "boodle" through jobs and contracts—from "muscling" in on his administrative responsibilities. The *Press* noted that Rush, when he was appointed, could not have been expected to know that his time in Cleveland would be largely consumed, not in running the library, but in keeping his own board from converting the institution into "a swill trough of patronage." It went on to speculate on the credentials of a brave new librarian:

Mr. Rush's successor must have, in addition to professional qualifications . . . steel nerves, cast-iron digestion and a brassy hide. He must love fighting for its own sake, and he must be able to handle politicians the way Clyde Beatty handles lions and tigers. Henceforth, these qualifications will be almost as essential in this post as the ability to read and write.

Jack Raper, witty and satirical columnist for the *Press*, suggested that an odd phenomenon named "Gameboy" Miller might be a possibility; his gambling room in Florida had been closed, but, according to Raper, he knew all about books.

Members of the Library Board reacted with unbecoming rage to this barrage of criticism. The youngest member claimed that the reputation of his father had been besmirched. Another wanted to dispose of Rush, whose resignation was effective two months later, by giving him an instant leave of absence with full pay. The major attack was mounted by a member who introduced a motion, which passed although it was both ultra vires and unsuccessful, to summon newspaper editors and Rush to a special meeting for the presentation of "facts, if they exist" to substantiate charges that had been made against the Library Board. The anticipated quiz turned out to be a "Hamlet without a Hamlet." None of the censured parties turned up; editors declined for understandable reasons, and Rush claimed that he would be elsewhere to attend a critical meeting on national defense. To Porter, in the *Plain Dealer*, this

> sudden rush of blood to the heads of several of the more mature members of the . . . board, . . . was as amusing as the consternation of a small boy caught with his hands in a jam jar. . . . it proved that they are not of broad enough caliber to be responsible for the policy of a large community institution.

The one-man minority, board member Samuel Kornhauser, told his colleagues by letter that he had no intention of attending the proposed special meeting; he notified them that "the truculent order on the editors to stand and deliver is not only unseemly, but extremely stupid." The editors would not attend, nor should they, when "assailed by petty creatures smarting under the lash of truth." His conclusion contributed to both the hilarity and the acrimony of the controversy:

Without hesitation, I assert that the people of Cleveland have lost confidence in the board of trustees as at present controlled. I therefore propose that all members of the board resign immediately and permit the appointment of a new board which will enjoy the confidence of the people of this city and which will be able to induce a librarian of distinction to assume the heavy responsibilities which the office now bears.

The board did not accept Kornhauser's suggestion of self-immolation. But, for most of the library's pressing difficulties, a solution appeared from an unexpected quarter several thousand miles distant.

The national disaster at Pearl Harbor in December 1941 created many new problems of global proportions. On the local front in Cleveland it solved a few, at least for the time being. It unravelled the problem of unemployment, which meant that the library was no longer a preferred place to work. For several years no one, including the Library Board, was looking for jobs; instead jobs were searching for takers to the extent that the library, for the first time since World War I, engaged girls to serve as pages. The worldwide conflict also involved so many of the citizenry in war service that the number of persons using the library declined as did the former close attention given by Library Board members to the time-consuming daily operation of the institution. There was new hope in 1942 when two vacancies on the board were filled by Mrs. Maude V. McQuate and Wayne L. Townshend. The *News* was so enthusiastic about the appointments that it entitled its editorial "The Library Turns a Corner." Townsend was a member of the faculty of the Law School at Western Reserve University; Mrs. McQuate had served well on the Civil Service Commission and as president of the Greater Cleveland Federation of Women's Clubs. Phil Porter, who had been a Jeremiah, finally concluded that remarkably little damage had been done to the library by the exasperating friction of the past three years:

The system built up by Brett and Linda Eastman has been big enough to stand a good deal without crumbling. The library still provides, as it has for years, a phenomenal service for special requests, and a wide and liberal range of general reading.

CHAPTER SEVEN

"MAKE NO LITTLE PLANS"

CLARENCE SHERIDAN METCALF

DURING THE LAST TWENTY-EIGHT YEARS of its first century, three librarians served the Cleveland Public Library. They were Clarence Sheridan Metcalf (1941–50), L. Quincy Mumford (1950–54), and Raymond C. Lindquist (1954–68).

In his first sixty years Metcalf had trained for two widely different occupations: music and business management. He was born in 1878 at McConnelsville, a village which was once a river port on the Muskingum in southeastern Ohio. His father, who was the prosecuting attorney of Morgan County, died when the son was twelve. At this point the family moved to Columbus where the lad attended high school and played the cello at night in theatre orchestras. His mother wanted him to be a dentist and, with this in mind, a year was spent at the Ohio Medical University in 1896. It was a mistake. As Metcalf later recalled it:

> I spent one horrible year in medical school cutting up cadavers, and I learned that I had a fussy heart. So, after that year I learned accounting.

He practiced first as a clerk for the Hocking Valley Railroad, ultimately became state examiner of public utilities (from 1908 to 1916) then auditor and finance director of the city of Cleveland under Mayors Harry Davis and William Fitzgerald. In 1921 a change of city administrations made it necessary to look elsewhere for employment with the result that (after interim positions in private business with the Lee Road Savings and Loan Company and the

Fidelity Mortgage Company) his employment with the Cleveland Public Library began in 1924 as secretary-treasurer or business manager until 1941, and after that as librarian for almost a decade.

Metcalf was a composer and instrumentalist of talent and virtuosity. The field of music became his avocation although he might well have made it his career. In McConnelsville his mother sang and his father directed the choir at the Methodist church. The son pumped the church organ and began taking violin lessons. Ultimately he would play the cello, violin, and piano expertly. His fondest wish was to compose a hymn that would stand the test of time. This ambition was never realized but throughout his life he maintained a dedicated interest in church music. In the 1940s throngs in Cleveland's Public Square heard and enjoyed at noon the organ chimes from the Old Stone Church; few knew that the man who often played them was the librarian from the institution nearby.

During the depression of the 1930s when many musicians were without regular jobs, Metcalf organized and directed the Friends of Music Symphony Orchestra. For its free concerts the orchestra rehearsed once a week in the carriage-house auditorium of the Museum of Natural History; its members "chipped in" five cents a week to pay the rent for the hall. Scores of classical music were borrowed from the Cleveland Public Library. The director wanted to present modern composers, but this was beyond the nonexistent budget of the orchestra. Metcalf was himself a composer and his two-act opera, "The Musicians of Bremen," based on a Grimm fairy tale, had its world premiere by a WPA Orchestra in Cleveland during 1939. He also wrote a setting for the Twenty-third Psalm and a chorus for mixed voices entitled "Israel Mourns Her Lost Splendor." Arthur Shepherd, himself a musician and composer of repute, thought the "Israel" was an estimable work, representing

> a composition of such outstanding and impressive merit as to cause one to wonder at the size of the bushel under which his light had been hidden. There was ample justification for the ovation that greeted the performance of the choral piece. . . . Here is a work of uncommon dignity and expressiveness, solidly constructed, sensitively imagined and colored with an appropriate Hebraic tinge in accordance with the text.

One of the results of Metcalf's avocational interests was that the Cleveland Public Library would become second only to its counterpart in New York in the number of music titles in its collection.

In April 1941, shortly after the resignation of Rush, Metcalf was named acting librarian in addition to his duties as business manager. Late in November the Library Board, by unanimous vote, made him librarian for a three-year term. At the same time certain members of the board, led by William Corrigan, tried to dictate the appointment of a vice-librarian who in due course would succeed Metcalf. He was to be Paul A. T. Noon, librarian of the State Library of Ohio at Columbus, who ultimately held the top position in smaller libraries in Lansing (Michigan), Jacksonville (Florida), and Canton (Ohio). There was a strong objection to this proposal from Samuel Kornhauser who introduced a resolution that it was the "sense of the Board" that all appointments, promotions, and terminations should be made on recommendation by the librarian rather than by Corrigan's Personnel Committee. For once Kornhauser enjoyed the unusual experience of voting with the majority, albeit a close one. His motion carried by a vote of four to three. The general effect of the resolution was to restore the librarian's power to choose his staff, a privilege that had been in abeyance for the past three years.

Later Metcalf would express wonderment at his appointment. He said:

> How in the world I ever became the Director of the CPL is more than I can explain. I certainly did not start out to make a career of librarianship.

Others were not only astonished but appalled by the designation of a person who was no bibliophile, who had not been trained as a professional librarian, and whose previous experience had been in accounting and business administration. Library Board member Maxwell J. Gruber, who was Metcalf's strongest supporter, counterattacked. He asserted that:

> The myth that the administration of a library must be a graduate of a library school is the bunk. The same opposition would not contend that to be an able administrator of a hospital one

must be a graduate of a medical school or that, to be an able editor of a newspaper, a graduate of a school of journalism.

It was his observation that there were poets and historians and individuals without library degrees who served very well:

> Let us say to those who might criticize, "What about Archibald MacLeish, librarian of Congress, Bernard Knollenberg, Yale librarian, and our own past librarians, William Howard Brett and Linda Eastman?"

The critics scoffed; they contended that Gruber's comparison was wide of the mark. One week after the board announced Metcalf's appointment, the Citizens League of Cleveland denounced it in vigorous language. To the league, the action was a violation of the principle of "merit and fitness" enshrined in the Constitution of Ohio (Article XI, Section 10) in the following language: "Appointments and promotions in the civil service of the state, and several counties and cities, shall be made according to merit and fitness." It noted that by following the state constitution the Cleveland Public Library previously had been designated by the eminent John Cotton Dana, the librarian at Newark, as the best in the United States if not in the world. In the past three years, however, the board—instead of restricting its jurisdiction to the determination of policies—had been administering the library in order to place favorites or relatives on the payroll. When Rush resigned, according to the league, the result was that news spread throughout the library world that the "model library" in Cleveland had fallen prey to personal and political spoils. When the board asked for applicants, the number from first-rank librarians in the nation at large was surprisingly small; when it finally offered the position to one of them he declined on the alleged ground that his wife preferred to stay where she was, but the real reason was that he did not want to serve in a library where board members dictated appointments. Under the circumstances, the league noted that Metcalf's appointment would be a great shock to the library world. It declared that the new librarian was a genial and pleasant fellow who had been an efficient and worthy finance officer both in the city and in the library but concluded that he was not "equipped by training or experience (and he recognizes it) to administer and progressively expand a great library system to meet the educational needs of a great educational community." The league saw only one glimmer of hope; Metcalf had a rare opportunity to "lay the groundwork before his retirement which is only three to four years away, for a successor who will not only meet all the requirements of merit and fitness, but who will be as distinguished in the library field as were Mr. Brett and Miss Eastman." In actual fact the librarian took his time in "laying the groundwork"; he served in the position for almost a decade, and did not retire until he was seventy-two years of age.

Metcalf was both conscious of and sensitive about this criticism. Shortly after his appointment he sent a formal letter to the board, thanking it for its action, recognizing that many believed him to be unqualified, and warning the board that this situation made it imperative to avoid the bickering that had destroyed Rush. He noted ingenuously:

> I cannot deceive myself from the belief that this staff would prefer a professionally trained Librarian, but that they accepted and welcomed the appointment because there has been such a fine spirit of cooperation between the Board and myself, and unless that same spirit can prevail I would be unable to go on.

Three years later he was still concerned enough about his lack of professional training that he received from the board permission to use the title of "director" in place of "librarian." The change of name accomplished little. In 1948 the professional librarians, through their Cleveland Public Library Workers Association, were asking the board to drop Metcalf as director because of low morale in the institution. By this time another factor was involved; Metcalf was seventy years of age and anxious to continue in the position as long as possible, in large part because of slender personal resources and inadequate retirement pay.

In 1947 the public was surprised by the disclosure that thirty active employees of the library who were past the retirement age of sixty-five, including Metcalf, were drawing pensions in addition to their salaries. They ranged in age from sixty-five to seventy-two. Some of the annuities brought the recipients only a few dollars a month, but a half dozen or so received monthly stipends in excess of $100. Metcalf was drawing $142.75 per month as pension in addition to his annual salary of $10,000. All were participants in the Prudential Insurance Company retirement plan which had been instituted by John G. White nineteen years earlier in 1928. Under this system participation was compulsory, with the employee contributing 4 percent and the library itself between 7 and 8 percent; after sixty-five the beneficiary received in each year one-half the total amount he paid into the plan.

Metcalf insisted that these pensions were justified because they cost the library nothing directly, and indirectly saved it money. Under the Prudential Insurance plan, payments by both employees and the library ceased when the beneficiaries reached sixty-five. If they continued as active employees the library saved the premiums that would have been necessary for younger replacements. Metcalf was delighted to quote precedent: Eastman herself had received annuity payments beyond salary for the six years she remained as librarian after reaching the age of sixty-five. Beyond these actuarial points, Metcalf's argument was weak in its contention that a personnel shortage required the retention of elderly employees who otherwise would have been "put out to pasture." In an economy that was absorbing fifteen million GIs after World War II, a personnel deficit was hard to find. At the same time, those who understood the situation were quite aware that the real reason for double payments to those over sixty-five was the pitifully small reserves and pensions commanded by most of them. Premiums of upwards of 12 percent on small salaries do not develop a large financial base for retirement. In the late 1940s the Cleveland Public Library had 800 employees of whom 450—more than half—received less than $3,000 a year; the minimum base pay for professional librarians was then $2,100. In Metcalf's own case, after seventeen years with the library he was earning $5,200 in 1941 when he was elevated to the top position.

SHUT-INS, HOSPITALS, AND INSTITUTIONS

In spite of the jeremiads about Metcalf's qualifications and administration and the decline in use of the library while the nation was preoccupied with World War II, there were three developments of particular significance during his regime in the 1940s: the Great Lakes Historical Society, the education of adults, and a new service to shut-ins which eventually led to a coordinated program for all the handicapped.

It will be recalled that Eastman had pioneered in providing library service for the blind and for patients in hospitals and institutions. There remained the shut-ins who were confined in their own or nursing homes—the chronically disabled, the temporarily convalescent, the many who lacked mobility for one reason or another—all shut off from contact with the outside world. In 1936 Eastman had begun a limited distribution of books to this group through the Girl Scouts. In 1940, shortly after she had retired, her dream of extensive service became possible for the first time by reason of two windfalls: a totally unexpected but welcome bequest from the Judd family and the appearance of Clara E. Lucioli, a library staff member who provided the dedication and the skill to get the job done. The Frederick W. and Henryett Slocum Judd Fund made available the income from an endowment of $450,000. The terms of the bequest provided that this fund was to be used for the city's homebound sick and disabled, to whom the library had not previously offered regular service because of lack of money. To this point in time, few had heard of the Judd family; now its name became both well-known and revered.

The Judds had lived quiet and uneventful lives. He was a machinist from England who had emigrated to Cleveland in 1880. In this city he established and was president of the Cleveland Stamping and Tool Company, retiring in 1924. Beyond this occupational information little is known of Judd and his wife. The childless couple were self-sufficient, had few friends, and were limited in their outside activities. The husband died in 1930, his widow in 1940. Their important bequest established the precedent, now copied in other cities, for providing a much-needed service to shut-ins who were homebound. A mystery still remains—what had motivated the Judds to do so? To this day no one knows why they happened to leave their fortune for the benefit of a segment of society which cannot enjoy one of the great pleasures available to civilized man, that of browsing in a public library. But no matter; the beneficial deed, that of providing a "Magic Carpet for the Shut-In," was more important than the incentive for it.

In 1942 the first income, $18,000, was received from the Judd bequest. It went a long way, making possible the purchase of a delivery truck, a first collection of some two thousand books, and the employment of Clara Lucioli, two clerks, and a driver for the truck. Lucioli already had more than one hundred shut-ins on her list; the names of eligible and interested clients came (and still do) from clergy, outpatient departments of hospitals, and welfare agencies. In addition to serving the homebound the fund also made it possible to establish special libraries in the Lowman Pavilion at City Hospital along with stations for children and adults at Sunny Acres Sanitarium—both for tuberculosis patients. At Sunny Acres the children were not only avid readers; as an added stimulus the library published the *Sunnyside News*, a mimeographed paper to which the youngsters contributed articles, book reviews, poems, and letters. For adults there has always been a steady demand for books on handicrafts, through which many have developed hobbies and skills. In popular literature, as the fund began its operations during the Second World War, the heavy demand was for books by Bill Mauldin and Ernie Pyle and Louis Bromfield and Margaret Bourke-White. By 1969, when the Judd Division Service to Shut-Ins was almost thirty years old, it reached more than twelve hundred readers with a total of 62,727 books in many languages. Most of them read 2, but some completed as many as 8 books a week. In years, only 5 percent were of public school age, 10 percent were from nineteen to forty, and 26 percent were from forty to sixty years. That left 60 percent with ages from sixty to one hundred one years (nine persons in this group were in their nineties; one other was one hundred one). The division was measuring up to its slogan: "So Those Who Cannot Run May Read."

Lucioli's background and achievements were both interesting and significant. Born in London in the British Isles, her father was Italian and her mother English. When she was nine the family came to Cleveland where she graduated from West High School and received the baccalaureate degree from Western Reserve University. She joined the Cleveland Public Library as a junior clerk in 1929, stating on her application that she preferred "varied work."

Her wish was to be realized in extravagant measure. She spent the 1930's as a children's librarian in Scarsdale, New York, and received her degree in library science from the Pratt Institute in that state. She resumed her career in the Cleveland library in charge of the Judd Fund Division in 1941, in time becoming head of the combined Hospital and Institutions Department. The Cleveland Public Library was the first to consolidate in her department its extramural services to hospitals, to correctional and welfare institutions, to shut-ins, and to the blind. For this distinctive service Lucioli achieved national recognition and honors; among them was the presidency (1959) and a Citation for Exceptional Service (1961) from the American Association of Hospital and Institutional Libraries, the chairmanship of the Adult Services Division of the American Library Association (1959), and the designation as Librarian of the Year by the Ohio Library Association (1960).

One of the interesting features of service on the part of both the Hospital and Judd divisions has been the use of special aids that make reading possible for the severely handicapped. Books in large type, plus large-print editions of *Reader's Digest* and the *New York Times*, have brought great satisfaction to those who have enjoyed books all their lives but have been cut off from them by failing eyesight. Machines that magnify type five times have been provided for those with even poorer eyesight. Special prism glasses (making use of a principle similar to the periscope) have been made available for those who must read lying down.

For those immobile in bed, "ceiling" books have been provided. Such projected reading came out of the Second World War where it had been a morale builder and an educational boon; Archibald MacLeish once said that this device was as vital to the immobilized as was Braille to the blind. Projectors for this reading were expensive, costing approximately $150 apiece in 1948, and the reading material had to be placed on microfilm at a cost of $2 to $6 per volume. Lions Clubs and the Cleveland *Plain Dealer* cooperated with the library in raising money for the Projected Books Fund, but all machines and microfilm were turned over to the library for distribution. The entire project was a nonprofit one from the manufacture of the equipment to the microfilming of the books. Publisher's royalties were also waived on all volumes used in the program. Not only current best sellers became available, but cartoon and sport books as well. The machines themselves were marvels of simplicity; an electric page-turner could move a page of print (forward or back) by a nod of the head or a click of the hand or the wriggle of a toe. For the first time, to cite an example, it became possible for Frank J. Kolodziej to read books again. At the age of twenty a dive into shallow water had left him with a broken neck and almost complete paralysis; in 1948, when he was thirty-one, he had been immobile and flat on his back for eight years in the nursing home of the County Relief Bureau. The book on the ceiling, which now became available to him, provided quite a contrast to the long and bleak stretches of time with little to relieve the monotony of bare ceiling and walls. There was a radio at his bedside, but he had been hungry for reading as well as listening.

The gratitude of the handicapped for the service was both pleasing and rewarding. One beneficiary wrote: "We have to have a few cabbages and roses to get along in this life. You certainly provide the roses." Her own particular "roses" came in the form of books of bird-lore, travel, and philosophy. It was soon obvious that shut-ins looked forward not only to receiving their books but also to the visits of the librarian, with whom personal friendships were a usual development. One lady, who had no other reason to dress up always did so on the day her books *and* the librarian arrived—normally at two-week intervals. Both the reading material and the personal visit did much to relieve the frightful loneliness that comes to the handicapped and the aged, and to give them once again a sense of belonging to society. Lucioli and her colleague Dorothy Fleak phrased it in this language:

> Unlike those who must snatch reading hours from a busy schedule, the shut-in is overwhelmed, almost drowned in an infinity of time which results in apathy, bewilderment, and even fear.
>
> Confinement brings to many a claustrophobia of self-concern. Insecurity, fear of poverty, and a feeling of worthlessness hang over those deprived of the ability to earn. The handicapped are plagued by a sense of inferiority and guilt; the elderly feel unwanted in a society that worships youth and

activity. All yearn for social recognition, independence, and self-respect.

The physical act of reading is in itself an attack on the endlessness of time. Books become topics of conversation, examples for understanding, suggestions for hobbies or home occupations. Time is valuable again. Whenever a shut-in becomes independent of family or institution for one of his needs, his morale moves skyward.

One of the texts in library gospel is "the right book for the right person at the right time"—an injunction that can have amazing consequences.

The decade of the sixties witnessed a major alteration in the financing of aid to the blind, and to those otherwise handicapped visually and physically, because of grants from the state of Ohio and the provision of books and mechanical devices by the federal government (through the Library of Congress). The Cleveland Public Library was thus able to offer greater service and was relieved of a substantial budgetary burden. Beginning in 1960 aid was granted in support of registered blind readers to the two public libraries which enjoyed regional status: Cleveland and Cincinnati. This amounted to an annual subsidy of thirteen dollars per reader. In 1967 Congress passed a major amendment to the basic act of 1931 which had provided reading materials for only the legally blind; the amendment established the principle of federal assistance to those visually *and* physically handicapped. The visually handicapped, estimated at 600,000 (in addition to 420,000 legally blind), were those with some vision but not enough to read ordinary print. The physically handicapped were those disabled to such a degree that the holding or reading of ordinary books and magazines was either impossible or extremely difficult. Such persons could receive aid at home, in schools, in hospitals, or in other institutions; by 1970 they would include almost 5,000 persons with the loss of both arms, 8,000 without any of their fingers, 1,600 in iron lungs or other respiratory devices, and more than 750,000 suffering from the results of strokes, cerebral palsy, multiple sclerosis, muscular dystrophy, polio, severe arthritis, Parkinson's disease, and other crippling ailments. For the first three years of its operation this new federal assistance was limited in large part to the provision of additional talking books and machines. With all of these developments, by 1969 the Braille and talking book service of the Cleveland Public Library circulated more than 232,000 books and magazines to almost 5,000 readers ranging in age from three to one hundred nine years. It had more than 60,000 individual items: 28,000 in Braille and 25,000 talking books on records plus 7,000 of them on tape.

Long since, this valuable service to the handicapped and the restricted had outgrown the once-adequate Room 47 in the main building. Beyond the ever increasing operations of the service to hospitals and institutions and shut-ins, the Library of the Blind had grown to such proportions that its talking books had to be shelved in the boiler room, where intrepid lady-librarians climbed high ladders to reach them. Fortunately, when the adjacent *Plain Dealer* building was acquired in 1959, its entire fourth floor was allocated to service to the blind, to hospitals and institutions, and to shut-ins. Among other advantages there is an extensive area for Braille and talking books. There is also an attractive reading room with a portrait in bronze bas-relief of Helen Keller. In Braille, are her significant words: "All sight is of the soul."

ADULT EDUCATION

In the early years libraries endeavored to serve, in equal measure, readers of all ages—the child, the youth, and the adult. After World War I emphasis shifted to the continuing education of those beyond school age. The term "adult education" came into general use in 1926 when the Carnegie Corporation of New York founded the American Association for Adult Education which encouraged a wide variety of programs in colleges, public schools, and libraries. In Cleveland the movement was particularly strong because of vigorous support from Newton D. Baker, a prominent lawyer who had been mayor of Cleveland and secretary of war under President Woodrow Wilson. Tent meetings with the charismatic Mayor Tom Johnson of Cleveland had introduced Baker to the enlightenment of adults; his later experience after World War I with the University of American Expeditionary Forces solidified his belief in the concept, with the result that he would become a trustee of the Carnegie Corporation, president of the American Association for Adult Education, and the "angel" (financial and spiritual) for Cleveland College of Western Reserve University which catered to adults as part-time students. In the mid-1920s the Cleveland Public Library swung into line as a "People's University" through the distribution of reading lists and a Reader's Advisory Service. For its effort it received enthusiastic and eager endorsement from the Cleveland *Plain Dealer*:

> A modern public library performs particularly intimate functions for its community. It is a great educational institution which confers blessings but no degrees, whose courses are all elective, whose students are never graduated because the pursuit of knowledge is unending, whose classes are open alike to the humblest and the proudest—an institute of democracy which recognizes no social distinctions but caters to everyone according to his thirst for knowledge.

In spite of this ardent testimonial, the movement was not without its critics. In 1928 John Cotton Dana of the Newark Public Library, who was noted for his barbed comments, saw adult education as the object of evangelistic worship in a quasi-religious frenzy. In 1952 Jesse H. Shera, dean of the Library School at Western Reserve University, wrote of the "willing, eager, and often misguided disciples of adult education." On the other hand there were many librarians who agreed with Baker that democracy was both the best and the most difficult form of government, and that its performance depended on the process of continuous education which they hoped to carry on with quiet restraint and in the absence of evangelical fervor.

In 1925 the American Library Association developed its "Reading with a Purpose" pamphlets, specifically planned to direct the dedicated reader through a succession of pertinent books in a specific field; the pamphlets were similar in principle to the "Five-Foot Shelf" sponsored by President Charles W. Eliot of Harvard, and to philosopher-historian Will Durant's list of one hundred books which would be helpful in achieving a broad education. In Cleveland the public library had long been doing the same thing through its publication the *Open Shelf*. Freeman, when she was the librarian at the main library, had an especial interest in adults; in 1926 she established the Reader's Advisory Service in an alcove off Brett Hall. Ultimately this service had more than a thousand books available for immediate referral and was serving more than three hundred inquirers a month, most of them general readers with hazy and hazardous notions of what was worth reading in a wide variety of fields.

In 1941 Cleveland Public Library established its first formal Office for Adult Education, devoted to the principle that a library was also a community center, and engaged in group programs both within and without the institution. During the closing years of the library's first century the new office had two directors—Munn (1941–44) and Long (1944–69)—whose backgrounds and training were particularly pertinent for the assignment. They developed the program to a point where it achieved and merited national recognition.

It will be recalled that Rush had brought Munn to Cleveland, and that there had been some opposition because he was an outlander (pp. 188–89). The local opposition to Munn made no sense from the standpoint of personnel policy, but it was certainly true that Munn's ancestral roots were not in Cleveland. A native of Newfoundland, he worked his way through college by picking oranges in California and apples in Canada, receiving his baccalaureate degree from the University of British Columbia in 1930 with honors in languages and literature. The day after graduation he took a job driving a bookmobile in Fraser Valley (British Columbia) which had been chosen by the Carnegie Corporation as an ideal spot to conduct one of its experiments in adult education. Around the lakes and the mountains of the valley's twenty-five municipalities he travelled daily in one of the first "libraries on wheels" to be met at desolate crossroads by book-hungry people, many of whom had walked miles to reach the rendezvous that had been specified. This experience of seeing gas stations, country stores, and even a large chicken coop converted into make-shift libraries was the deciding factor in Munn's final choice of a profession. With the aid of a Carnegie Fellowship he received his second degree in 1932 from the School of Library Service of Columbia University. He became the first librarian in the new town of Norris in the Tennessee Valley when it was little more than a camp established for the construction of the famous dam. He also served as the village's first newspaper editor, first motion picture manager, and first supervisor of adult education. In 1937 he moved to Passamaquoddy Bay in Maine, where he became the librarian of the nation's first regional camp of the National Youth Administration. "Quoddy" had begun as a tidal-power project but was turned into an experimental station to provide unemployed youth with study, work, and vocational guidance. There Munn saw many groups learn to use and to appreciate books, both for entertainment and for educational value.

When Munn became the librarian of the Akron Public Library in 1944, he was succeeded as head of the Adult Education Department by Fern Long. Born of Czech parents on Denison Avenue in Cleveland, she was fluent in both French and Czech, and her training and experience was even more cosmopolitan than that of Munn. After graduating magna cum laude with election to Phi Beta Kappa at Radcliffe College, she received her doctorate in comparative literature from Charles University in Prague and her degree in library science from Western Reserve University. Among her publications were translations into English of four prominent Czech writers. After a four-year period of service as executive secretary of the Social Service League in Ames, Iowa, she became a field worker and then head of the Adult Education Department in the Cleveland Public Library. Her service was so distinguished that in the late 1960s she was first deputy and then acting director of the library. In a city where a large proportion of the potential clientele of the library has an ethnic background, her unique understanding of their problems and interests was of especial value in the development of programs for adults. Her credo was based on Plato and Aristotle, that is, that the end of education—which is wisdom—cannot be achieved by youth. She said that the age of fifty, rather than twenty-five, was a more valid demarcation for the beginning of intellectual maturity. In 1960 Radcliffe presented to her the Alumnae Achievement Award, the highest honor which it bestows; that college cited her as the librarian and civic leader

> whose warm understanding has brought new interest and opportunity to thousands of people; an imaginative woman

who has realized the dynamic role of the public library in the community and works with tireless energy for the betterment of mankind.

The fundamental idea behind the Adult Education Department was to extend the library's influence by encouraging groups to study and read. These organizations were myriad in kind. During World War II Long organized a Navy Mothers Club whose common interest was simply that of having sons in the Navy; nearly every nationality in Cleveland was represented in its membership. Most organizations were not that esoteric; they represented traditional groups which reflected the particular interests of labor, senior citizens, aliens (for elementary English and citizenship), social service, foreign language, and general education. These groups were attracted by a variety of programs, the most dramatic of which were built around the Speaker's Bureau, the Live Long and Like It Club, the Film Bureau, and the Great Books Program.

The germ of the Speaker's Bureau was planted in the early 1890s by Brett when local luminaries spoke at nine o'clock in the morning because the library was both open and quiet at that hour. The annual lectures, less than ten in number, varied all the way from *Macbeth* to George Eliot to the influence of poetry on politics. Fifty years later the bureau had a panel of local speakers, including a cadre from the staff of the library, who spoke to discussion groups without charge. In 1947 this service was provided to almost two hundred organizations on subjects varying from atomic energy to the four hundredth-anniversary of the birth of Cervantes.

The Cleveland Public Library was the first in the nation to experiment successfully with a program for senior citizens primarily interested in an educational experience rather than programs of pure recreation. The Live Long and Like It Club, whose members were over sixty, began in 1946 with an enrollment of twenty-five; within two years its registration was almost two hundred. On its third birthday in 1949 Louis B. Seltzer, editor of the *Cleveland Press*, promised a party when the club's membership passed the five-hundred mark. The club "made good," and so did Seltzer; in 1950 he gave the members an impressive book-shaped birthday cake with four tall candles. The club membership represented a cross section of the community. There were men and women who lived on old-age pensions and a few who arrived for the meetings in chauffeur-driven automobiles, with every shade of prosperity between the two extremes.

Its intrepid members tramped through blizzards and ninety-degree heat to meetings held semimonthly or weekly. Once, for a sightseeing tour on a hot June day, a regular participant came prepared as usual for any emergency: two coats, an umbrella, and overshoes. Programs dealt with a variety of topics, among them popular books, travel, health, retirement, world government, and city planning. Sometimes there were presentations of original poems and essays, musical recitals by talented members, and on one occasion a play. The club adopted for its motto the encouraging words of Michelangelo at ninety: "I Am Still Learning."

Documentary films can present social problems in dramatic form, and the showing can be followed by stimulating discussions and supplemental reading. With assistance from the Carnegie Corporation the Cleveland library began participation in an experimental film-forum program as early as 1941. At first the small collection of films was easily housed in a single drawer of a steel file. Later more than two thousand 16-millimeter films, most of them in color and sound, were available for loan or programs in the library itself and were viewed by tens of thousands of people. Growth was phenomenal and a striking illustration of what could be done with a cinematic medium which had originally been developed, in quite another way, by Freeman. Because of its long association with films as a conveyor of information and ideas, in 1948 the Cleveland Public Library received a Carnegie grant which made possible the development of a model regional film circuit for the libraries of northern Ohio. This novel pattern was later adopted by libraries throughout the nation.

There were also the groups, numerous in the decade after World War II, which discussed those books considered basic to a liberal education. A national Great Books Foundation conducted leadership-training programs, from which a number of discussion groups emerged on what many considered to be a "high literary" level. By 1947 the Cleveland Public Library had more than fifty "Great Books" groups in Cuyahoga County with a total enrollment of al-

most two thousand dedicated students. In 1952 a very special co-
terie of "Great Books Players" reached back more than two thousand years to stage *The Clouds* by Aristophanes; the production in
the auditorium of the Cleveland Public Library proved that the
classic Greek comedy had a relevant wit that was amazingly current and appropriate.

GREAT LAKES HISTORICAL SOCIETY

Throughout his life Metcalf had an avocational interest in boats
and shipping as well as in music. When he was young he enjoyed
trips on Muskingum River steamboats; later he built his own sail-
boat for cruises on Lake Erie. As a resident of Cleveland he had
long been shocked by the lack of source materials and awareness
by the general public of the vital role played by the Great Lakes in
national as well as local history. To stimulate interest he conceived
the idea of a Great Lakes Exhibit at the library, with contributions
coming from private collectors, shipping companies, and the Western Reserve Historical Society, as well as the library. The exhibit
opened in the winter of 1942 with a response that exceeded the
fondest expectations; planned as a local affair, enthusiastic visitors
came from afar to see it.

With this encouragement, two years later (in 1944) Metcalf put
the wheels in motion for a long-cherished idea—a continuing organization devoted to the preservation of the history of the Great
Lakes. Sponsored by the library, this organization was called the
Great Lakes Historical Society. Its euphoric motto was "To Preserve a Great Past for a Great Future." The organization appealed
to a wide variety of members: lake captains, college professors,
shippers, marine editors, owners of sailboats of varying types and
shapes, and members of the U.S. Coast Guard; its membership
also included libraries, museums, historical societies, colleges and
universities.

The first president of the society was Alva Bradley, grandson
and namesake of Cleveland's pioneer lake shipper from whom
Thomas Alva Edison derived his middle name. Metcalf was executive vice-president of the new organization, and other members

of the staff of the Cleveland Public Library would serve as editors, consultants, and vice-presidents. In 1945 Volume 1, Number 1 of *Inland Seas* appeared. It is a scholarly quarterly devoted to the history of the Great Lakes, past and present. For a decade the publication, always impressive in text and in content, was edited by Donna Root, head of the History Department of the Cleveland Public Library.

The entire effort was a unique and significant contribution; the Cleveland Public Library had been the first to sponsor a regional historical society and an impressive publication. Both evoked a long period of history that was exciting and memorable by reason of its grandeurs and mysteries and tragedies. There were impressive names, running the gamut of time from Sieur de La Salle to Oliver Hazard Perry to Alexander McDougall (the shipbuilder who ran away from home in Canada to become a sailor on the Great Lakes and whose interest in ship design led him to develop the "whaleback" freighter in 1888). There were the puzzling tragedies which began in 1679 with the *Griffon*. Built at Niagara by La Salle, she was the first ship to sail the Great Lakes, but not for long; the little vessel disappeared mysteriously on her initial voyage and no one, to this day, knows what became of her. There were the commercial triumphs; by World War II the Great Lakes were carrying almost a billion tons of shipping over busy lanes, and the "Soo" was the busiest canal in the world. Unfortunately, by 1970 there was a gnawing doubt whether some of the same lakes would survive the new menace of pollution, a situation which presented still another and a unique problem—that of obliteration—to those interested in the inland seas.

In time, the society, with financial support from the family of Commodore Fred W. Wakefield, would establish a museum at Harbor View in Vermilion (west of Cleveland) on a bluff overlooking Lake Erie and the Vermilion River. There is an eighty-five-foot flagpole familiar to all sailors who cruise the southern shore of Lake Erie. There is also a timber from one of Perry's craft that fought in the War of 1812 as well as a gyrocompass from a modern freighter. The museum displays notable collections of ship models, paintings, photographs, and relics, plus the Clarence Metcalf Library of reference books and memorabilia. Shortly after his retirement in

Cleveland, Metcalf became the curator of the Great Lakes Museum in Vermilion and continued in that capacity from 1953 to 1957.

LAWRENCE QUINCY MUMFORD

Lawrence Quincy Mumford's original appointment in 1945 as assistant librarian in Cleveland was made with the virtual assurance that he would become the director. It was the only promise of this kind in the first hundred years of the institution. The members of the Library Board were careful to point out that it was impossible for them to make an unequivocal guarantee because their membership changed from time to time. Nonetheless the appointment was made with the understanding that "among the present members of the Board you will succeed the Director when he retires." The letter went on to say that in appointing Mumford the board felt that it was "making an investment for the future and providing an insurance for the interim period." The intervening years turned out to be longer than anticipated. Metcalf was already sixty-seven when his successor was appointed; he was expected to resign within three years. He managed to stay on as director until 1950, when he was seventy-two.

Mumford's credentials were indeed brilliant and promising. His career was authentic in the American tradition of lowly origin, hard work, and estimable achievement. He was born on a "non-gentlemanly" farm in North Carolina; there he worked with his hands, during school terms and vacations, to help pay for his early progress in preparatory institutions and from this experience learned about the inherent dignity of all work. He was graduated magna cum laude and elected to Phi Beta Kappa from Duke University in 1925 and three years later received his master of arts degree from the same institution; as both an undergraduate and graduate student he was a staff member of the University Library, serving as acting chief of the Reference and Circulation Department in 1927–28. On graduation from the School of Library Service at Columbia in 1929 he was appointed to the staff of the New York Public Library, where he ultimately became coordinator of the General Service Division. In this position, which he left to come to

Cleveland in 1945, he had a staff of 700 and a budget of upwards of $2 million. In 1940 Archibald MacLeish, who had recently become head of the Library of Congress, wanted an experienced administrator to supervise the reorganization of its Acquisitions and Preparations Division into one great Processing Department; he prevailed upon the New York Public Library to lend Mumford for a year. Later MacLeish would testify that Mumford effected a "minor—perhaps a major—miracle" in the revision and improvement of technical procedures and methods. In time, Cleveland would also benefit from this administrative knowledge and skill. Mumford established a new processing department here, one that sped the preparation of books and resulted in notable economies in administrative costs in the Cleveland Public Library.

Promoted in 1950 from assistant to head librarian, Mumford's tenure in the top position at the Cleveland library was destined to be brief. In 1953 he was elected president of the American Library Association (ALA)—the same year that Dr. Luther H. Evans, then the Librarian of Congress, resigned to become the director general of the United Nations Educational, Scientific, and Cultural Organization (UNESCO). President Eisenhower asked the ALA to present a list of nationally recognized librarians from which Evans' successor would be nominated. The name of the ALA's own president was obviously included, and Mumford was designated as the eleventh head of the largest library in the nation, with its thirty-one million items including ten million books and pamphlets. He was the first "librarian's librarian"—that is, the first graduate of a library school—to achieve the position.

Mumford possessed a rare combination of administrative ability, a sense of humor, and courageous support of the right to read and to learn. Nominated Librarian of Congress when Senator Joseph McCarthy was at the apogee of his crusade against alleged radicals and "Comsymps," Mumford was ready to stand on principle. Preceding confirmation of his post he appeared before the Senate Rules Committee, whose ultraconservative Chairman William E. Jenner of Indiana asked a long list of prepared questions. At one point Jenner suggested it should be the librarian's duty to screen out subversive literature before it could be placed on the library's shelf. Mumford replied that not only would this be an impossible administrative chore because of the sheer number of books and pamphlets coming into the institution, but that it was the prime function of a library to have material on both sides of every issue because people should have the right to choose what they wanted to read. At this point Senator Thomas C. Hennings of Missouri broke in with the commendation, "I am glad to hear you say that you do not intend to set yourself up as a censor." When Mumford finally took the lengthy oath of office, in which he gave repeated assurances that he did not belong to subversive organizations and would not engage in strikes against the government, his sense of humor overcame him. He was heard to say: "It's longer than the marriage oath."

RAYMOND CHARLES LINDQUIST

Mumford's successor was Raymond Charles Lindquist, the eighth and last librarian to serve the Cleveland Public Library in its first century. His family was of Scandinavian origin with deep roots in the north central region of the United States, where he earned his baccalaureate and law degrees from the University of Minnesota in 1927 and 1930. At this point in his career Lindquist had no interest in becoming a librarian, but the Great Depression of the 1930s changed his mind, as it did for many of his generation. His background in law led to the successful completion of a federal civil service examination and to his appointment as librarian at the U.S. Bureau of Prisons at Fort Leavenworth in Kansas. With the help of a fellowship from the Carnegie Foundation, his lack of formal training for the position was remedied by the award of baccalaureate and master's degrees in library science at Columbia in 1935 and 1943. With professional training in two fields, for a decade after 1935 he served successively as librarian or consultant with the Department of Correction in New York City, with the New York Law Institute, and with the Public Library Commission of New Jersey. In 1946 he became the head of the Cuyahoga County Library, a position he held for nine years. His thirteen-year service as director of the Cleveland Public Library began in 1955. After his "retirement" at sixty-three in 1968 he returned to his ancestral base in Minnesota, where he became the first director of the new Minnesota Legislative Research Library in the capitol building in St. Paul. This "do-it-yourself" post, whose staff consisted of himself and one assistant, presented a quiet contrast to the busy position in Cleveland where he had supervised 850 employees.

The major achievement during Lindquist's tenure was the acquisition of the *Plain Dealer* building adjacent to the main library, a transaction which solved space problems that were immediate and critical. More than a quarter century earlier, when the institution had occupied its impressive main building at Third and Superior streets, there were optimists who claimed that the library's space problems had been solved for the next fifty years! It soon developed that the estimate should have been five rather than fifty years. As early as 1929 Eastman wished there was some way to expand the walls of the structure, and as an alternative, space for storage was rented in nearby buildings. In 1939 the Carnovsky Report noted that in the past fourteen years the book-stock had more than doubled and that the shelving problem was acute in the Division of Technology, the Business Information Bureau, the County Department, and the Library for the Blind. The difficulties became more critical in the 1940s and 1950s, by which time the number of books in the building had tripled. The situation was also exasperating since floors could not be added because the library was part of the municipal Group Plan for the Mall, and walls could not be expanded because of streets on three sides and a minuscule park on the fourth. Then the miracle happened; the six-story *Plain Dealer* building became available at an attractive price.

The *Plain Dealer* originally asked $2 million for the building and site. When an appraisal established the "fair market price" at $1,880,000 the newspaper unselfishly reduced its figure to $1,800,000. Still later, it further lowered its asking figure to $1,600,000 because of a unique legal problem.* It also held the

---

* The second reduction of $200,000, on the part of the *Plain Dealer*, arose from a very unusual development. There was a strip of land twenty feet wide under the western part of the newspaper building which was owned by the Cleveland Trust Company (in trust for five beneficiaries) and leased to the *Plain Dealer*. The newspaper had expected to purchase this strip and include the cost in its asking price

building off the market for a year—meeting from its own pocket
the added expense of another $100,000 for taxes, maintenance, in-
surance, and watchmen—until a bond issue could be passed. It was
a remarkable windfall for the library. When Mrs. Robert H. Jamison, the president of the Board of Trustees who was most active
and effective in the entire transaction, finally presented the *Plain
Dealer* with a check for $1,600,000 she expressed very special
thanks for the newspaper's generous gift to the library and to the
city of Cleveland.

The library asked the Cleveland electorate for $3 million to pur-
chase and remodel the *Plain Dealer* building. Lindquist's campaign was ably conducted. It was the first library bond issue in
thirty-five years and passed by a majority of 66 percent, a safe
margin over the required 55 percent. In addition, the interest rate
was the lowest for any local municipal issue for some time; it cost
the library only 2.66 percent to retire the bonds over fifteen years.
The acquisition was equivalent in area to the main building, doubling the floor space and providing housing for a number of additional operations, including almost a million additional books.
There was now adequate space for the Business Information and
the Science and Technology departments. What had been hopelessly overcrowded quarters for the Library for the Blind and the
Hospital and Institutions Department was alleviated when the entire fourth floor of the newly acquired building was assigned for
this purpose. There were enlarged quarters for the Adult Education Department and Film Bureau with classrooms and meeting
rooms and a 375-seat auditorium which was air-conditioned. A
functional tunnel between the two buildings created the semblance
of one structure. There was the added dividend of the Eastman
Reading Garden in the small park between the two buildings.

but found that the trust was so drawn that the land might not be sold
even though the beneficiaries were willing. The strip was appraised at
$160,000; the *Plain Dealer* generously knocked an additional $200,000
off its price. This meant that the library could take over the ninety-
nine year renewable lease, paying $7,400 a year in rental and taxes for
the strip. This annual expenditure would be offset, at least for a number of years, by the *Plain Dealer's* special reduction of $200,000 from
the original price of the property.

READERS DROP OUT

During the last twenty-five years of its first century, the Cleveland Public Library was confronted with three exasperating problems, one new and the others old. The new one was the alarming drop in readers and circulation. The remaining problems were the two M's—Money (whence derived?) and Merger (into a county or regional system?).

The decline in readers and circulation is portrayed graphically in the table for the years 1935, 1955, 1970:

TOTAL BORROWERS' CARDS ON HAND	1935	1955	1970
Main Library	82,868	80,814	100,291
Branch Libraries	225,676	185,995	150,871
Bookmobiles	5,689	7,841	7,772
TOTAL	314,233	274,650	258,934

TOTAL CIRCULATION (Adult & Juvenile)	1935	1955	1970
Main Library	1,566,104	692,756	734,904
Hospitals & Institutions	440,080	324,263	270,459
Library for Blind	21,915	71,981	242,728
Branch Libraries	5,794,952	3,215,814	1,971,925
TOTAL	7,623,051	4,304,814	3,220,016

These figures reveal that, at the main library, the number of borrowers has increased but circulation has decreased by one-half —not unexpected for a main library which is becoming a great research institution rather than a lending library. The disturbing drop has been found in the thirty-six branches; there borrowers' cards have fallen by one-third and books in circulation by two-thirds.

The causes for this development are elusive but, for whatever reasons, an increasing number of potential book borrowers either *will not—or cannot read.* Those disinclined to do so are representative of the competition facing book-reading from television and broadened recreational possibilities, from boats to cars to snow-mobiles to comic and picture magazines. It is the increasing num-ber of those who cannot read which presents frightening prob-lems for the future, not only for libraries, but for American democracy as well. A study completed at Harvard University in 1970 estimated that half of America's adults appear to lack the lit-eracy required to read such basic items as newspapers, job appli-cations, driving manuals, or the simplest exposition. Its conclusion was that more than half of the adult men and women in this coun-try may well be "functionally illiterate." Much of the essential reading required in a democracy assumes reading ability at the tenth- to eleventh-grade level, but the Harvard study contended that an astonishing number of adults have not maintained even fourth- or fifth-grade reading skills and are therefore "to all intents and purposes unable to read and write or absorb information from print." The communications editor of the *Saturday Review*, Rich-ard L. Tobin, wondered whether the nation was drifting into two classes of adults—not divided by social position or income or reli-gion or color—but "into those who can read and write and do so habitually and those who, for all practical purposes, cannot." Read-ing is a habit and reading muscles require practice and use, as all muscles do. Reading is also communicable; children read if their parents do and if they have books and magazines and newspapers around the house for reading rather than show. TV is no substitute because the coverage is too skimpy; the entire broadcast of the average dinner-hour news program can be printed on a single page of a daily newspaper. Walter Cronkite, the eminent news analyst, expressed his own concern about the consequences of all this; he noted that "since a democracy cannot flourish if its people are not adequately informed on the issues, the problem becomes one of the nation's survival."

In the closing years of its first hundred years the Cleveland Pub-lic Library was acutely aware of this issue. It would ponder new means of reaching the 75 percent of the population of the inner city which avoids the libraries—those who are not self-starters, who do not have a tradition of using a library, and the increasing number of those who do not read well—all of whom present an ominous problem at both national and local levels. After World

War II the United States had become concerned with adult illiteracy in the backward nations of the "Third World." It had assumed, in nostalgic recollection of the "melting-pot" concept from the Civil War to World War II, that the only people in the United States who could not read and write were immigrants, many of whom were literate enough in their own languages to learn English without too much trouble. But the 1960s brought a rude awakening. The nation tumbled to the fact that it had its own problems of adult illiteracy; in the city of Cleveland a survey in 1965 indicated that almost half of the adults over twenty-five read at, or below, the sixth-grade level.

During most of its first century the Cleveland Public Library concentrated on those who read with dedication and purpose, from the devotees of general reading to scholars in specialized fields—people who *sought* the library. In the 1960s the library found it advisable to make its own overtures to *reluctant* readers. Through a grant from the Ohio State Library Board it was able to open three experimental reading centers for the purpose of developing those persons limited educationally because their reading muscles had deteriorated through lack of use. This project involved the library for the first time in a teaching function that was direct rather than indirect. The library also became concerned with teaching materials—unconventional printed material, filmstrips, slides, records—which were quite a contrast to the usual stock-in-trade on library shelves.

In 1968, as the library evaluated the results of its first direct-teaching experiment in reading skills, it had reason for some satisfaction and considerable disappointment. It learned, as many teachers do, about the smallness of result in proportion to the magnitude of effort. This was reflected in the library's film about the project, realistically entitled *Step a Little Higher*; the cinematic portrayal was sensitive and purposeful and realistic enough to achieve national attention. There were many who questioned, for understandable reasons, whether the teaching of reading was the proper function of a library. They felt strongly that libraries should serve those who could and wanted to read. Pragmatists agreed in principle but dissented on practice; they noted that democracies and libraries can hardly function without a plenitude of readers.

If the schools and the society failed to provide the skill and motivation required for reading, the library must accept the challenge and do something about it.

WHENCE MONEY?

As far as money was concerned the library had known the meaning of poverty from its first year, but this embarrassing condition was to become acute with the Great Depression of the 1930s and in the years that followed.

Prior to 1931 all libraries in Ohio, along with other political subdivisions, received their income from the real-property tax. The economic depression which began in 1929 brought on a crisis in the funding of local and state governments. To alleviate the mounting financial problems of taxpayers, amendments to the Ohio Constitution ultimately imposed a limit of ten mills on all real property. When this happened in the early 1930s, many libraries found themselves without adequate financial support because the limited revenue from the property tax was no longer sufficient to support them *and* all other political agencies. Some libraries closed entirely, others struggled on with volunteer help or with reduced staff on half salary. Between 1930 and 1933 the income of the Cleveland Public Library declined by nearly $750,000, more than one-third of its former revenue.

In 1933 Robert A. Taft, then a state senator, engineered the passage of legislation designed specifically for the succor of distraught libraries. It provided for a tax on intangible property (by contrast with real property intangible assets, such as stocks and bonds, cannot be perceived by the senses) the proceeds from which were to be devoted primarily for use by libraries. Taft's bill stated that any library board which made its services available to all residents of a county would have first consideration in the distribution of income from the state tax on intangibles. After library needs were met, any money remaining was to be allocated to park and sanitary districts and to municipalities.

It seemed clear that the original intent of the Ohio legislature was to make the free libraries of the state secure and self-supporting by earmarking a tax for this special use. But the law's language was foggy and municipalities were pressed for funds. The law provided that public libraries should get the tax funds they "need" from the tax on intangibles; the municipalities contended that libraries did not "need" nearly as much as they claimed, and that municipalities should get more. It was not long before an annual tug-of-war began between all the library systems and all the mayors in Cuyahoga County, over the distribution of the tax. In 1937 a member of the Cleveland City Council, which was faced by mounting deficits for poor relief, contended that the budget of the Cleveland Public Library was too high by $200,000; in his judgment the library preferred that people "starve while they read." In 1952 the law director of Shaker Heights, a wealthy suburb which paid much more in taxes on intangibles than was returned to it by the county authorities, claimed that he would "rather have . . . streets patrolled than to buy 6,000 books for someone else's library." On one occasion the Ohio State Board of Tax Appeals, which was petitioned frequently for relief, asserted that "even King Solomon might experience some difficulty in arriving at actual need as distinguished from claimed need."

This unedifying donnybrook went on for decades, from time to time involving appeals to the Ohio Supreme Court and the legislature, as well as the Board of Tax Appeals. Ultimately libraries established their prior claim, but the annual struggles had been costly and worrisome. In the early 1940s, 76 percent of the tax on intangibles in Cuyahoga County was going to libraries and 24 percent to municipalities; a decade later, in 1955, it was 96 percent for libraries and 4 percent for municipalities—specifically $5.9 million in intangible-tax dollars for libraries and $275,000 for cities and villages (from $2 for tiny Woodmere to $83,848 for the city of Cleveland.)

This seemed to be a triumph; actually there was no victory. The Cleveland Public Library lost ground because the enlarged percentage of income from the tax on intangibles was not enough to compensate for increasing costs for books and personnel and services. In the late years of its first century the library was spending more each year for new books, but acquisitions remained constant because of rapidly increasing prices. Even so, in 1969, the Cleveland Public Library ranked as the second largest public institution in the nation in the number of books owned, but below Chicago, Brooklyn, and Philadelphia in the amount spent on new books. Salary scales had not been high enough to keep vital employees; in 1955, as an example, the scale for teachers in Cleveland was significantly above that for its librarians—in spite of the fact that teachers could be employed after four years of college training, whereas professional librarians require five. By 1968 the starting salary for beginning librarians had risen to $7,184 (from $3,660 in 1955). This increase of almost 100 percent, long overdue, helped reduce the previous rapid turnover of personnel but added materially to the size of the payroll. Because of developments such as these, during two months in 1970 the library would be forced to close on Wednesdays in order to balance its budget.

How could this happen? The answer was obvious. The tax on intangibles, noble in intent, was not productive of enough money to meet adequate library budgets anywhere in Ohio. There were several reasons. One was that the tax was not raising nearly as much money as it might. It was being evaded or ignored by many citizens, and little effort was expended on a state-wide basis to collect from many who were derelict in their legal obligations. Over the state as a whole the tax, collected on the county level, produced large revenues for some counties and caused poverty for library services in others. In modern society it is axiomatic that intangible property is dispersed in a random pattern which coincides only accidentally with the need for a public service. Within a county, however, the intangible tax provided a reasonably equitable distribution of the county's wealth for the benefit of the entire area. In 1969 Shaker Heights in Cuyahoga County paid almost $4 million in taxes on intangibles and got back about $375,000, by contrast with the residents of the city of Cleveland who paid $1.7 million and received in return almost $6.8 million for their library budget. In the state as a whole, however, there could be great inequality. In 1965 the per capita collections from the tax on intangibles varied from 57 cents in one county to $8.13 in another; the "fifty-cent" county allocated 100 percent of its income from the tax to its libraries whereas the other allowed 82 percent—but that 82 percent amounted to more than $6.40 per capita. In 1965 the average for the state from the tax on intangibles was $3.11 per capita, but there were eleven counties with less than $1.00 per capita for library services.

The tax on intangibles had obviously been welcomed by libraries because its proceeds were especially dedicated to their use. Unfortunately the law also made it so easy to establish new libraries that they frequently appeared without much thought or planning beyond the confines of a school district. It had become possible for any small community to establish a library, with no community expenditure, because the cost of the new library would come from the tax on intangibles by the county. In Cuyahoga County alone there were 6 libraries when the intangible-tax law was passed in 1932; by 1938 7 additional ones had been added. In Ohio the number of libraries mushroomed from 197 in 1934 to 280 in 1947, a growth of 42 percent in a thirteen-year period. This development was so haphazard and disturbing that in 1947 the legislature was compelled to take action. It passed a bill, sponsored by the Ohio Library Association, providing that thereafter any new public libraries in Ohio must be established on a county-wide basis. This meant that libraries already established by cities, townships, and school districts would be permitted to continue, but no taxing authority other than the county could establish new ones.

For all of these reasons, by 1970 libraries in Ohio, including the giant Cleveland Public Library, were caught in a financial bind. They found it awkward, if not impossible, to project growth on the basis of the uncertain intangible-tax collection. Voters had shown an unmistakable aversion to adding libraries to the list of beneficiaries of real-property taxes; they regarded the real estate tax as too high already. Perhaps economies were possible through better planning or new devices. Libraries might find that fewer branches were necessary if they were distributed on the basis of current imperatives rather than tradition and history. Perhaps new technology might help; as an example, some librarians were enthusiastic about the potentialities of UMF (ultramicrofiche) libraries which make possible as many as eight hundred photo-reduced pages on a four-by-five-inch card. But pending such savings or some revision of the tax structure, by 1970 all libraries in Ohio found themselves "locked in" financially at the same time the greatest publishing explosion in history was upon them.

There was some comfort, but not much, in the fact that this financial bind was national in scope. In 1970 the Library of Congress, with the greatest collection of books ever assembled, was facing its worst crisis since 1814 when the British burned the Capitol and destroyed the infant library's entire stock. The chief problem of the Library of Congress was lack of space; its expansion had been so rapid and extensive in recent years that (like the Cleveland library in the early 1900s) books lined the floors in front of stacks, a stopgap productive of inevitable difficulties in locating them. The New York Public Library, surpassed as a research facility only by the Library of Congress, was also in a precarious situation. By late 1970 when the Cleveland Public Library had found it necessary to close on Wednesdays, the New York institution had already been shut on weekends for a year. Although the library in New York had been closed to conserve fuel during World War II and to commemorate the death of public figures, it had never before been forced to close for budgetary reasons. The problem was an exasperating one because the research collections in New York, as with the White Collection in Cleveland, were supported largely from endowments which were no longer adequate to sustain the service. It was apparent that, among other means of subsistence, increased gifts—large and small—would be vital, and in both New York and Cleveland organizations called Friends of the Library performed yeoman service in raising money. But the large individual gifts and endowments for public libraries, those from the Astors, the Tildens, the Andrew Carnegies, and the John Griswold Whites, had declined with the passing years. This was regrettable because, as a New York writer noted:

> The public library is the one institution of a community which is open and has something to offer all of the people, all the time. It is for the well and for the sick, for the rich and for the poor, for the old and the young, for those seeking practical help in the business of life and for those seeking needed escape from that business. It is the one institution by which the life of the entire community is enriched.

WHITHER MERGER?

In the early 1920s separate libraries were serving *some* of the residents of Cuyahoga County, that is, those who happened to live in the municipalities of Cleveland, East Cleveland, Cleveland Heights, Lakewood, Westlake, and Bay Village; the remainder were without library facilities. Eastman was so concerned about this inequity that she lobbied effectively in the state legislature for the establishment of a supplementary county library system to serve deprived areas. In 1921 the Ohio legislature authorized the creation of county libraries with seven-member boards of trustees, three appointed by the judges of common pleas courts and four by the county commissioners. The first such library in Ohio was established in 1922 by a majority vote of the people in Cuyahoga County residing outside the districts which already had libraries. When it opened in 1924 the Cuyahoga County Library had no books, no staff, no organization, only the interest of those areas of the county which were lacking in library facilities. Within a year it was distributing 29,000 books in branches, stations, and classrooms. Some were makeshift in character; in Bedford, as an example, a reading room was created by using half of the study hall in the school building. Its equipment was furnished by the Bedford School Board; the County Library provided books and a thousand dollars toward the cost of service. Hours were extended so that such libraries could be opened to the public after school hours. By 1969, with more than a million books and twenty-five branches, the Cuyahoga County Library ranked third in size in Ohio.

Although the County Library had separate and independent tax support, during its first eighteen years (1924–42) it was so closely integrated with the Cleveland Public Library that the two institutions were virtually one. The county institution was housed in the basement of the Cleveland Public Library which furnished both space and administrative services under contract. This arrangement worked very well until 1942 when the contract was terminated. The County Library withdrew books, periodicals, records, supplies, furniture, fixtures and motor stock—and set up its own independent operation on West Third Street. The official reason given for the abrupt change was that the Cleveland Public Library needed the space in its main building then occupied by the County Library. By 1942 the Cleveland library *was* short of space, but this was not the complete story. As mentioned earlier, the Library Board had approved of neither Charles Rush, its librarian, nor Amy Winslow whom he had brought to Cleveland to be vice-librarian. When Winslow became librarian of the County Library in 1941, the Cleveland Library Board saw a solution for two problems by jettisoning both Winslow and the County Library. For those who favored the merger of city and county library facilities this was an exasperating setback.

Over the past half century the administration of libraries on a county or regional pattern has been advocated by organizations and groups at the national, state, and local levels. As early as 1923 the American Library Association stated that the county or region (several counties) was the logical unit for library service in most parts of the United States. In 1947 the Ohio State legislature, alarmed by the proliferation of school-district libraries financed by the county tax on intangibles, decreed that from that point in time all new public libraries must be established on a county-wide or regional basis. Since 1933 upwards of a dozen studies and reports from a variety of research organizations—including the Citizens League, METRO (Cleveland Metropolitan Services Organization), the Cleveland Commission on Higher Education, and Ernst and Ernst—have advocated the consolidation of school-district libraries (eight of them in 1969) into one system for Cuyahoga County.

Proponents of the county system have asserted that the school-district pattern is anachronistic, that desirable economies would follow the adoption of a single county library, and that the unified system would make possible the elimination of inequalities and inequities in current salary scales. In the early days school-district libraries made sense because financial support came from a tax on property within the district, and primary emphasis was on service to school children. In recent decades this has no longer been true. Because money for school-district libraries now came from the county tax on intangibles, these libraries were in effect petitioning the county commissioners for funds which often exceeded the amount paid by citizens of a particular district. Under current archaic procedures, however, library budgets must first be approved by boards of education and filed by them with the County Budget Commission. But the Cleveland Public Library no longer served *primarily* either school children or residents of Cleveland. By the close of its first century two out of three book borrowers at the library were suburbanites, reflecting the fact that by 1970 two-thirds of the population of Cuyahoga County lived outside the city of Cleveland.

At the same time the Cleveland Public Library was withdrawing from the school-library business. This was a result, in large part, of the Ross County Decision of the Ohio Supreme Court in 1958 which upset school-library arrangements all over the state, including Cuyahoga County. Basically the decision was to the effect that a board of education should pay the entire cost of school-library service if it could afford to do so; prior to this time, in Cleveland, the Cleveland Public Library was paying the major part of such costs. By 1969, however, the Cleveland library's School Department had been dissolved and the library was no longer supervising or building school libraries as it had done in the days of Brett and Eastman. School libraries continued to draw books from those remaining in the Cleveland Public Library's school collection, but the central library no longer purchased new books for school libraries. By the time of the Cleveland Public Library's centennial the pattern had changed so significantly that, as in most places in the United States, school libraries were operated by boards of education rather than by public libraries. The term "school-district" library had become an anachronism.

There was no question that economies would result from a single county library—from the coordinated planning of new branches, central purchasing of books and supplies, and by elimination of time-consuming and costly duplication of effort in book selection, space, personnel departments, cataloguing, budgeting, public relations, and printing—although estimates of the amount of these savings varied over the years. In the selection of new books, as an example, the *Cleveland Press* noted in 1962 that librarians in the County and Cleveland systems, frequently sitting only a few blocks apart, were reading and reviewing the same books for their shelves. The Cleveland Public Library and the County Library were each holding three all-day meetings every month for this purpose, obligating upwards of thirty thousand librarian man-hours every year, a substantial part of it duplication of effort. Another example was the annual dog-eat-dog struggle between numerous libraries, all competing for funds from a common pot, in an exercise that was frenetic and time-consuming and needless. In November 1943 the Citizens League noted the yearly battle between fourteen library boards and thirteen suburban mayors before the County Budget Commission over the allocation of the revenue from the tax on intangibles. The league observed that the "struggle each year grows more intense—the guns used are of large calibre—and the ammunition is in the form of tabulated data and charges and countercharges." By 1969 the municipalities were largely out of contention, but nine libraries, each one walking a financial tightrope, were asking the budget commission for considerably more money than was available, wasting time and effort in the preparation of nine budgets rather than one.

The league's conclusion was that "either library users are receiving less service than they are entitled to or there is a waste of economic resources in the form of higher taxes than are needed to render the service." In 1943 the league reported that the cost for library service, in fifteen separate and independent libraries then existing in Cuyahoga County, was $2.27 per capita; in Hamilton County (which includes Cincinnati), with a single unified county library system, the cost was $1.00 per capita. At the same time the American Library Association noted that per capita costs of library service were $0.92 in Boston and $0.63 in San Francisco; only one metropolitan library system, outside of Cleveland, was then above one dollar—Rochester with $1.14. The league was quick to point out that it did not find library staffs wasteful; in fact it was happy to report that they were performing magnificently in spite of low salaries. It did find a solution for raising these salaries through economies resulting from a single county system in place of the current "disintegrated and duplicating . . . system, or rather lack of system. . . ." In addition the elimination of inequities between libraries, possible under a county system, would provide a unified salary schedule built upon logic and fairness for the entire staff. This coordination was all the more necessary by reason of the fact that all taxpayers in the county contributed to the maintenance of its libraries; continuation of wasteful duplication was unfair to them. One study, that of Ernst and Ernst in 1970, noted that $117,000 would be saved by consolidation into a single county library, but the net gain would amount to only $37,000. This was because $45,000 would be needed for salary adjustment and upwards of $35,000 to equalize employee fringe benefits—certainly worthy and legitimate use of money saved by the elimination of unnecessary duplication.

Opposition to a county-wide library was based in part on geography (Cleveland vs. the suburbs) and in part on library size (large vs. smaller libraries). Some suburbanites feared that their library funds would be spent in Cleveland; some Clevelanders felt that the central city would be neglected while the suburbs flourished. Some partisans of the Cleveland Public Library, justifiably proud of the institution as the largest in the state of Ohio and one of great national prestige, were not anxious to lose its name and its identity in a bibliothecal conglomerate. Some disciples of small libraries feared that these institutions would be swallowed up. In 1941 the president of the Cleveland Heights PTA characterized a proposed county-wide library as follows:

This is the first step toward annexation. It will rob the smaller libraries of their rights.

It was the story of the Constitutional Convention of 1787 all over again, albeit in microcosm. New York and Virginia had looked down on Rhode Island and Delaware; the latter had feared absorption, even sacrifice, at the hands of colossi. At the regional level Cuyahoga County was a metropolitan community in every respect except government, balkanized into dozens of conflicting political subdivisions many of which were seeking their own benefit at the expense of others—really at the expense of taxpayers who paid dearly for the overlapping of jurisdiction and the duplication of both personnel and services.

Interestingly, in 1939 Samuel J. Kornhauser, president of the Cleveland Public Library's Board of Trustees, came within one vote of merging the Cleveland library into a county system. In an attempt to convince his colleagues that the existing "waste, duplication, overlapping and inefficiency" in the fourteen-library setup had to be ended if libraries in Cuyahoga County were to survive, the histrionic Kornhauser presented a ten-page statement in which he asked the board to immolate itself:

> Nothing we could possibly do as trustees of this library for its benefit and for the benefit of the people for whom it exists would be so eminent a service as this act which I now ask you to perform. . . . Greater love you cannot show than to lay down your political existence in their behalf.

The board almost succumbed to this eloquence but ultimately turned it down by a vote of four to three. One of the opponents, of Czech derivation, asked, "Is this the American way?" and declared that Adolf Hitler had also claimed that in unity there was strength. Another antagonist, this time Irish by descent, contended that the county-wide library might be good for the Germans in Cincinnati but was inappropriate for the more varied population of Cleveland.

A CENTURY OF SERVICE

Every institution of age and fame has had its ups and downs, its *grandeurs et misères*. The Cleveland Public Library, like most centenarians, has acquired a few aches and pains along the way. Fortunately, throughout most of these years the quality of the staff and of its service has been sustained.

Many readers have asserted that, although the New York Public Library has more books, the service in the open-stack Cleveland library is much more efficient and satisfying. William F. McDermott, a bibliophile, was the nationally known drama critic of the Cleveland *Plain Dealer* from 1921 to 1958; in his world travels he studied in many libraries. He noted that the British Museum had more books than the Cleveland library, but by comparison the London institution was a "chill and cheerless place." In Paris, McDermott was inclined to applaud five million volumes in the Bibliothèque Nationale, but was less than impressed to find that "it would take an act of Parliament to obtain approval for a private citizen to withdraw a book . . . for home reading." He concluded that there was no library in the world which performed so greatly and so variously, as did the Cleveland Public Library, for the benefit of the community. In 1957 the distinguished historian and biographer, Catherine Drinker Bowen, visited Cleveland. She was trustee of the Philadelphia Free Library and research for her many books had been done all over the world, from libraries in Moscow and Paris to Berlin and London and Washington and New York. She testified that the Cleveland Public Library compared so well with all other libraries that it made them blush.

Eastman, who served the Cleveland Public Library with heart and soul for many years, was a great admirer of Daniel H. Burnham, the imaginative architect who designed the Cleveland Mall. Eastman liked to quote Burnham's famous injunction:

Make no little plans; they have no magic to stir man's blood and probably themselves will not be realized. Make big plans; aim high in hope and work, remembering that a noble, logical plan once recorded will never die, but long after we are gone will be a living thing asserting itself with growing insistence.

This was a moving observation more than half a century ago. It is just as pertinent now, after one hundred years, when the Cleveland Public Library—"high in hope and work" is fully justified in letting the past speak to the future.

NOTES

THESE NOTES do not presume to provide a bibliography in depth for the legion of topics discussed in this volume. They are designed to provide the inquisitive reader with an indication of the sources which were used directly or indirectly (as general background) in the writing of this particular narrative.

It is understood that all references cited are available at the Cleveland Public Library, unless otherwise specified in these footnotes.

In order to avoid repetition which could only be boring and profligate of space, the following abbreviations have been used:

AR	Annual Report of the Cleveland Public Library
CPL	Cleveland Public Library
CWRU	Case Western Reserve University
News	*Cleveland News*
PD	Cleveland *Plain Dealer*
Press	*Cleveland Press*

The use of the term Annual Report must also be explained. The annual reports on the library were included in the reports of the Board of Education through 1878; after that date they were included in the annual reports of the Library Board. The reports seldom reflect a calendar year; usually they were for a fiscal period ending on 30 April or 31 August—or some other artificial date within a calendar year. For the purposes of this study the annual reports of the library, from whatever basic source, will carry an abbreviated designation which is indicative of the *close* of the library's reporting period, for example, Annual Report of 1879.

I am indebted to Frank Joseph for providing the papers of his father, to Mrs. Sigvald Refness for making available the scrapbooks about her father, William J. Corrigan, and to Tom Barensfeld for permitting me to read the files of the *Penny Press*.

Among staff members of the Cleveland Public Library who are now retired, conversations or correspondence have been helpful with the following: Edith Case, Rose Vormelker, Varelia Farmer, Emilia Wefel, Carl Vitz, Lucy Duker, and Donna Root. Those now active in the library have given me every assistance, but special commendation must go to Mrs. Alice Loranth in the John G. White Collection and to Ethel Robinson in General Reference. Mrs. Loranth provided the specialized scholarship and the basic materials essential for the analysis of an esoteric area of knowledge. General Reference is omniscient, in part because it has a collection of newspaper clippings which is invaluable.

CHAPTER 1, Out of Small Beginnings

SMALL BEGINNINGS IN OHIO

William Bradford, *Of Plymouth Plantation, 1620–1647* (Alfred A. Knopf, 1959), p. 236; Frederic D. Aldrich, *The School Library in Ohio with Special Emphasis on Its Legislative History* (Scarecrow Press, 1959), p. 15 —on the Coonskin Library; Grace Goulder, "Some Early Ohio Libraries," *Serif, Kent State University Library Quarterly*, Mar. 1966; Wilfred Henry Alburn and Miriam Russell, *This Cleveland of Ours* (S. J. Clarke Publishing Co., 1933), 1:370 ff.; Vinnie J. Mayer, "The Coonskin Library," in *An American Library History Reader: Contributions to Library Literature*, ed. John David Marshall (Shoe String Press, 1961), pp. 45–49; Harlan Hatcher, *Lake Erie* (Bobbs-Merrill, 1945), p. 206, quoted in "One Out of Four Clevelanders in 1811 Holds Card in Library," *Christian Science Monitor*, 4 Feb. 1946; William Ganson Rose, *Cleveland: The Making of a City* (World Publishing Co., 1950), pp. 155, 161, 162, 173, 198, 202, 211, 228, 234, 238–40, 252, 264, 292, 346,

371, 409; Russell H. Davis, *Memorable Negroes in Cleveland's Past* (Western Reserve Historical Society, 1969), pp. 18–19; *Dictionary of American Biography*, s.v. "Case, Leonard, Sr." and "Case, Leonard, Jr."; Egbert Cleave, *Cleave's Biographical Cyclopaedia of the State of Ohio, City of Cleveland and Cuyahoga County* (J. B. Lippincott & Co., n.d.), pp. 6 ff. —particularly on William Case; Walter B. Hendrickson, *The Arkites and Other Pioneer Natural History Organizations of Cleveland* (Press of Western Reserve University, 1962), pp. 1, 10; David Mead, *Yankee Eloquence in the Middle West: The Ohio Lyceum, 1850–1870* (Michigan State College Press, 1951), p. 218 —on Case Hall; Elbert Jay Benton, *Cultural Story of an American City: Cleveland*, 3 vols. (Western Reserve Historical Society, 1942–46), 3:87 ff. —on Cleveland Library Association; "Cleveland's Other Libraries," *Open Shelf*, CPL Bulletin, Sept.–Oct. 1920. For obituaries on Leonard Case, Jr.— *Penny Press*, 6, 7, and 8 Jan. 1880; *Cleveland Leader*, 7 Jan. 1880; *Cleveland Evening News*, 6 Jan. 1880; *Cleveland Weekly Leader*, 10 Jan. 1880; *PD*, 6 Jan. 1880.

The circumstances surrounding the death of Leonard Case, Jr. were so unusual and dramatic that there was considerable speculation whether it was a natural demise or whether he took his own life. A frail child at birth, his health deteriorated rapidly in the late 1870s from ailments affecting his stomach and his lungs. He was weakened by chronic diarrhea and by emphysema which produced symptoms of "asthmatic consumption." He was troubled with frequent paroxysms that came from shortness of breath and a "winter cough." To relieve the paroxysms, in an era without the tranquilizers which are now so common, physicians (Case's personal one was the famous Dr. Henry K. Cushing) regularly used injections of morphine and permitted patients to inhale chloroform from a sponge or cloth. All of this affected his nervous system, resulting in periods of pessimism and depression. In his last year, Case was quite broken down—to the point where he required constant attention, frequently had to be carried about, and was restricted to the area of his house and yard. Mr. and Mrs. William Rattle (she was a cousin of Mr. Case) lived in the house with him.

On the evening before his death he entertained close friends at whist, and they found him in surprisingly good spirits. At two o'clock the next morning Mr. Rattle heard him coughing, but the "spell" was of short duration. An hour later Rattle noted a light in Mr. Case's room, investigated, and found him dead. Beside the still warm body, according to the *Cleveland Weekly Leader*, was an empty chloroform vial and a saturated handkerchief. The details varied in the *Penny Press*, which stated that Rattle found a saucer of chloroform on the table and Case with the bed clothing over his head. It was presumed that he had put the cover over his head to better inhale the chloroform, lost consciousness, and fell to the floor. When the bed clothing was removed, there was a strong odor of chloroform.

The obituary in the Cleveland *Plain Dealer* had this headline:

THE DEATH OF LEONARD CASE
RELIEF FROM LONG YEARS OF SUFFERING

The article went on to say that "Mr. Case would have preferred to die rather than to live, life having become so great a burden." The *Cleveland Weekly Leader* noted the presence of chloroform and "supposed that yesterday morning he took an overdose, which in his low state of health caused almost immediate death." The summary by E. W. Scripps in the *Penny Press* appears to have been the most judicious of all commentaries. Scripps noted that, by reason of the declining state of Case's health, the cause of his death would always remain a mystery. Physicians testified that the death might have been caused from the direct effect of chloroform, or from a paroxysm caused by the influence of the chloroform as it came into contact with weak lungs. Whether the chloroform was administered purposefully, or by accident, Scripps did not believe anyone would ever know.

SMALL BEGINNINGS IN THE UNITED STATES

Jesse H. Shera, *Foundations of the Public Library: The Origins of the Public Library Movement in New England, 1629–1855* (University of Chicago Press, 1949), pp. 32, 49, 56, 74–75, 226 ff., 234; W. R. Rose, "Cleveland's First Public Library," *Open Shelf*, July–Aug. 1921; Edwin Wolf II, "Franklin and His Friends Choose Their Books," in *American Library History*, ed. Marshall, pp. 19, 20, 40;

Carl Bode, *The American Lyceum: Town Meeting of the Mind* (Oxford University Press, 1956), pp. 8 ff., 165 ff., 191, 201, 239, 241; William I. Fletcher, *Public Libraries in America* (Roberts Brothers, 1894), pp. 20–21, 94; C. Dewitt Hardy, "The Foundations of Library Government," in Oliver Garceau, *The Public Library in the Political Process* (Columbia University Press, 1949), pp. 16–17, 20–21; Walter Muir Whitehill, *Boston Public Library: A Centennial History* (Harvard University Press, 1956), p. 5; Arthur E. Bostwick, *The American Public Library* (D. Appleton and Co., 1910), pp. 6 ff., 19–20; Benton, *Cultural Story*, 2:8, 38 ff.; Cecil B. Hayes, *The American Lyceum: Its History and Contribution to Education* (U. S. Government Printing Office, 1932), pp. viii, xi, 3, 22, 24, 28, 31 ff., 36 ff., 51 ff.; George E. Condon, *Cleveland: The Best Kept Secret* (Doubleday, 1967), p. 93.

It has been noted that a major founder of the lyceum was Josiah Holbrook. Interestingly, it was in the Western Reserve that he hoped to establish the center of his movement. In 1837 he moved from the East to Berea (a holy city near Cleveland named for a village near Jerusalem) in order to "assist in spreading knowledge and holiness over our globe and to redeem man from ignorance and vice." In this effort, which may come as something of a surprise to the more materialistic citizens of modern Berea, Holbrook was associated with John Baldwin, a young man with deep religious convictions and some fortunate business happenings. The utopian village of Berea then consisted of a tract of five hundred acres, all property of the lyceum corporation held in the form of stock which was sold at fifty dollars a share "to young persons of good moral character; families who desire to move there; influential friends of science and the moral enterprises of the age; to Lyceums and institutes." Holbrook was a graduate of Yale, an idealist who was enough of a pragmatist to know that those who followed the program of the lyceum would require scientific equipment for the study of chemistry and physics and astronomy, plus cabinets containing rocks for geology. For that reason he set up his own plant for the manufacture and sale of this paraphernalia—an early attempt to provide visual education in teaching methods. By 1842 Berea, with its dozen buildings and a school with fifty students, was a transplanted New England community. In that year Holbrook's noble experiment for the one and only lyceum village collapsed. It had not prospered in spite of splendid objectives to redeem men from ignorance and vice and "to engraft education upon business, and not business upon education."

Baldwin fared better. Originally he had bought in Berea two hundred acres of land which he had never seen. On them he developed a gristmill and a sawmill, but was forced into bankruptcy in 1842 as a result of the Panic of 1837 and expenditures for the lyceum. After this debacle he discovered a fragment of sandstone on which he happened to sharpen a knife. He realized it was excellent material for a grindstone and discovered a plentiful supply of the same rock under his own land. In time, the products of Baldwin's quarries provided industry for Berea, subsequently known as the "Grindstone City" rather than the "Holy One." Ultimately these sandstone operations would give Cuyahoga County its first college in Baldwin Institute, later a part of Baldwin-Wallace College. See Mead, *Yankee Eloquence*, pp. 16–17; Rose, *Cleveland*, pp. 159, 1068 ff.; *Dictionary of American Biography*, s.v. "Baldwin, John" and "Holbrook, Josiah."

SHOULD LIBRARIES BE FREE?

Sidney Ditzion, *Arsenals of a Democratic Culture: A Social History of the American Public Library in New England and the Middle States from 1850 to 1900* (American Library Association, 1947), pp. 12, 22–23, 36–37, 66, 103, 114–17, 121, 134–35; M. D. O'Brien, "Free Libraries," in *A Plea for Liberty: An Argument Against Socialism and Socialistic Legislation*, ed. Thomas Mackay (John Murray, 1891), pp. 329–30, 343–45; Thomas A. Bailey, *The American Pageant* (D. C. Heath and Co., 1956), pp. 333–34; AR 1897, p. 10; Clyde H. Farnsworth, "West Europe Attributes Continuing Technology Lag Behind the U.S. to Inferior Management," *New York Times*, 13 Dec. 1967 —on Servan-Schrieber; Cleveland Public Schools, "Report of the President, 1867–1868," p. 14; George S. Bobinski, *Carnegie Libraries: Their History and Impact on American Public Library Development* (American Library Association, 1969), pp. 35–37, 92.

THE FIRST PUBLIC LIBRARIES

Ditzion, *Arsenals*, pp. 4–5, 30; Hardy, in Garceau, *Public Library*, pp. 24–27, 38; Fletcher, *Public Libraries*, pp. 21–24; Whitehill, *Boston Public Library*, pp. 13, 103; Aldrich, *School Library in Ohio*, pp. 34, 70 ff.; AR 1879, pp. 18 ff.; Benton, *Cultural Story*, 2:88; *Open Shelf*, Oct.–Dec. 1969 —on Anson Smyth; "Plans, Views, and Descriptions of the Free Public Library of Cleveland, Ohio," 1893.

It should be noted that at about the time the Boston Public Library opened in 1854, several endowed institutions also came into existence: the Astor Library in New York, the Peabody Library in Baltimore, the Grosvenor Library in Buffalo, and the Watkinson Library in Hartford—all bearing the names of their benefactors. Still later would come the Newberry in Chicago. See George B. Utley, "An Early 'Friend' of Libraries," *Library Quarterly*, July 1942.

Interestingly, in 1817 Ohio established a State Library in Columbus, theoretically to assist the legislature. In that year Governor Thomas Worthington, with money from a contingent fund, bought 509 books for a sum that amounted to almost one thousand dollars. In presenting these books to the legislators the governor, perhaps with tongue in cheek, said he was doing so to provide such information as would aid them in the discharge of their important duties. The next year (1818) the legislature recognized the importance of this institution by providing a salary of $200 a year for the librarian, plus an annual appropriation of $350 for the purchase of "useful books and maps." From this point of time the State Library received annual appropriations. In 1882 it was opened to the public and became a regional counterpart of the Library of Congress. See Aldrich, *School Library in Ohio*, pp. 30 ff.

A CLEVELAND PUBLIC LIBRARY

"The Public Library," *Cleveland Herald*, 19 Feb. 1869; W. R. Rose, "All in a Day's Work," *PD*, 18 Jan. 1917; John H. Clarke, "The Public Library," in *A History of Cleveland*, 3 vols., ed. Samuel P. Orth (S. J. Clarke Publishing Co., 1910), 1:583; W. R. Rose, "Cleveland's Public Library"; Morris Bishop, "The Lower Depths of Higher Education," *American Heritage*, Dec. 1969 —on college libraries in the nineteenth century.

CHAPTER 2, The First Fifteen Years:
Two Librarians Succumb to Pressure

TWO LIBRARIANS, 1869–84

Minutes of the Library Board, 3 Nov. 1884, in script, p. 243 —on janitors and lights; "The Board of Education," *PD*, 26 Jan. 1875 —on provision of spittoons.

LUTHER MELVILLE OVIATT

General Catalogue of the Officers and Students of Adelbert College of Western Reserve University (originally Western Reserve College), 1826–1895, p. 46, CWRU Archives; Andrew Freese, *Early History of the Cleveland Public Schools* (Robison, Savage and Co., 1876), p. 108; Clarke, in *Cleveland*, ed. Orth, 1:584; "The Public Library," *Cleveland Leader*, 2 July 1872 —on quality of Oviatt's education; William J. Akers, *Cleveland Schools in the Nineteenth Century* (W. M. Bayne Printing House, 1901), p. 99; William H. Brett, "The Rise and Growth of the Cleveland Public Library," *Magazine of Western History*, Nov. 1887; AR 1878, pp. 94–95 —for poetry by Oviatt; AR 1869, pp. 12, 14–15, 98, 140 —for salary scales, first classification system, contribution of German books; *Cleveland Herald*, 19 Feb. 1869 —for rules of library; Sam Walter Foss, *The Song of the Library Staff* (John R. Anderson, 1906), p. 4 —for verse on Dewey.

WHAT SHOULD PEOPLE READ?

Lyman Bryson, "Educating the Community," in *The Library of Tomorrow: A Symposium*, ed. Emily M. Danton (American Library Association, 1939), pp. 155 ff.; Ernestine Rose, *The Public Library in American Life* (Columbia University Press, 1954), pp. 185, 203; Josephine A. Rathbone, "Pioneers of the Library Profession," in *American Library History*, ed. Marshall, pp. 294–96 —on Dewey;

Hardy, in Garceau, *Public Library*, pp. 22, 34 —on concern by Jefferson and the clergy about novels; Detroit *Free Press*, 10 June 1877, quoted in Frank B. Woodford, *Parnassus on Main Street: A History of the Detroit Public Library* (Wayne State University Press, 1965), pp. 255 ff.; AR 1869, pp. 102–3 —on high quality of juvenile books; AR 1874, p. 104 —justification for purchase of novels; AR 1875, p. 38 —on Watterson's concern about novels; Bessie Kelsey to Freeman, 11 Oct. 1940.

OVIATT VS. BOARD OF MANAGERS

AR 1873, p. 209; AR 1872, pp. 85–86, 92; Archer H. Shaw, *The Plain Dealer: One Hundred Years in Cleveland* (Alfred A. Knopf, 1942), pp. 107–8, 127, 245; *Dictionary of American Biography*, s.v. "Cowles, Edwin"; Charles E. Kennedy, *Fifty Years of Cleveland, . . . 1875–1925* (Weidenthal Co., 1925), p. 26; AR 1874; p. 103; *Cleveland Herald*, 18 June, 2 July, and 6, 20 Aug. 1872, 15 July 1873, 10 Mar. 1874; *Cleveland Leader*, 2 and 16 July, 6, 12, and 20 Aug. 1872, 29 and 30 June 1875; *PD*, 18 June, 2 July, 6 and 20 Aug., and 22 Oct. 1872, 4 Feb., 15 July, and 26 Aug. 1873, 10 Mar. 1874, 29 June 1875, 10 Aug. 1889; Foss, *Song*, pp. 12–13.

Until the 1920s the official name of the Cleveland institution was the Public Library of the City School District of the City of Cleveland, and the official name for the board was even longer—the Board of Trustees of the Public Library of the City School District of the City of Cleveland. In 1923 enough members of the Ohio legislature found this so tautological that it authorized, at long last, the change to the present designations: the Cleveland Public Library, and the Board of Trustees of the Cleveland Public Library. See AR 1924, pp. 9–10.

IRAD L. BEARDSLEY

AR 1875, p. 37; Archer H. Shaw, "P.D. Partner Was Librarian," *PD*, 13 June 1950; *PD*, 3 and 5 Nov. 1901 —obituaries on Beardsley; *Cleveland Leader*, 14 and 15 July 1875 —on alleged reason for appointment of Beardsley; AR 1876, p. 5.

William H. Brett, who succeeded Beardsley as librarian, testified that his predecessor had an extensive knowledge of books as well as wide business experience. John H. Clarke, a long-time resident of Cleveland who later became a justice of the Supreme Court of the United States, said the same thing. It was rumored that just before his death Beardsley had completed a historical novel dealing with life in western New York. This testimony on the intellectual activity and virtuosity of Beardsley seems less than convincing. Brett was writing in 1887, in his third year as the new librarian. It is understandable that, at this early point in his career, he would hesitate to tell the whole truth about his predecessor. Clarke was writing a quarter of a century after Beardsley had ceased to be librarian; over that period of time Clarke's memory had become so dim that he repeated Brett almost word for word. The quality of Beardsley's putative novel can never be tested because it was never published. See Brett, "Rise and Growth"; Clarke, in *Cleveland*, ed. Orth, 1:583; *Annals of the Early Settlers Association of Cuyahoga County, Ohio*, 4, no. 4 (1901): 390–91.

OVIATT AND BEARDSLEY: A COMPARISON

AR 1875, p. 37; AR 1880, p. 5; AR 1876, pp. 5–6, 9 ff.; AR 1877, p. 135; AR 1879, p. 6; Clifford K. Shipton, "John Langdon Sibley, Librarian," in *American Library History*, ed. Marshall, p. 183.

The story about Sibley has been repeated over and over again as an example of primitive ideas about libraries and books. This is not fair to the librarian at Harvard. In actual fact the rules there, similar to those at most other libraries of that generation, ordered the librarian to close the institution each year for an inventory, the goal of which was to locate every book. Sibley was merely trying to carry out this order, for better or for worse. In the attempt to persuade a faculty member to return books, the result was frequently discouraging—then and now.

NEW QUARTERS AND FINANCIAL CRISIS

Rose, *Cleveland*, pp. 277, 401; AR 1875, p. 37; AR 1876, pp. 4, 7–8, 15; AR 1885, p. 5; AR 1878, pp. 6, 46; AR 1877, pp. 30–31; AR 1879, pp. 9 ff., 18 ff.; "The New Library Rooms," *Cleveland Leader*, 18 Jan. 1875; Anne C. Granger, "Early Days in the Library," *Open Shelf*, July–Aug. 1921.

BRECKENRIDGE VS. BEARDSLEY

Minutes of the Library Board, June–Aug. 1884, in script, pp. 170–217; *Penny Press*, 10 Jan. 1880, 2 and 5 Aug. 1884; *PD*, 19, 22, and 31 July 1884; *Cleveland Leader*, 19 and 31 July 1884.

The problem of books lost or strayed, which so concerned Oviatt and Beardsley and their library boards, has been a perennial and exasperating one. By the close of the Cleveland institution's first century many libraries had found it necessary to install turnstiles to facilitate examination of briefcases, shopping bags, and the inner folds of capacious greatcoats. A few had adopted electronic devices—one of them a metallic bookplate (in reality an electromagnetic field pasted in each volume in the library). At the checkout counter, sensing screens five feet in height automatically locked the turnstiles if one of the special bookplates went through it. The system was not perfect; a thief could get a book through by carrying it on his head or kicking it along the floor.

Clients of the library purloin or keep books because they want to collect them as cheaply as possible or are forgetful or are loath to pay fines. There was the classic example of the delinquent lady who told a librarian: "I don't see why I should be fined when I didn't have time to read the books." In the 1940s the Cleveland Public Library had a special officer whose duty it was to see that overdue books were returned; he bore the interesting and historic name of Mark Anthony. A city ordinance provided that books must be returned within thirty days after the library had notified a borrower that they were overdue. Those flagrantly delinquent could end up in court, and some did. In the 1930s and 1940s about a thousand negligent borrowers received summonses each year. Interestingly there were four times as many careless or conniving adults as there were careless or conniving children. In 1939 a borrower was fined twenty-five dollars in a Cleveland municipal court for keeping a copy of *Gone With the Wind* for eighteen months; the delinquent stated that he intended to work out the fine at the Warrensville Workhouse because he would not pay in cash even if he was kept in jail for one hundred years.

In the Cleveland Public Library's first century the record for filching books was held by a professor of business administration at Cleveland College and Akron University who was arrested after nearly a thousand books—stolen from public libraries in New York, Chicago, Detroit, Toledo, and Cleveland—were found in his apartment. One hundred fifty of them were from Cleveland Public Library. This came as no surprise to university librarians who are frequently confronted by professors who forget or decline to return books. One exasperated college librarian commented sardonically: "Every now and then a professor dies and leaves his collection to a library, and we will find several of our own books in it."

The return of books after a lapse of many years usually involves forgetful borrowers who left the city and did not receive notices from the library. The record was forty-nine years. Don P. Mills borrowed a book from the Cleveland Public Library in 1889 when he was ten; he returned it in 1938 when he was fifty-nine. The family had moved to Spokane shortly after he borrowed the volume but later returned to Cleveland. Mills, an attorney, finally happened on it while he was "rummaging around" the house. Accompanied by a reporter he returned the volume "to see what would happen." According to the newspaper report, "both men went unarmed." The Cleveland library treated him like a prodigal son; Marilla Freeman (then in charge of the main library) announced, with tongue in cheek:

> This really makes some kind of statement of policy necessary. The decision is that for anybody who returns a book after five years and within fifty years we will wipe the slate clean. Also, we would be very happy to receive any donations of new books such a person might like to make.

Ironically, Mills' lost book, which happened to be *The Whispering Pine* by Elijah Kellogg, was taken to the Treasure Room and placed in a glass case; as the years had gone by it had become a rarity. According to the author, the volume illustrated "what a boy who has wasted himself may accomplish, when he rallies and resolves to redeem misspent hours."

In 1968 a book forty-one years overdue arrived from London, England; the borrower explained that it was so fascinating he had never managed to finish it! The next year the Cleveland Public

Library designated the date of its centennial as "Forgiveness Day"; forgetful borrowers could return, without fines, all overdue books, records, and films that had been gathering dust for years in some forgotten corner. One was twenty-two years late; a young architect had borrowed this volume, titled *Dynamic Chemistry*, and soon afterward took a new wife and the book to Arizona. On 17 February 1969 he returned the book—but not the wife—just in time for the library's one-in-a-century fine-free day.

Not only books are returned. Librarians find everything in them from sandwiches to scissors. One found a strip of bacon in a returned copy of *Gone With the Wind*. Other items discovered have included a marriage license, bankbooks, court summonses, nail files, razor blades, a magnifying glass, love letters, bus and streetcar tickets, social security cards, endorsed checks, and photographs. The most satisfying collateral item was returned in a novel by Charles Dickens; it was a hundred-dollar bill.

See "Libraries Combat Rising Book Thefts," *New York Times*, 9 Jan. 1971; "Library Investigator Is Kept Busy Chasing Books," *Press*, 17 July 1944; "He's 'Gone With Wind' to Works," *News*, 7 Dec. 1939; "Professors Take Books Too," *PD*, 8 Mar. 1940; Ted Robinson, Jr., "Takes Back Library Book 49 Years Late," *PD*, 13 Feb. 1938; "At 100, Library Is Forgiving," *Press*, 15 Feb. 1969; "Book Returned 22 Years Late," *PD*, 18 Feb. 1969; Jack Warfel, "Bacon Makes a Handy Bookmark, or Does It?," *Press*, 17 July 1940.

CHAPTER 3, The First of the Great Triumvirate:
William Howard Brett

ALWAYS A BOOKMAN

Carl Vitz, "William H. Brett," in *American Library History*, ed. Marshall, p. 244; *National Cyclopaedia of American Biography*, s.v. "Brett, William Howard"; Linda A. Eastman, *Portrait of a Librarian: William Howard Brett* (American Library Association, 1940), pp. 3–14, 73–74; William H. Brett, lecture notes on "The School and the Library," n.d., for the School of Library Science —about schooling in Warren; Harriet Taylor Upton, *A Twentieth-Century History of Trumbull County, Ohio*, 2 vols. (Lewis Publishing Co., 1909), 1:382; Rose, *Cleveland,* pp. 255, 394, 496 —on Cobb and Andrews; J. D. Cox to Carl Vitz, 20 Nov. 1923 —on Brett's interest in the West; Minutes of the Library Board, 5 Aug. 1884, p. 219; *aide-mémoire* on Brett's salaries, Folder No. 2, 1918; J. G. White to M. L. Brett (son), 29 May 1925 —on election of Brett as librarian; "Merit Recognized," *PD*, 2 July 1895 —on comparative salaries.

THE OPEN SHELF

White to M. L. Brett, 29 May 1925; Rose, *Cleveland,* pp. 466, 507–8, 513–14, 763; Eastman, *Portrait,* pp. 20 ff., 78; Roscoe Rouse, "The Libraries of Nineteenth-Century College Societies," in *Books in America's Past,* ed. David Kaser (University Press of Virginia, 1966), p. 31; Bostwick, *American Public Library,* pp. 9 ff.; William H. Brett, lecture notes on open-shelf system [about 1911] for the School of Library Science; "After 100 Years: The Past Speaks to the Future," CPL, *Branch Newsletter,* Jan. 1969 —on Brett's faith in humankind and freedom of choice; Granger, "Early Days"; "E" to the editor of *New York Sun,* 25 Aug. 1895 —about situation in Astor Library; AR 1890, pp. 8, 9; AR 1891, pp. 5, 9; AR 1892, p. 5; AR 1894, p. 5; *Press,* 21, 23, 24, and 25 Mar. 1895; AR 1895, p. 11.

CLASSIFICATION AND ORGANIZATION

Vitz, in *American Library History,* ed. Marshall, pp. 245, 251; "E" to *New York Sun,* 25 Aug. 1895; Carl L. Cannon, *American Book Collectors and Collecting from Colonial Times to the Present* (H. W. Wilson Co., 1941), pp. 40–41 —on Jefferson as classifier; Charles K. Bolton, "The First One Hundred Years of Athenaeum History," in *The Influence and History of the Boston Athenaeum* (Boston Athenaeum, 1907), p. 48; Report of the Library Board, 3 Mar. 1885, in script, pp. 260–61, Director's Office; William H. Brett, *Alphabetic Catalogue of the English Books in the Circulating Department of the Cleveland Public Library: Authors, Titles, and Subjects* (Cleveland Printing and Publishing Co., 1889), pp. iii–viii; Eastman, *Portrait,* p. 18; AR 1890, p. 5; Gordon W. Thayer, "Cleveland's Public Library, 1869–1944," clipping [sometime in 1944], Western Reserve Historical Society.

The Dewey system, or modifications thereof, is still used by most libraries in the United States. A few large libraries, however, have found it tempting to change to the Library of Congress system, which provides greater variation and flexibility for large or special collections. As an example, more than five thousand volumes have been published on Abraham Lincoln, a situation that invites classification by class and subclass; the Dewey system has no special number for this most studied of Presidents. The Library of Congress system was developed by two great cataloguers—J. C. M. Hanson and Charles Martel—who found themselves confronted, at the close of the nineteenth century, by a million books. They proceeded to develop classes and subclasses by both letters and numbers. This permitted many more combinations than was possible with numbers alone. The Library of Congress system, as one example, has twenty major classes by single letters—contrasted with the ten major classes in the Dewey Decimal System. Furthermore, an extensive list of subclasses is provided by double letters, and additional refinements are possible by the addition of numbers.

CUMULATIVE INDEX TO PERIODICALS

Vitz, in *American Library History*, ed. Marshall, p. 246; Eastman, *Portrait*, p. 25.

BRETT AND CHILDREN

"The Children's Day," *Open Shelf*, July–Aug. 1921; Harriet G. Long, *Public Library Service to Children: Foundation and Development* (Scarecrow Press, 1969), pp. 10, 26, 45–47, 85–93, 104, 126–28, 132, 136, 141–42; Foss, *Song*, p. 8; AR 1899, pp. 25, 57 ff.; Philip Arthur Kalisch, *The Enoch Pratt Free Library: A Social History* (Scarecrow Press, 1969), p. 126; Margaret B. Becker, "Effie Louise Power: Pioneer in the Development of Library Service to Children" (Master's thesis, School of Library Science, Western Reserve University, 1950), pp. 18, 20, 22, 25, 59–60, 72, 141–42; Carolyn E. Werkley, "Mister Carnegie's 'Library,'" *American Heritage*, Feb. 1970; Whitehill, *Boston Public Library*, p. 166; Bostwick, *American Public Library*, pp. 11 ff.; Aldrich, *School Library in Ohio*, p.

Wakefield Museum of the Great Lakes Historical Society, Vermilion, Ohio

Lawrence Quincy Mumford, Librarian (1950–1954)

Raymond Charles Lindquist, Librarian (1954–1968)

Reading from Braille, Blind Division, Cleveland Public Library

A service made possible by the Judd Fund

Martin Luther King, Jr., Regional Branch Library

Solid research at the Cleveland Public Library

Traffic in the main lobby, Cleveland Public Library (1969)

82; AR 1890, p. 7; AR 1898, p. 19; Vitz, in *American Library History*, ed. Marshall, pp. 247–48; AR 1897, pp. 21–22; Linda A. Eastman, "The Library and the Children: An Account of the Children's Work in the Cleveland Public Library," *Library Journal*, Apr. 1898; AR 1901, p. 26; AR 1908, pp. 51–53; AR 1926, pp. 101–2; "Interpreting America," *Open Shelf*, Apr. 1921; Alvin Beam, "200 Choice Words from Singer," *PD*, 7 Mar. 1970; Effie L. Power, *Work with Children in Public Libraries* (American Library Association, 1943), p. 179 —for quotation from Morley; R. R. Bowker, "Some Children's Librarians," *Library Journal*, 1 Oct. 1921; Power to Elizabeth D. Briggs, 18 Sept. 1944 —on compensation for Power in early years; Alice D. Martin, "Miss Effie L. Power," CPL, *Branch Newsletter*, Nov. 1969.

Brett and other librarians may have frowned on *Little Lord Fauntleroy*, but his soul marches on. The volume is still in print and by 1955 passed the million-mark in sales. Hollywood has twice lavished its extraordinary talents on the story. In the silent movie of 1921 Mary Pickford portrayed both Fauntleroy and his devoted mother known as "Dearest"; in the talking version of 1936 Freddie Bartholomew played the child but not the mother. It is claimed that even the undemonstrative William Ewart Gladstone succumbed to the literary charm of Fauntleroy; he was alleged to have said that the romantic novel about the little American boy who inherited a British title and went to live in an elegant castle would "have great effect in bringing about good feeling between the two nations." If so, historians have missed a significant fact in the relations between England and the United States. See Tom McCarthy, "The Real Little Lord Fauntleroy," *American Heritage*, Feb. 1970.

The nationality diversity in the population of Cleveland was reflected in the books ordered for the public library. By 1909 Brett would note:

> The foreign language collections present some interesting problems, a few of which are being solved, and more of which will have to be considered during the coming year.
>
> The revision of the German catalogue was begun in the summer and is progressing steadily, if slowly. The Italian collec-

tion is being both classified and catalogued. . . . The Danish, Norwegian and Swedish books are being regularly classified and catalogued.

The collections in Bohemian, Hungarian, Polish, Slovenian, and Yiddish afford the unsolved problems. . . . As these collections grow it becomes more difficult for assistants who do not know the languages or the literatures to help the foreign readers find what they want. The foreign-speaking assistants are usually untrained and often without much knowledge of their own literature.

By 1912 the library required a typewriter with keyboards in Russian and Yiddish to complete the catalogue in these languages. In 1914 the Cleveland Public Library was issuing books in twenty-one languages, and they comprised 8 percent of the total circulation for the year. See AR 1909, p. 32; AR 1910, pp. 31, 32; AR 1912, p. 44; AR 1914, p. 47.

SCHOOL LIBRARIES

AR 1885, pp. 9–10; AR 1890, p. 9; AR 1891, pp. 7, 11–12; Lloyd Vernor Ballard, *The Public Library* (American Library Association, 1937), pp. 5 ff.; Bostwick, *American Public Library*, pp. 1–15; Arthur E. Bostwick, ed., "United States of America," in *Popular Libraries of the World* (American Library Association, 1933), p. 289; AR 1913, p. 26; Citizens League, *Greater Cleveland*, 22 Dec. 1928, CWRU Archives.

SAINT ANDREW AND THE BRANCHES

AR 1890, p. 9; AR 1891, p. 6; AR 1892, p. 5; AR 1893, p. 12; AR 1895, p. 9; AR 1896, p. 84; AR 1897, pp. 18–20, 27; AR 1903, p. 15 —for letter from Carnegie to Brett, 4 Apr. 1903; AR 1905, p. 6; AR 1907, p. 17; AR 1913, p. 27; AR 1928, p. 10; Clarke, in *Cleveland*, ed. Orth, 1:579–83; *Open Shelf*, Oct.–Dec. 1912 —on deposit stations; Bostwick, *American Public Library*, pp. 15, 211–12; "Reaching Out," *Open Shelf*, July–Aug. 1921; Eastman, *Portrait*, pp. 32–33, 68–69; Carnegie to Brett, 9 Dec. 1891; Ditzion, *Arse-*

nals, pp. 114–15, 161 ff.; Carnegie to Brett, 19 Nov. 1914; Eastman to Dr. Frank P. Hill, 30 Sept. 1935 —on close relations between Carnegie Corporation and Brett on building plans for libraries; Hardy, in Garceau, *Public Library*, pp. 42–43; Vitz, in *American Library History*, ed. Marshall, p. 253; Bobinski, *Carnegie Libraries*, pp. 3, 13, 31–32, 57–58, 91, 95, 99, 103, 105, 108, 190; Burton J. Hendrick, *The Life of Andrew Carnegie*, vol. 2 (Doubleday, Doran and Co., 1932), p. 207; Joseph F. Wall, "The Rich Man's Burden— and How Andrew Carnegie Unloaded It," *American Heritage*, Oct. 1970. On repeated requests for gifts— AR 1892, p. 13; AR 1893, pp. 7, 12–15; AR 1914, pp. 41–42; AR 1925, pp. 16–17; and H. L. Mencken, *Baltimore Sun*, 7 May 1939, quoted in Kalisch, *Pratt Free Library*, p. 162.

TRAINING AND LIBRARY SCHOOLS

AR 1891, p. 11; AR 1893, pp. 12–13; AR 1897, pp. 22–23, 27; AR 1898, pp. 10–11; AR 1904, p. 30; AR 1912, p. 35; Brett to Carnegie, 10 Feb. 1905, CWRU Archives; Long, *Library Service to Children*, pp. 124–25; Bobinski, *Carnegie Libraries*, pp. 151–52; Eastman, *Portrait*, pp. 47 ff.; Alice Tyler to Carnegie Corporation, 30 Mar. 1917, CWRU Archives; Eastman to Alice Tyler, 2 Dec. 1916, CWRU Archives; *Open Shelf*, Jan.–Mar. 1968.

A "PERMANENT" HOME?

Bobinski, *Carnegie Libraries*, p. 34; Granger, "Early Days"; AR 1891, pp. 5–6, 51 ff.; Long, *Library Service to Children*, p. 132; AR 1901, pp. 51 ff.; E. Frank Carmody, Memoirs, in pencil, written at CPL in summer 1969, pp. 1–2, Director's Office; Clarke, in *Cleveland*, ed. Orth, 1:578 ff.; AR 1905, p. 24; Woodford, *Parnassus*, pp. 149–50; AR 1910, pp. 38–39; AR 1908, p. 29; AR 1913, pp. 24–25, 33–34, 42, 52, 71; Rose, *Cleveland*, p. 689; *PD*, 26 June 1970 —on Halle Bros.; Linda A. Eastman, "Library Service to a City," in *Essays Offered to Herbert Putnam*, eds. William W. Bishop and Andrew Keogh (Yale University Press, 1929), p. 132; Eastman, *Portrait*, pp. 57 ff.; "The Main Library—Some Passages in Its History," *Open Shelf*, July–Aug. 1921; AR 1896, p. 85; AR 1898, p. 11; AR

1904, pp. 30–31; Condon, *Cleveland*, p. 184; Harlan Hatcher, *The Western Reserve* (World Publishing Co., 1966), p. 285; AR 1912, p. 28; AR 1916, p. 2.

Blaming deterioration of books on the vapors emanating from gas lights was an easy, but inaccurate, explanation for the phenomenon. Regardless of the quality of paper, that is, whether it was made from rags or wood, after 1870 it showed a distressing tendency to disintegrate with increasing rapidity. The cause was in the sizing—the water-resistant substance which gives paper a hard surface that prevents ink from being absorbed; by contrast, a blotter is made of unsized paper. Until the second quarter of the seventeenth century the principal sizing agent was gelatin or glue made from animal hides and tendons. This produced an alkaline paper that was durable and long-lived. Then alum was added to the gelatin to make the paper more resistant to ink. Unfortunately alum is highly acid with the result that from 1750 on, it was noted that paper disintegrated faster than it had before. Two centuries later, in the 1850s, a new sizing was introduced that eliminated entirely the animal gelatin that had previously been the base. The new alum-rosin sizing was more easily applied than gelatins and glues, and was generally adopted. This compound has been fatal to the longevity of paper. Alum, combined with the sodium resinate of rosin, decomposes into components of sulphuric acid which can literally burn up a book in thirty years. The acid is pervasive; recently it has been discovered that it migrates readily from acidic papers to acid-free ones! Frazer G. Poole, whose responsibility is preservation of books at the Library of Congress, says that this problem is the most serious one confronting the library world. He notes that in collections as large as those in the Library of Congress and metropolitan public libraries, where many books are used infrequently, some are found to have "disappeared" into a crumbling mass at their reputed position on the shelves. See David G. Lowe, "The Case of the Vanishing Records," *American Heritage*, Aug. 1969.

BRETT AND CENSORSHIP

The Rev. Samuel Osgood, *Librarian's Convention, 1853*, quoted in Harriet Price Sawyer, ed., *The Library and Its Contents: Reprints and Addresses* (H. W. Wilson Co., 1925), p. 33; J. Christian Bay, *The John Crerar Library, 1895–1944* (Chicago, 1945), p. 24; Kalisch, *Pratt Free Library*, pp. 82, 121 —quoting Mencken; C. H. Cramer, *Royal Bob: The Life of Robert G. Ingersoll* (Bobbs-Merrill Co., 1952), p. 171 —on Comstock: Bostwick, *American Public Library*, p. 80; Edmund Lester Pearson, *The Library and the Librarian: A Selection of Articles from the Boston Evening Transcript and Other Sources* (Elm Tree Press, 1910), pp. 66–67, 71; Charles Ammi Cutter, "What Are the Best Books?," *Library Journal*, Feb. 1901, quoted in Sawyer, *Library and Contents*, pp. 24, 27; William H. Brett, "Books for Youth," *Library Journal*, June 1885; AR 1887, pp. 7–8; AR 1891, p. 9; AR 1900, p. 131; White to Brett, 5 and 12 June 1899, 2 July 1901; Thos. A. McCaslin (law partner of White), "Meminisse Juvabit," *Open Shelf*, June 1929 —on range of White's reading; AR 1918, passim; William H. Brett, "Libraries and the Great War" (Founder's Day Address delivered at Library School of Western Reserve University, 11 June 1918), pp. 7–10; Minutes of the Library Board, 17 Jan. 1940, pp. 5–6; *National Cyclopaedia of American Biography*, s.v. "Brett, William Howard" —on Brett's attempts to enlist in the Civil War; Eastman, *Portrait*, pp. 9–10, 84 ff.

BRETT AS ADMINISTRATOR

Carmody, Memoirs, p. 3; Gordon W. Thayer, "Cleveland's Public Library—1890–1944," clipping from *PD*, n.d., Western Reserve Historical Society —on dress regulations; Linda A. Eastman, "The Whole Duty of a Librarian" (Founder's Day Address delivered at School of Library Science, 16 June 1931), CWRU Archives; Eastman, *Portrait*, pp. 85 ff., 94; testimonial by Eastman, Cutter, White, and Vormelker, "Memorial Book, 1884–1914," Director's Office; Kennedy, *Fifty Years*, p. 174; White to Charles E. Kennedy, 17 Jan. 1925; Brett to Kennedy, 9 July 1914 —on travel expenses; White to Helen Norton, 7 Dec. 1918 —on Brett's estate.

Brett was so generous toward all others that he neglected to think of those immediately dependent on him. After his death Charles Belden, librarian at the Boston Public Library, wrote to Eastman (on 2 Nov. 1918) about a check for $350 which was to be made out to Brett for service on a survey committee. Brett had told Belden that he did not wish to keep it but wanted the money devoted to the Children's Department of the Boston Public Library —or for some other special need there. Eastman replied that the money should be sent to Mrs. Brett,

> as the provision for her is very limited. Mr. Brett was so young in spirit and was so full of energy, that he had counted on continuing to provide for her himself; and he was always so generous in his dealings with others that it left little for himself.

This was certainly true. Mrs. Brett had the potential support of four grown sons and a married daughter, but her late husband's estate of little more than a thousand dollars was encumbered by debts. Fortunately the Carnegie Foundation was able to be of limited assistance; in 1919 it awarded Mrs. Brett an annual pension of $600. The foundation noted, in a statement to President Thwing of Western Reserve University, that "in communicating this action to Mrs. Brett we beg you say to her that the Executive Committee holds in the highest esteem the work and record of your husband." See Belden to Eastman, 2 Nov. 1918; Eastman to Belden, 20 Nov. 1918; Henry S. Pritchett of the Carnegie Foundation to Thwing, 13 May 1919.

A TRAGIC DEATH

AR 1916, p. 2 —on Brett's five-year contract; "Books vs. Boredom," *Open Shelf*, Apr. 1919 —on CPL staff members in library service overseas; *Cleveland Sunday Leader*, 24 Mar. 1918 —on war service of members of Brett's family; Brett, "Libraries and War," passim; AR 1918, passim; Eastman, *Portrait*, pp. 85 ff., 92; Sophie K. Hiss to Eastman, 4 June 1918 —on situation at Newport News; Linda A. Eastman, statement made to John Griswold White on Brett's death; Dr. Hubert Carleton, statement made to members of the Brett family on his death; PD, 25 Aug. 1918; *Cleveland Sunday Leader*, 25 Aug. 1918.

White was outraged by the law's delay and the punishment— or lack of it—for the irresponsible driver who killed Brett. He was John M. Warner, who was charged with manslaughter and driving while intoxicated. Leaving the scene of the accident might have been added to the charges because—according to witnesses—after striking Brett, Warner drove on at an increased speed, leaving his victim lying on the street. When he crashed into the lamp post, he backed a few feet and then drove the automobile forward along the curb for a short distance before deciding that the vehicle was inoperable. The son of well-to-do parents, he was released on bond of $3,300, furnished by his father. More than three years later the unpunished Warner was still free on bail. In White's judgment the trial and the subsequent handling of the case was a public scandal, one that played an important, if negative, role in a later survey of the administration of criminal justice in Cleveland.

Warner had a previous record of similar accidents. Once he had driven his automobile on a joyride with a married woman and collided with a railroad train; his automobile was demolished and the lady passenger killed. Later, in one memorable night on the streets of Cleveland, he established the unenviable record of running into two different streetcars; after the second and last impact he was taken to the hospital, arrested, and convicted of intoxication. The incident involving Brett was therefore a fourth offense. In White's opinion Warner belonged to the class of reckless and irresponsible young men who, when entrusted with automobiles, were a menace to every pedestrian and vehicle within range.

A trial followed. It was an authentic judicial farce. A juror was taken sick, and the judge declared that he must be excused and the jury discharged. As a result the case had to be heard before a new jury. Warner's attorney requested the judge to proceed with eleven jurors, stating that he would waive any future claim of error in the trial. The judge agreed reluctantly, but the damage had been done. Under this procedure Warner's attorney could not lose, at least in the court of first resort. If his client won, he was free. If his client lost, the lawyer could appeal, forgetting his waiver, on the procedural ground that there had been eleven instead of the statutory twelve jurors. Warner did lose, and on this procedural basis appealed all the way to the Supreme Court of Ohio, where he lost again. By this time upwards of four years had elapsed before he was finally sent for two years to the Ohio Reformatory. There he appealed for parole after only part of his mild sentence had been served. By this time White was beside himself; he stated in un-equivocal terms that he felt a two-year detention—considerably delayed—was light punishment indeed for reckless driving of a homicidal character on Cleveland's busy streets. See White to N. W. White (superintendent of Paroles and Pardons), 20 Jan. 1922; and White to Ohio State Board of Administration, 5 Mar. 1923.

A WARRIOR'S BURIAL

American Library Association, "Memorial Minute," n.d., Director's Office; Eastman, *Portrait*, pp. 61–62, 71, 77 ff., AR 1896, p. 85 —on Brett's presidency of ALA; White to State Board of Administration, 5 Mar. 1923; Library Board Resolutions, 5 Sept. 1918; Brett, "Libraries and War," p. 27.

CHAPTER 4, John Griswold White

FAMILY AND EDUCATION

White to Mrs. Gertrude Wickham, 30 Dec. 1912; Vital Statistics, form completed in White's own hand [sometime between 1920 and 1928], Alumni Office, Adelbert College of Western Reserve University; "John G. White," *Reserve Alumnus*, Oct. 1928, CWRU Office of Development; White to Brett, 13 May 1899; "The John G. White Evening of Reminiscences," typescript of recording by White's friends at the home of Mrs. Richard Watt, 28 Nov. 1966, passim; McCaslin, "Meminisse Juvabit"; Roscoe Rouse, in *Books*, ed. Kaser, pp. 32–33; White to C. S. Metcalf, 14 Feb. 1927; White to Arthur C. Ludlow, 26 Mar. 1924.

LAWYER

"White Evening," passim; McCaslin, "Meminisse Juvabit"; testimonial by White on James W. Stewart [sometime after Stewart's death on 5 Nov. 1927]; Gordon W. Thayer, "A Few Reminiscences of John G. White, 1845–1928," typed manuscript in White Collection, n.d., passim; "White," *Reserve Alumnus*; White to Gleason L. Archer, 27 Dec. 1927; obituary on White, *PD*, 28 Aug. 1928; George A. Peck, "Alumni Sketches," *Reserve Weekly*, 14 Feb. 1928,

CWRU Office of Development; White to Charles J. O'Connor, 20 July 1912.

INDIVIDUALIST AND "CHARACTER"

"John G. White," *Open Shelf*, June 1929; Sam Hook, "John G. White," *Press*, 28 Aug. 1928; John G. White, Last Will and Testament, passim; "White Evening," passim; White to Alexander Hadden, 20 Aug. 1925; statement to the author by Mrs. William A. McAfee —for verse about food on White's vest; Carmody, Memoirs, p. 7; McCaslin, "Meminisse Juvabit"; Thayer, "Reminiscences," passim; John W. Love, "The By-Product: The White Collection of Folklore and Orientalia," *PD*, 29 Aug. 1928.

Newton D. Baker, who was squiring Lloyd George around Cleveland, wrote White a conciliatory letter in which he presented another explanation for the tardiness of the Welshman in arriving at the dedication ceremonies. He said that Lloyd George was weary from his travels, and his aides had decided to avoid exposure to chilly air on the platform while the preliminaries of the program were being conducted. Unfortunately the calculations on the schedule left something to be desired. Baker noted, with his usual charm: "I know that I, myself, regretted not hearing what you had to say and seeing you say it, but being impresario for a prima donna, I was rather coerced into giving first consideration to his comfort. . . ." There is no record that White was mollified by Baker's letter, and it is likely that he was not; he was scarcely the kind of person who would be impressed by a plea from anyone who admitted that he was an impresario for a prima donna. See Baker to White, 24 Oct. 1923.

White had an interesting observation on the formation of the Union Club, of which he was more than a charter member. He wrote:

> The origin of the Union Club was this: A number of us formed a club,—I don't remember now the name, which met in a building on the southeast corner of Ontario and High Street in 1870–71. Some of the members began gambling for high stakes. Under the laws, as they stood, we could not stop it, so a number of us withdrew and decided to organize another

Club. The Union Club was the result. It came mighty hard for a young lawyer, without much practice, to cough up $600.00, but all good things come high.

See White to William F. Michalske (secretary of the Union Club), 24 Nov. 1924.

SERVICES AS BOARD MEMBER

Theodore Blegen, "A Glorious Court," in *Book Collecting and Scholarship* (University of Minnesota Press, 1954), p. 8; articles on White as benefactor, *Open Shelf*, June 1929 and July–Dec. 1968; Linda Eastman, "The Passing of a Great Trustee," *Open Shelf*, June 1929; "White Evening," passim; "City Pension Rate Cut Under Study," *PD*, 7 Apr. 1928; Eastman, *Portrait*, p. 65.

CHESS AND CHECKERS

Peck, "Alumni Sketches"; McCaslin, "Meminisse Juvabit"; Herman Helms, editorial, *American Chess Bulletin*, Sept.–Oct. 1928, quoted in *Open Shelf*, June 1929; article on fortieth anniversary of White's death, *Open Shelf*, July–Dec. 1968; Thayer, "Reminiscences," passim; Thomas J. Holmes, "Notes on the John Griswold White Collection of Chess and Checkers," *Open Shelf*, June 1929; Cannon, *American Book Collectors*, pp. 139 ff.

ORIENTALIA AND FOLKLORE

Eastman, *Portrait*, pp. 14–15; AR 1899, pp. 11, 19; "White Evening," passim; White to Brett, 11 Apr. 1899; editorial on White on the fortieth anniversary of his death, *Open Shelf*, July–Dec. 1968; Love, "By-Product: White"; White to Brett, 24 Feb. 1899; "The Main Library," *Open Shelf*; editorial on White, *PD*, 28 Aug. 1928; White, Last Will and Testament, passim; White to Brett, 12 July and 28 Dec. 1900, 22 Aug. 1901, 20 Nov. 1906, 19 Feb. and 3 Nov. 1908; Cannon, *American Book Collectors*, pp. 139 ff.; Wes Lawrence, "Why Travel? It's All Here," *PD*, 27 May 1965.

BOOK COLLECTOR

"White," *Open Shelf*; Kennedy, *Fifty Years*, pp. 177 ff.; Thayer, "Reminiscences," passim; White to Brett, 26 Apr., 9 and 12 June, and 7 Dec. 1899, 26 Feb. 1902, 25 Mar., 7 May, and 22 Oct. 1904, 14 Dec. 1905, 16 Nov. 1906, 14 Oct. 1914; White to Messrs. Kegan, Paul, Trench, Trubner & Co., 28 Mar. 1928; Peck, "Alumni Sketches"; "White Evening," passim; "Pershing's Librarian Dreams of Better War," *PD*, 25 Dec. 1929; White to Brett, 17 Sept. 1900 and 3 Apr. 1901; Faith Corrigan, "Korean among 94 Tongues Known to Local Linguist," *News*, 8 Aug. 1950; Larry Hawkins, "Cleveland's Mr. Polyglot," *PD*, 15 Mar. 1953; "Done to the King's Taste!" *News*, 27 Aug. 1931; "F. E. Sommer," *Latin World*, Nov. 1929; F. E. Sommer, "Celebration of the Arrival of the 5,000th Language in the John G. White Collection of the Cleveland Public Library, 10 January 1939," scrapbook of recollections and documents collected by Sommer as an *aide-mémoire* on the planning and execution of the dinner, passim; "They'll Eat Words at Library Dinner for New Languages," *News*, 5 Jan. 1939; "Five-Thousandth Language Banquet," *Press*, 4 Jan. 1939.

NATURE LOVER

Thayer, "Reminiscences," passim; "White Evening," passim; John G. White, "Narrative of Fishing Trip to Jackson Hole, Summer of 1905 (Parties: T. A. McCaslin, James W. Stewart, John G. White, S. N. Leek, George Goodrich, and Various Horses)," pp. 1, 2, 18; John G. White, "In the Mountains of Wyoming, 1923: A Diary," pp. 5, 7–8, 24, 56–57, 72, 79–80; John G. White, "Diary of a Fishing Trip to Jackson Hole and Yellowstone National Park, July 1919," pp. 2, 60, 93; McCaslin, "Meminisse Juvabit."

CONTRIBUTION

White, Last Will and Testament, passim; Love, "By-Product: White"; "The Last Tribute," *PD*, 1 Sept. 1929; "White," *Open Shelf*; Louis B. Wright, "American Book Collectors," in *Book Collecting and Scholarship*, pp. 53–54.

Chapter 5, Linda Anne Eastman

EARLY YEARS

Qualifications of Librarians of Public Libraries in Middle Western States, questionnaire completed in Eastman's hand [sometime after

1938]; William Miller, "Linda Eastman—46 Years of Service," *Press*, 24 May 1938, CWRU Archives; Cecil Olen Phillips, "Linda Anne Eastman: Librarian" (Master's thesis, School of Library Science, Western Reserve University, 1953), pp. 2–3, 5 ff., 9–11, 20, 35; Rose, *Cleveland*, p. 466; Eastman to Brett, 2 May 1892; Examination for Library Work, 1892, in Eastman's hand; Howard Beaufait, "A Woman Gives Her Life to Books," *News*, 14 May 1937; Grace V. Kelly, "Linda A. Eastman Quits Library Post," *PD*, 24 May 1938; Kennedy, *Fifty Years*, p. 178; Worthington C. Ford, ed., *Writings of John Quincy Adams*, 7 vols. (Macmillan Co., 1914), 4:183–84.

A PERMANENT HOME

"The Main Library Housing Problems," *Open Shelf*, Sept.–Oct. 1921; Kelly, "Eastman Quits Library"; AR 1929, p. 14; AR 1926, pp. 8, 13; AR 1930, p. 6; Rose, *Cleveland*, pp. 821–22, 887, 893, 911; "Public Library Will Accomodate Four Times As Many Books As at Present," *PD*, 10 May 1925; Linda Eastman, "The Cleveland Library Bond Issue," *Library Journal*, 15 Nov. 1921; Phillips, "Eastman," p. 25; AR 1924, p. 10; "Lloyd George Speech Will Be Broadcast," Cleveland *Times*, 19 Oct. 1923; "City Will Be Paid Honor Today by Lloyd George," *PD*, 23 Oct. 1923; "Irish Protest Appearance of Lloyd George," *PD*, 19 Oct. 1923; CPL dedication brochure, "The New Cleveland Public Library, May the Sixth 1925, passim; Gordon W. Thayer, "Cleveland's Public Library—1869–1944," *PD*, 11 Oct. 1944; Pearson, *Library and Librarian*, p. 55; AR 1929, p. 13; Ethel Robinson (head of CPL General Reference) to the author, July 1970; "If You Don't Know Ask the Library," excerpt from *Boston Transcript*, quoted in *Cleveland Women*, 1 Dec. 1917, CWRU Archives.

MARILLA FREEMAN

Who's Who in Library Service (American Library Association, 1933), s.v. "Freeman, Marilla"; Howard Beaufait, "Here Today," *News*, 1 Sept. 1938 —on contrast between Eastman and Freeman; Gerald D. McDonald, "Marilla Waite Freeman," *Bulletin of Bibliography*, Jan.–Apr. 1947; Marilla W. Freeman, "Tapping the Underground," *University of Chicago Magazine*, Oct. 1944; "Lists and the Cleveland Public Library," *Christian Science Monitor*, 27 July 1927 —on bookmarks; Marilla W. Freeman, "Tying Up with the Movies: Why? When? How?," *Library Journal*, 15 June 1929; W. Ward Marsh, "Movies Helping to Swell Libraries' Circulation," *PD*, 4 Aug. 1935; Marilla W. Freeman, "Censorship in the Large Public Library," *Library Journal*, 1 Mar. 1928; obituary on Freeman, *Open Shelf*, Nov.–Dec. 1961; "Sees Library as Community for Social Service," *PD*, 20 Oct. 1922; obituary on Freeman, *Press*, 31 Oct. 1961; "Miss Marilla Freeman Resigns Library Post," *PD*, 16 May 1940; Freeman to E. E. Wefel, 20 July 1943 —on importance of keeping readers busy in a library; Floyd Dell, *Moon-Calf: A Novel* (Macaulay Co., 1920), pp. 172–81; Floyd Dell, *Homecoming: An Autobiography* (Farrar & Rinehart, 1933), pp. 90–91, 149; Dale Kramer, *Chicago Renaissance: The Literary Life in the Midwest, 1900–1930* (Appleton-Century Co., 1966), pp. 15–16, 18, 97–98; "Masefield on Air, Hails Friend Here," *PD*, 13 May 1937; Lucy M. Buker (assistant to Freeman, 1922–36) to the author, 10 July 1970.

The author is also indebted for background and anecdotal material to a number of CPL staff members who knew Freeman, among them Edith Case, Emilia Wefel, Fern Long, Adeline Corrigan, Eleanore Hartman, Evelyn B. Balzer, Helen Inglis, Varelia Farmer, and Ethel Robinson.

CONCERN FOR THE BLIND

The Cleveland Society for the Blind: 1906–1960 (Cleveland Society for the Blind, 1961), pp. 7, 8, 29, 66; Helen G. Sheffield, "A Report on the History and Development of the Library for the Blind of the Cleveland Public Library" (Master's thesis, School of Library Science, Western Reserve University, 1951), pp. 1–8, 10–11, 21; Kelly, "Eastman Quits Library"; "A New World for the Blind," *Open Shelf*, Feb. 1929; "Library of the Month—Cleveland," *Talking Book Topics*, 5 Sept. 1967.

SERVICE TO HOSPITALS

Linda A. Eastman, "Here We Are!," *Modern Hospital*, Apr. 1922; AR 1925, p. 30; AR 1926, pp. 97–98; AR 1928, p. 17; Citizens

League, *Greater Cleveland*, 22 Dec. 1928, CWRU Archives; Helen Toland, "What Do They Read When They're Sick?," *PD*, 22 Nov. 1936; Edna P. Moody, "Books Bring Hope," *Library Journal*, 1 Mar. 1952; Moody to the author, 18 Aug. 1970.

BUSINESS INFORMATION BUREAU

AR 1928, p. 18; Agnes O. Hanson, "The Business Library: Its Services and Functions," *Ohio State University Bulletin of Business Research*, Apr. 1968; Marilla W. Freeman, "My First A.L.A.," *Wilson Library Bulletin*, Jan. 1946; *Dictionary of American Biography*, s.v. "Dana, John Cotton"; "Library Service," *Cleveland Club Woman*, Mar. 1930 —on Vormelker; "Library Unit Big Asset to Business," *Press*, 26 Mar. 1948; Carmody, Memoirs; CPL Business Information Bureau Annual Report for 1956, p. 6; "Establishment of the Business Information Bureau," *News*, 13 Jan. 1930; CPL Business Information Division pamphlet, "Where to Get Business Information in Cleveland."

Among other things Dana devised an interesting slogan on the importance of reading. There were twelve rules:

1. Read
2. Read
3. Read some more
4. Read anything
5. Read about everything
6. Read enjoyable things
7. Read things you yourself enjoy
8. Read and talk about it
9. Read very carefully—something
10. Read on the run—most things
11. Don't just think about reading, but
12. Just read.

> (Quoted in Vermont-New Hampshire, *North Country Libraries*, Sept. 1958)

TRAVEL SECTION

AR 1926, pp. 35, 36; "Travel and the Public Library," *Cleveland Topics*, 17 Apr. 1926; "Library Offers Travel Advice," *PD*, 22 Apr.

1926; "Library Aide in New Post," *News*, 22 Sept. 1944 —on Donna Root; Mildred Rauschkolb, "File Cabinet Grows into Travel Room," *PD*, 21 Feb. 1960; "Library Travel Bureau Aids Public, Agents," *Travel Trade*, 3 Feb. 1969; "Travel Unit Tops Library Expansions," *News*, 19 Nov. 1959; "Library to Lose Experts in Language, Travel," *Press*, 19 Mar. 1966.

THE GREAT DEPRESSION

AR 1928, pp. 7–8; AR 1929, p. 7; *Parade*, 26 May 1932; AR 1930, p. 23; Leon Carnovsky, "An Apprasial of the Cleveland Public Library: Evaluations and Recommendations," mimeographed, 1939, pp. 9, 14 ff.; "What Cleveland Asked For," *Open Shelf*, Mar. 1931; "Crisis Feared by Miss Eastman If Library Budget Is Slashed," *News*, 7 Mar. 1932; CPL pamphlet, "Your Library in 1931"; Citizens League, "The Public Library Appropriations," *Greater Cleveland*, 9 Dec. 1937; AR 1910, p. 16 —on tax situation; Ralph Blasingame, *Survey of Ohio Libraries and State Library Service— A Report to the State Library Board* (State Library of Ohio, 1968), pp. 21 ff.; "Says Libraries Will Be Closed without Tax Aid," *Press*, 9 Nov. 1931; "Outlines Plans for Library Economies," *PD*, 17 Dec. 1931; "Meets Today on Library Cost Cut," *PD*, 15 Dec. 1931; CPL pamphlet, "Saved Through Its Savings, the Library in 1932"; Linda Eastman, "We Are a City of Readers," *PD*, 7 July 1923; "Economy in Order," *PD*, 2 Feb. 1932; "Closed on Sunday," editorial, *Press*, 9 Sept. 1932; "A Lot of Bunk," editorial, *Press*, 7 Feb. 1933; "Librarians Pay Cut 10 Percent," *News*, 15 Jan. 1932; "Library Borrows Funds to Carry On," *Press*, 14 May 1932; "Saving the Library," *PD*, 24 Sept. 1932; "Library Funds," *PD*, 16 Sept. 1932; "900 at Library Get Past Due Salaries," *PD*, 29 Sept. 1932; "Intangible Tax Law Void, Library Is Hit," *News*, 7 Feb. 1933; "Practical Suggestion," *PD*, 8 Jan. 1932 —on voluntary payment of fines; "Don't Shut Out the Light," *PD*, 23 Dec. 1931; "The Library Stays Open," editorial, *Press*, 14 July 1933; Citizens League, "Suburban Mayors Want a Part of the Library Funds," *Greater Cleveland*, 6 Feb. 1936 —on breakdown of salaries in CPL; CPL pamphlet, "Gains and Losses in Your Library, 1936"; "WPA Helps Library," *Press*, 25 Jan. 1937 and *PD*, 7 Apr. 1938; Grace V. Kelly, "Library's Murals Tell City's

Story," *PD*, 11 Dec. 1934; William Sommer, Description of Mural in Brett Hall, typed statement; White to Charles E. Kennedy, 18 Jan. 1925; "To Miss Linda Eastman," *Press*, 11 June 1938; John W. Love, "Miss Eastman's Library," *Press*, 31 Aug. 1938; William J. McDermott, "McDermott on Service," *PD*, 7 Jan. 1938; Cable Robbins, "An Outsider Looks at Our Library," *Bystander of Cleveland*, 28 Sept. 1929; "Talk of the Town," *New Yorker*, 29 Mar. 1969 —on Polykarp Kusch.

RESIGNATION AND HONORS

Eastman to the Library Board, 18 May 1938; Jack Warfel, "Nearly 50 Years of Service as Librarian Recalled As City Honors Miss Eastman," *Press*, 27 Aug. 1938; *Open Shelf*, May–June 1960 —for tabulation of honors and comment by Benesch; "Librarians of America Pick Her for President," *PD*, 24 Feb. 1928; Phillips, "Eastman," p. 13; Eastman to Thwing, 4 Mar. 1919, CWRU Archives; typed copy of Eastman's remarks at the public testimonial in Music Hall, 1 Sept. 1938 —on pride in her colleagues.

In an open letter to the *Plain Dealer* on 13 May 1933, Benesch expressed his dismay over the burning of books in Hitler's Germany, along with his consternation that so many liberals had remained silent about it:

> It is passing strange that thus far the voices of but two eminent Americans have been heard crying in the wilderness in condemnation of this refinement of medieval barbarism— those of Helen Keller and Linda A. Eastman. All honor to those courageous liberals for their fearless stand.

In a competition that was both unique and unusual, the title of "Cleveland's Most Valuable Woman" was conferred on Eastman in 1930. Six prominent men were to name five women who were eligible for the award. The men were Samuel G. Mather, R. B. Robinette (president of the Chamber of Commerce), Rabbi Barnett R. Brickner, Judge Homer G. Powell, the Reverend Dan Bradley, and "a leading educator who asked that his name be withheld." Eastman was the only one mentioned by all six men. Mrs. Adella Prentiss Hughes and Miss Belle Sherwin were nominated three times, Mrs. Chester C. Bolton, Mrs. E. F. Prentiss, and Mrs. Dudley S. Blossom twice. See Alice Kuehn, "Title of 'Cleveland's Most Valuable Woman' Is Conferred," *Cleveland Sunday News*, 28 Dec. 1930.

THE EASTMAN GARDEN

City Record, Cleveland, 15 Sept. 1937; "Reading Room with Sky Top Lures Curious," *News*, 8 July 1937; Roelif Loveland, "Open Air Library to Mark Miss Eastman's Library," *PD*, 16 June 1937; "Reading Garden Opening Set by Library," *PD*, 1 May 1960; "Quiet Beauty Overtakes Old Eastman Park, 1960," editorial, *PD*, 6 May 1960; Bill Dvorak, "Sights and Sounds," *Press*, 21 May 1960, Emerson Batdorf, "Lunching on Soul Food," *PD*, 21 June 1964.

In the Eastman Garden recorded music is played during the summer at noontime. At the first concert each year Mrs. Jamison is always present to hear the initial selection which opens the new season. It is Chopin's *Les Sylphides,* her particular favorite because of associations going back to the courting days of the Jamisons.

CHAPTER 6, Nadir

CHARLES EVERETT RUSH

CPL Personnel File on Rush; *Who's Who in America, 1954–55,* s.v. "Rush, Charles Everett"; Kelly, "Eastman Quits Library."

LIBRARY BOARDS — "OLD AND NEW"

"Library Board, 1871–1921," *Open Shelf,* July–Aug. 1921; Philip W. Porter, "The Inside of the News in Cleveland," *PD*, 23 July 1939; "Defends Policies of Library Board," *PD*, 5 Feb. 1940; George J. Barmann, "Thompson Is Named to Library Board," *PD*, 1 Mar. 1955 —for quotation from Benesch; Frances P. Bolton, "The Cleveland Public Library," *Congressional Record*, 16 May 1950 —on small-town trustee; "Library Board Member Feted as a 'Good Guy,'" *PD*, 13 Aug. 1948 —on non-reading habits; E. Marcus, "The Trustee of the Future," in *Library of Tomorrow*, ed. Danton, p. 120; "An Unearned Honor," editorial, *PD*, 7 July 1939; Alvin Silverman, "Consider Five for Library Trustees," *PD*, 4 July 1939; Grace V. Kelly, "Name F. W. Dorn to Head Library Board," *PD*, 23 June 1938; Ralph Kelly, "Politicians Decry New Library Coup," *PD*, 9 July 1939; Alvin Silverman, " 'Unknown' Is Elected to Library Post," *PD*, 6 July 1939; "Guardian of Our Books," editorial, *News*, 7 July 1939; "No Compliment," editorial, *Press*, 5 July 1939; Eugene Segal, "Board Member Is Bewildered by His Sudden Fame," *Press*, 6 July 1939; "Rebuilding the Library Board," editorial, *PD*, 9 Apr. 1942.

In 1884 an antilabor novel, titled *The Bread-Winners* (Harper and Brothers, 1884), was published anonymously. Its author was actually John Hay and the locale was Cleveland—called Buffland with Euclid designated as Algonquin Avenue. Hay had been a member of the Library Board. In the novel he manifested contempt for politicians as well as labor leaders and stated that the staff of the Cleveland Public Library was appointed as a result of political pressure. The librarian—Oviatt or Beardsley or a composite of both—was portrayed as the "doddering Dr. Buchlieber." See *The Bread-Winners*, pp. 53 ff., 148 ff.

JOBS FOR CLEVELANDERS

"Bradley Defends Home Town Hiring," *PD*, 10 July 1938; Philip W. Porter, "Clean-Out," *PD*, 6 July 1938; "Poor Appointments," editorial, *Press*, 6 July 1938; Eugene Segal, "School Board Member Intervenes in Girl's Behalf," *Press*, 29 July 1939; "Corrigan's Bid for Library Job Stirs Surprise," *News*, 4 July 1938; "Report W. J. Corrigan Will Get Library's Labor Chairmanship," *News*, 2 Sept. 1938; "Emil Joseph, Library Board Veteran," *Press*, 21 June 1937; "Emil Joseph Is Dead at 80," *Press*, 11 June 1938; Library Board Proceedings, 22 June 1938, p. 62 —on death of Joseph; "W. J. Corrigan Dies: Sheppard Trial Star," *PD*, 31 July 1961.

THE INVESTIGATIONS

Eugene Segal, "Wright Must Quit One of His Jobs," *Press*, 22 July 1939; "The Library Report," editorial, *Press*, 27 July 1939 —on Turner; "Wearing the Wright Label," editorial, *Press*, 22 July 1939; "Col. Alexander to Aid Library Study," *PD*, 25 Apr. 1939; Alvin

Silverman, "Alexander Gives Library Findings," *PD*, 15 Oct. 1939; John M. Johnson, "Koubek Brands Library Report as a 'Dud,'" *Press*, 16 Oct. 1939; Alvin Silverman, "Name Three for Library Appraisal," *PD*, 8 Feb. 1939; Carnovsky, "Appraisal of Cleveland Public," passim; "Carnovsky Report Confirms What Every One Knew," editorial, *Press*, 4 Aug. 1939; "Favorable Report," editorial, *PD*, 5 Aug. 1939; "Looking at the Library," editorial, *PD*, 16 Oct. 1939.

HOWELL WRIGHT

Rose, *Cleveland,* pp. 517, 611, 699 —on Robert C. Norton; "Wm. J. Corrigan and Howell Wright Elected to Board," *Press*, 6 July 1938; "Put Wright, Corrigan at Library," *PD*, 6 July 1938; "Keep the Corrupting Grasp of Spoils Politics Out of Our Public Library," *Press*, 19 July 1939; "Poor Appointments," *Press*; "Charge Attempt at Bribery on Library Awards," *Press* and *News*, 30 Sept. 1939; "Max Zinner Dies; Headed Bindery," *PD*, 16 Mar. 1942 —on bribery by, and conviction of, Wright.

LIBRARIAN VS. LIBRARY BOARD

"Woe!" editorial, *PD*, 22 Oct. 1939; Minutes of the Library Board, 17 Jan. 1940; Rush to L. H. Wieber, 1 Mar. 1940; Rush to Library Board, 1 and 21 May, 5 Sept. 1940; *Who's Who in Library Service, 1966,* s.v. "Munn, Russell," *1955,* s.v. "Winslow, Amy," and *1933,* s.v. "Prouty, Louise"; Metcalf to Library Board, 23 Sept. 1940; Minutes of the Library Board, 25 Oct. 1945; CPL Personnel Files on Munn, Prouty, Rush, and Winslow.

RESIGNATION OF RUSH

"They Asked for It!," *Press*, 7 Feb. 1941; "Congratulations, Mr. Rush," *PD*, 8 Feb. 1941; "Rush Resigns as Library Head in Surprise Move," *News*, 6 Feb. 1941; Jack Raper, "Most Anything," *Press*, 7 Feb. 1941; "Rush Sacrifices $4092 Yearly for Library Harmony," *Press*, 12 Feb. 1941; Phil Porter, "The Inside of the News in Cleveland," *PD*, 12 Feb. 1941; Kornhauser to Members of the Library Board Attending the Meeting Called for 12 Feb. 1941, Director's Office; "Rush's Exit Stirs Library Friends," *PD*, 7 Feb. 1931;

"Library Appointments," editorial, *PD*, 24 July 1942; "The Library Turns a Corner," editorial, *News*, 23 July 1942; "Mrs. McQuate Is First Woman to Become Library Board Head," *News*, 20 July 1944.

CHAPTER 7, "Make No Little Plans"

CLARENCE SHERIDAN METCALF

Norris F. Schneider, "Head of Cleveland's Celebrated Library Tells of Boyhood in Morgan County," Zanesville *Sunday Times-Signal*, 26 Oct. 1947; obituary on Metcalf, *Press*, 16 Nov. 1961; *Who's Who in America, 1952–53*, s.v. "Metcalf, Clarence Sheridan"; "Clarence Sheridan Metcalf," *Open Shelf*, Nov.–Dec. 1961; "Clarence S. Metcalf," editorial, *Press*, 18 Nov. 1961; "Funeral Rites Are Today for C. S. Metcalf," *PD*, 18 Nov. 1961; Ben Wickham, "They Played for Fun—Symphony Was Born," *News*, 1 Oct. 1937; Ruth Gordon, "Clarence Sheridan Metcalf," *Bulletin of Bibliography*, Jan.–Apr. 1950; Arthur Shepherd, "Large Audience Enthuses over Music Festival," *Press*, 19 June 1929; James D. Hartshorne, "Library's Chiefs Put Metcalf In," *PD*, 29 Nov. 1941; Minutes of the Library Board, 28 Nov. 1941; John M. Johnston, "C. S. Metcalf Appointed as Library Chief," *Press*, 28 Nov. 1941; "Gruber Proposes Metcalf for Library Post," *Press*, 13 Nov. 1941; Citizens League, "Merit and Fitness Must Determine Appointments," *Greater Cleveland*, 4 Dec. 1941; Minutes of the Library Board, 19 July 1944 —authorization of title of Director; Metcalf to Library Board, 5 Dec. 1941; Wilson Hirschfeld, "30 at Library Draw Pensions and Pay," *PD*, 24 Dec. 1947; James Gorman, "Library Workers Call on Board to Dismiss Metcalf," *News*, 14 Oct. 1948; "Public Library Has Earned Acceptance of Its Budget," editorials, *Press*, 17 Nov. 1947 and 16 Dec. 1949.

Over the past quarter century there has been a considerable amount of talk about a putative femme fatale named Edith Woodburn, and some speculation about what influence she might have had on vital decisions concerning the library. Her formal education included a high school diploma and upwards of two years of credits toward a college degree when she was a part-time student at Cleveland College. She began her career in the library in 1926 as a typist and served in the 1930s as a secretary for Marilla Freeman, who gave her strong recommendations as an intelligent, alert, and poised individual. She had no library degree but attended the annual meetings of the American Library Association regularly and became president of a prominent business and professional woman's club in Cuyahoga County. In 1939 she was appointed secretary in the office of Librarian Charles Rush and, for a decade after 1945, occupied the dual positions of secretary-treasurer of the Library Board and assistant to Librarians Clarence Metcalf and L. Quincy Mumford.

Her doll-like face was pert and attractive. She dressed well and had a way with men, except the one she wanted to marry; he jilted her in a manner that was reported to have been both brazen and traumatic. After this shock she manifested an increasing attraction for the bottle and, according to rumor, for a Library Board member or two. In 1955 her employment with the library was terminated at the height of a controversy about money and her private life. Among other things it was found that she had borrowed, unwisely and without authorization, the small but significant sum of $673.03 from a number of minor funds entrusted to her care: the Victory Book Campaign Funds of 1942 and 1945, the ALA Fund (supposedly controlled by its Tours and Square Dance committees), and the Staff Welfare Fund. Fortunately an audit revealed that the John G. White Fund of $280,000, which she also handled, was in satisfactory condition. Subsequently she worked as a secretary in two Cleveland industries, but in 1964 she was bold enough to ask Librarian Raymond Lindquist if she could return to the Cleveland Public Library as his personal secretary. His reply was both compelling and sensitive, recalling Thomas Wolfe's novel *You Can't Go Home Again*. Lindquist wrote that the same principle was apropos of her request: "Once a person has made a break with the past—whether at home or from an important position in the past—he really can't go back to it as if he had never gone away." She died in 1966 at the age of fifty-seven.

There is no question that she hobnobbed with people of influence in institutional and corporate milieus. There is no question that her opinions and judgments were considered and that she had some influence on important appointments. There is also no question, in the judgment of the author, that her enduring influence on the Cleveland Public Library was nil. Her years of potential influence were scarcely golden ones in the institution's long history, and it is not possible to prove that the library's chronicle would have been changed materially had she never served it. It is undeniable, had she never been employed, that the library would have been deprived of a perennial subject for lively discussion and that many of its officers would have been spared a great deal of exasperation and irritation. See Noel Wical, "High Library Position May Be Left Vacant," *Press*, 13 Jan. 1955; Woodburn to Library Board, 8 Jan. 1955; Stanley J. Klonowski (president of Library Board) to Woodburn, 18 Jan. 1955; Woodburn to Lindquist, 1 June 1964; Lindquist to Woodburn, 18 June 1964; obituary on Woodburn, *PD*, 15 Apr. 1966.

SHUT-INS, HOSPITALS, AND INSTITUTIONS

"Map Library Fund's Use," *PD*, 27 Oct. 1940; Howard Preston, "Judd Foundation Shut-Ins' Pal," *PD*, 29 Jan. 1968; "Library Starting Book Deliveries at Doors of Shut-Ins," *PD*, 19 Feb. 1942; "So Those Who Cannot Run May Read," *Cleveland Foundation*, Mar. 1942; Marion B. Gross, "Aid to Shut-Ins," *PD*, 28 July 1945; Clara E. Lucioli, "Library Goes to the Handicapped," *Crippled Child*, Feb. 1944; Claire MacMurray, "Do You Need This Help?," *PD*, 9 Jan. 1954; Bob Seltzer, "Books Travel to the Reader," *Press*, 16 Oct. 1969 —biographical on Lucioli; Jesse Borocz, "Lakewood Woman Chosen Ohio Librarian of the Year," *Lakewood Sun Post*, 24 Sept. 1970; J. A. Wadowick, "Ceiling Books to Give Joy to Invalid Clevelanders," *PD*, 4 Jan. 1948; "Electric Page Turner Boon to Polio Victim," *Press*, 14 Nov. 1960; Stephanie Mackey, "Books Open Doors for Shut-Ins," *Press*, 10 Aug. 1959; CPL Judd Fund Division Annual Report for 1969, passim; Clara E. Lucioli and Dorothy H. Fleak, "The Shut-Ins—Waiting for What?," *ALA Bulletin*, Apr. 1964; "Beginning a Second Century of Books," typescript in files of Katherine Prescott, CPL Braille and Talking Books Department; "Library of the Month," *Talking Book Topics*; Blasingame, *Survey of Ohio Libraries*, p. 77; CPL Braille and Talking Book Service Annual Report for 1969; "New Developments in Library Service," *Talking Book Topics*, Jan. 1967.

ADULT EDUCATION

Ballard, *Public Library*, pp. 10, 11; Margaret E. Monroe, *Library Adult Education: The Biography of an Idea* (Scarecrow Press, 1963), pp. 7, 12, 32, 54; Alvin Johnson, *The Public Library: A People's University* (American Association for Adult Education, 1938), pp. 31, 37–38; CPL Adult Education Office Annual Reports for 1941 and 1947, passim; Martha Lee, "Read for Pleasure and Profit," *News*, 18 July 1940; Elizabeth Jacobson, "Library Ushers Groping Clevelanders through Magic Portals," *PD*, 6 Dec. 1936; "The Fruition," editorial, *PD*, 5 May 1925; Virginia Strange, "In and about Cleveland," *PD*, 24 Mar. 1940 —on Munn; "Happy Birthday," *Akron Beacon Journal*, 7 Sept. 1950 —on Munn; CPL Personnel File on Munn; Fern Long, "I Am Still Learning," Lake Erie College, *Bulletin*, Nov. 1959; "Radcliffe Award to Long," *PD*, 7 July 1960; *Who's Who in Library Service, 1955*, s.v. "Munn, Russell" and *1966*, s.v. "Long, Fern"; AR 1891, pp. 10–11 —on early lectures; "Four Candles Salute Live Long and Like It Club," *Press*, 16 Nov. 1950; Fern Long and Clara Lucioli, "Live Long and Like It Club," *Wilson Library Bulletin*, Dec. 1948; Fern Long, "The Live Long and Like It Club—The Cleveland Public Library," *Library Trends*, July 1968; Fern Long, "The Story of a Club," *Golden Age Center News*, Mar. 1958; Fern Long, comments on reception of Alumnae Award, *Radcliffe Quarterly*, Aug. 1960 —on Film Bureau; "Great Books Plan Calls for Leaders," *PD*, 21 Apr. 1949; Glenn C. Pullen, "Library Group Romps in Greek Classic Comedy," *PD*, 31 Oct. 1952; Fern Long, "The Growing Edge," unpublished manuscript, 1958.

GREAT LAKES HISTORICAL SOCIETY

Gordon, "Clarence Sheridan Metcalf"; Great Lakes Historical Society, frontispiece, *Membership Roster, 1968*; Donna L. Root, "A Twenty-Fifth Birthday, *Inland Seas*, 1945–1970," Spring 1970; A. F. and W. R. Wakefield, "Property Brief Prepared on Harbor View," brochure, passim; Donna L. Root, "The Great Lakes Historical Society," *Ohio Archaeological and Historical Quarterly*, Apr. 1947; Rose, *Cleveland*, p. 351; Great Lakes Historical Society brochure on its museum; Kenneth Colvin, "New Museum at Vermilion to House Great Lakes Lore," *PD*, 15 Mar. 1953.

In 1965 because the demands of the growing organization for space and staff-time were becoming too heavy, the library terminated its formal sponsorship of the society, and Root resigned as editor of *Inland Seas*. Fortunately her colleague in the History Department of the Cleveland Public Library, Janet Coe Sanborn, agreed to edit the journal from her own residence. Under her guidance the magazine has continued to grow and prosper, and has increased in size from the original forty-eight to eighty-eight pages.

LAWRENCE QUINCY MUMFORD

Louis H. Wieber (chairman of Personnel Committee of Library Board) to Mumford, 12 June 1945; speech by Mumford to CPL Worker's Association, 28 Nov. 1945, Personnel Division; "L. Quincy Mumford Seen as Next Library Director," *PD*, 9 Sept. 1950; "L. Quincy Mumford," *Open Shelf*, June–July–Aug. 1954; Paul North Rice, "L. Quincy Mumford Nominated Librarian of Congress," *Library Service News*, Columbia University School of Library Service, June 1954; "New Librarian of Congress, Lawrence Quincy Mumford," *Illinois Libraries*, May 1954; "Mumford Airs Philosophy: Weighs Both Sides of Issues," *PD*, 27 July 1954; Eve Edstrom, "Mumford Sworn as U.S. Librarian," *Washington Post*, 2 Sept. 1954.

RAYMOND CHARLES LINDQUIST

"Raymond C. Lindquist," *Open Shelf*, July–Dec. 1968; Harry Hite, "Librarian 'Retires' to New Job," *St. Paul Dispatch*, 1 Jan. 1969; Raymond C. Lindquist, "Thirteen Year Report, 1955–1968," pp. 5 ff.; CPL, "Background Material on Proposed Bond Issue for Purchase of the *Plain Dealer* Building," mimeographed release, 24 May 1957; "Syndicate Gets Library Bonds," *News*, 11 Dec. 1957; Doris Linge, "Voters OK New Schools, Approve Bonds for Library," *News*, 6 Nov. 1957; "Library to Open Annex in 1958," *PD*, 22 Dec. 1957.

Whether there was a ninth librarian, for the last day of the library's first century, depends on the definition of the Anniversary Day—17 February 1969. Was it the last day of the first century or the first of the library's second hundred years? Whatever the decision, on 17 February 1969, the Board of Trustees appointed Edward A. D'Alessandro as Lindquist's successor. D'Alessandro had spent his entire career with the Cleveland Public Library. He started as a fourteen-year-old page in the Brownell Junior High School Library, then a part of the Cleveland Public Library's system. He continued to hold student library jobs while attending John Adams High School and John Carroll University (from which he graduated in 1937) and the Library School at Western Reserve University, where he earned a professional degree in 1938. In 1941 he became assistant librarian at the Euclid-East 100th Street branch, the first male appointed as an assistant branch librarian in the Cleveland system. After serving in a number of other positions at library branches, he became assistant librarian of the main library in 1954, business manager in 1956, and deputy director in 1968. Nine months after his appointment as director, D'Alessandro suffered a heart attack which necessitated his resignation in January 1970 after forty years of service in the system.

In some ways the twelve months marking the One Hundredth Anniversary constituted "the year that was." It saw two acting directors and one director, three different presidents of the Library Board, plus the untimely death of one trustee and the resignation of two. See Ann Skinner, "D'Alessandro Gets Top Library Post," *PD*, 18 Feb. 1969 and "Library Director Here to Resign," *PD*, 29 Jan. 1970; Robert L. Merritt, "Remarks at Board of Trustees Meeting," 2 Feb. 1970.

READERS DROP OUT

Statistics on borrowers and circulation by Virginia Aroson (CPL statistician); Richard L. Tobin, "News and the Functional Illiterate," *Saturday Review*, 13 June 1970; Fern Long, "Impatience and the Pressure of Time: Cleveland's Reading Centers Project," *Ohio Library Association Bulletin*, June 1966; CPL Adult Education Department, Reading Centers Project, Final Report (1968), passim.

WHENCE MONEY?

Blasingame, *Survey of Ohio Libraries*, pp. 21 ff., 102 ff.; Citizens League, "The Public Library Appropriations," *Greater Cleveland*, 9 Dec. 1937; CPL, "The Tax Funds Which Support the Library and How These Funds Are Obtained," mimeographed release, Nov. 1937; Ralph Kelly, "Council $30,000 to Aid CCRA in Crisis," *PD*, 9 Feb. 1937; "Library Fund Demand Faces Budget Ruling," *Press*, 23 Dec. 1952; Paul Brokaw, "Foggy Legislation Is Basis of Scrap about Tax Revenue for Libraries," *News*, 17 Dec. 1945; Edward Lucy, "Libraries Given 96% of Intangible Taxes," *Press*, 18 Feb. 1955; "Raps Mayors' Efforts to Get Library Funds," *Press*, 5 Nov. 1943; "Library Independence," editorial, *News*, 2 Nov. 1944; Lindquist, "Thirteen Year Report," pp. 3, 17, 30, 32; "Public Library Expenses Bring Drop in Acquisitions," *PD*, 3 July 1969; "Your Great Library System Deserves Fair Budget Share," editorial, *Press*, 19 Dec. 1952; "Boost Library Salaries Now," editorial, *Press*, 16 Oct. 1946; "Little Fiche Eat Big Librarians—One Whale of a Story," *Wilson Library Bulletin*, Feb. 1970; "Libraries Need New Dollar Source," editorial, *PD*, 7 Nov. 1970; Paul Brokaw, "Libraries Wasteful, Municipalities Charge in Protest on Tax Division," *News*, 18 Dec. 1945; "The Plight of the Libraries," editorial, *PD*, 3 Aug. 1969; Howard Preston, "Money and the Libraries," *PD*, 29 June 1970; "Why Support the Public Library," *New York Libraries*, adapted in *Open Shelf*, Mar. 1921; "Cluttered and Cramped, Library of Congress Faces Worst Crisis since 1814," *New York Times*, 3 Jan. 1970; Ada L. Huxtable, "Library as Friend," *New York Times*, 24 Jan. 1971; Emanuel Perlmutter, "Rally Protests Library Closing," *New York Times*, 18 May 1969.

WHITHER MERGER?

Cleveland Bureau of Governmental Research pamphlet, "Public Library Service in Cuyahoga County," 1960, pp. 5 ff., and passim; Phillips, "Eastman," p. 33; "Merger Action Begun on Library Systems," *PD*, 25 Feb. 1955; AR 1924–25, pp. 11, 21, 103–4; AR 1929, p. 18; Arlene Theuer, *Public Libraries in Cuyahoga County* (Cleveland Metropolitan Services Commission, 1959), passim; Citizens League, "A Unified Library System Is Needed," *Greater Cleveland*, 23 Nov. 1938; "The Libraries Should Merge," editorial, *Press*, 10 Aug. 1962; Lindquist, "Thirteen Year Report," pp. 13 ff.; CPL, "Staff Information Bulletin," mimeographed, Jan. 1968, passim; Citizens League, "The Library Problem Still Unsolved," *Greater*

Cleveland, 23 Mar. 1943; "Let's Vote on It," editorial, *Press*, 14 May 1963; Citizens League, "Another Proof of the Need of Unification," *Greater Cleveland*, 24 Nov. 1943; "For One Great Library," editorial, *Press*, 21 Aug. 1969; Citizens League, "The Public Library Appropriations," *Greater Cleveland*, 9 Dec. 1937; Michael Kelly, "Library Merger to Save $37,000," *PD*, 8 Oct. 1970; "Cry 'Annexation' at Library Plan," *Press*, 19 Feb. 1941; Alvin Silverman, "County Library Unity Plea Loses," *PD*, 14 June 1939; Library Board Proceedings, 1939, pp. 45–46; "Continue Efforts to Unite 14 Library Units in County," *Press*, 14 June 1939.

This controversy over mergers was not unique to Cleveland. In the late nineteenth century Allegheny, Pennsylvania, had a library which was privately endowed by almost a half million dollars from Andrew Carnegie, who had spent his early years in the municipality. The dedication of the Allegheny Library became a national event in 1890 because President Benjamin Harrison made the main address.

When Allegheny became a part of Pittsburgh in 1909, all governmental units were amalgamated except the library. There the merger was successfully prevented until 1956, when the Allegheny Library was finally combined with the Pittsburgh Public Library.

During all these intervening years, a great deal of opposition against the merger had come from older residents who objected because of local pride. Some of it, however, was derived from local politicians who used appointments in the library as part of the "loaves and the fishes" which they expected as one of their perquisites. See Bobinski, *Carnegie Libraries*, p. 77.

A CENTURY OF SERVICE

"The Bookish Centenarian," editorial, *PD*, 9 Feb. 1969; William F. McDermott, "McDermott on Library," *PD*, 15 Oct. 1954; "City Library Gets Foreigners' Praise," *PD*, 2 May 1971; "Best-Selling Writer Calls Cleveland Library 'Superb,'" *PD*, 12 Oct. 1957 —referring to Bowen; Rose, *Cleveland*, p. 606 —for quotation from Burnham.

Figures on the relative size of libraries vary depending on whether books alone, or books plus pamphlets and papers and other bits and pieces, are counted. In 1969 the *World Almanac* (p. 634), using the U.S. Office of Education as its source, listed the first ten public libraries as follows on the basis of the number of volumes in them:

New York	17,490,650
Cleveland	3,305,759
Los Angeles	3,189,122
Chicago	3,124,686
Brooklyn	2,604,112
Philadelphia	2,408,341
Cincinnati	2,344,166
Boston	2,306,711
Buffalo	2,120,020
Queens	2,084,997

INDEX

This book was set in eleven-point Caledonia and printed by
Oberlin Printing Company, Oberlin, Ohio.
It was bound by John H. Dekker & Sons, Inc., Grand Rapids, Michigan.
The book was designed by Edgar J. Frank.